KV-577-693

Morphological Productivity

Walter de Gruyter   1749   250   1999   Berlin · New York

Topics in English Linguistics 28

Editors

Bernd Kortmann
Elizabeth Closs Traugott

Mouton de Gruyter
Berlin · New York

Morphological Productivity

Structural Constraints in English Derivation

by

Ingo Plag

W DE G

Mouton de Gruyter
Berlin · New York 1999

Mouton de Gruyter (formerly Mouton, The Hague)
is a Division of Walter de Gruyter & Co. KG, Berlin.

⊗ Printed on acid-free paper which falls within the guidelines of the
ANSI to ensure permanence and durability.

Library of Congress Cataloging-in-Publication-Data

Plag, Ingo.
  Morphological productivity : structural constraints in Eng-
lish derivation / by Ingo Plag.
      p.   cm. − (Topics in English linguistics ; 28)
  Includes bibliographical references and index.
  ISBN 3-11-015833-7 (cloth : alk. paper)
  1. English language−Morphology.   2. English language−
Word formation.   I. Title.   II. Series.
PE1171.P57   1999
425−dc21   98-51325
                                                             CIP

Die Deutsche Bibliothek − Cataloging-in-Publication-Data

Plag, Ingo:
Morphological productivity : structural constraints in english
derivation / by Ingo Plag. − Berlin ; New York : Mouton de
Gruyter, 1999
  (Topics in English linguistics ; 28)
  ISBN 3-11-015833-7

Printing: Arthur Collignon GmbH, Berlin. − Binding: Lüderitz & Bauer, Berlin.
Printed in Germany.

Preface

Many people have played a part in the writing of this book. First and foremost, I would like to thank Rüdiger Zimmermann, who has supported me as a mentor and friend over the past ten years and has promoted this project from the beginning. His help and encouragement has been simply invaluable.

Many thanks are due to Michael Job and Richard Wiese for their constant interest in my work and the many useful remarks on earlier drafts of the manuscript. I am also very grateful to Birgit Alber for the many discussions we had on phonological theory and for her detailed critical comments on various draft versions of chapters 6 and 7. Many other people provided useful comments or information at various stages of the project: Laurie Bauer, Geert Booij, Ellen Broselow, Harald Baayen, Heinz Giegerich, Martin Haspelmath, Martin Hummel, Bernd Kortmann, Jaap van Marle, Wolfgang Kehrein, Paul Kiparsky, Thomas Klein, Martin Neef, Renate Raffelsiefen, Franz Rainer, Elizabeth Traugott, the participants of the 'Sprachwissenschaftliches Kolloquium' at my university, the audiences at several conferences, and a number of anonymous reviewers. Many thanks to all of them. They are, of course, not responsible for the errors and follies that remain.

I am also grateful for the help provided at different stages of the project by our student assistants Marcus Callies, Stefan Hügel, Sabine Lappe, Birgit Sasse, Kristine Scholz and Christian Uffmann and our secretary Annette Heberle. Special thanks to Christian Uffmann for his assistance with the Cobuild word lists and to Stephanie Hellmuth for her helpful suggestions concerning my style. I also would like to thank the students in my seminars on word-formation who tentatively explored some of the terrain covered in this book.

Finally, I am grateful for the moral support I received from my friends and my family. Everyone always told me that I would be able to write this book, so that in the end I started believing it myself. Many thanks to Hannah, Jonas and Claudia for distracting me from my work, thereby helping me concentrate on it.

Marburg, October 1998

Contents

Abbreviations and symbols

A	adjective
Adv	adverb
I	pragmatic potentiality
LCS	lexical conceptual structure
LMBM	Lexeme-Morpheme-Base-Morphology
LMH	Lexical Morpheme Hypothesis
N	noun
NP	noun phrase
OT	Optimality Theory
P	productivity in the narrow sense
P*	global productivity
SPE	Chomsky and Halle 1968 (see references)
UBH	unitary base hypothesis
UOH	unitary output hypothesis
V	verb
V	extent of use
WFR	word formation rule

!	precedes possible, but unattested forms
*	precedes ungrammatical forms
?	precedes doubtful forms
σ	syllable

1. Introduction

In his 1983 introduction to English word-formation, Laurie Bauer remarks that "word-formation is such a confused area of study at the moment that it would not be possible to write an uncontroversial introduction to the subject" (1983:xiii). Although a lot of research has been done since the publication of Bauer's book, many of the old controversies remain, though sometimes restated in more fashionable terminology. Some of the still unanswered questions include the following: is morphology word-based or morpheme-based? What is the nature of morphological rules and how do they interact with phonology, syntax and semantics? How can we account for allomorphy? How do rival morphological processes interact?

Needless to say, this study will not provide the reader with an all-embracing answer to these questions. What the study does provide, however, are some new insights into these problems and a number of suggestions how to tackle these questions in order to arrive at satisfactory results. The purpose of the investigation to be presented here is twofold, empirical and theoretical. Firstly, and maybe surprisingly, many well-known English derivational processes are still poorly described and more adequate accounts of the facts are needed. The empirical problems and their solutions as proposed in this book open up new and, hopefully, interesting perspectives on some of the morphological problems mentioned in the preceding paragraph.

I am thoroughly convinced that any account of these problems should be judged on the basis of its empirical adequacy. In general terms, the central empirical problem theories of word-formation have to deal with is productivity. Thus, an ideal theory of word-formation must be able to account for the (possible) existence or non-existence of morphologically complex words by positing mechanisms that can correctly predict the combinatorial properties of morphological elements. A study of the existing literature reveals that these mechanisms have often remained obscure, which brings us back to Bauer (1983), where it is stated that "productivity remains one of the most contested areas in the study of word-formation" (Bauer 1983:62). Not much has happened in the meantime to invalidate this statement.

Research on the issue of productivity can be characterized by two diverging trends. On the one hand, linguists working in the generative tradition have tended to propose generalizations that, however, have often been based on a rather shallow analysis of a rather limited range of data. On the other hand, standard handbooks of English word-formation like Marchand (1969), or Jespersen (1942) contain an incredible wealth of material, but the analyses often remain vague and do not arrive at significant generalizations, let alone predictions.

The present study is an attempt to bridge this gap between important theoretical insights and broad empirical coverage. In doing so, I argue against the common assumption that (derivational) morphology tends to be "inherently messy" (Hooper 1979:13) and rather unpredictable. To some extent this is true, since, as is well-known, complex words, once in more general usage, can adopt all kinds of idiosyncrasies that opacify their original semantic, morphological or phonological structure. However, as pointed out for example by Plank (1981), there is a lot of regularity in the apparent irregularity of derivational morphology. It is one aim of this study to show that many derivational processes are much more regular than previously conceived.

As just mentioned, the present investigation tries to clarify the nature of the mechanisms that govern the combinatorial properties of morphological elements. This will be done through a survey of the combinatorial properties of a broad range of English suffixes, followed by the in-depth analysis of the rival morphological processes by which verbs can be productively derived, i.e. the suffixation of *-ize, -ate, -ify* and conversion. Derived verbs have been selected because comparatively little is known about their semantic, morphological and phonological properties although they are often dealt with in the linguistic literature. Furthermore, the distribution of verbal affixes is an unsolved empirical problem, i.e. it is yet unclear what makes a given base choose a specific suffix (or conversion) to derive a new verb. Chapters 5 through 8 will provide a solution to this problem.

The thorough empirical analyses presented in the following chapters lead me to the central claim of this study, namely that the structural restrictions on the productivity of derivational processes are primarily the result of the individual properties of these processes and not due to more general mechanisms of the various kinds proposed in the literature (for example, by proponents of Lexical Phonology/Morphology (e.g. Kiparsky 1982b, Mohanan 1986, Giegerich 1995) or in the work of van Marle (1985, 1986), Fabb (1988), Lieber (1992) or Beard (1995)). Given a detailed adequate description of a particular derivational pattern, constraints on the distribution of this pattern turn out automatically, and only little additional machinery is necessary. The results also speak for an output-based model of morphological rules and against the separation of meaning and form in morphology.

This study also addresses some important methodological questions, such as the use of text corpora and dictionaries in the study of word structure. The empirical investigations presented in part II of the book are largely based on data extracted from the *Oxford English Dictionary on Compact Disc (OED)*, accompanied by data from the Cobuild corpus, which contained approximately 20 million words at the time.

The book is structured as follows. In the next chapter the reader will find a discussion and clarification of the notion of productivity, which appears often to be a controversial or incoherent concept. I will not only deal with the question what productivity is, but also how it can be measured, which is an intriguing methodological problem. Chapter 3 deals with the nature of productivity restrictions and reviews the mechanisms as proposed in existing models of (English) morphology. One of these models, Fabb (1988), is empirically tested in chapter 4 and an alternative account is proposed, which sets the scene for the following chapters (5 through 8), in which the focus is narrowed down to one of the central empirical and theoretical problems in derivational morphology, rival morphological processes. Finally, the main results are summarized in chapter 9.

2. Productivity: Definitions and measurements

The central aim of general morphological theory is to define the notion of 'possible complex word in natural language', or, in the case of theories about a specific language, the notion of 'possible complex word in language A'. Such a theory would ideally not only describe existing complex words but also non-existing, but equally possible derivatives, as they could be formed by the speakers according to the regularities and conditions inherent in their morphological competence. In other words, any morphological theory should make predictions which words are possible words of a language and which words are not. Assuming the existence of morphological rules according to which complex words are structured or formed, one can easily observe that some rules are often used to create new words, whereas others are less often used, or not used at all for this purpose. In this sense, some rules can be called productive and other rules unproductive or less productive. The obvious question now is which mechanisms are responsible for the productivity of morphological processes. Is the productivity of a rule the result of structural factors, conditioned by pragmatic factors, or an inherent non-derivable property of any morphological rule? And how can we measure the productivity of a rule?

This book is an attempt to shed some new light on this problem by investigating the nature of some of the mechanisms that condition the productivity of morphological processes in English. However, before we turn to the empirical side of the matter we will first take a closer look at the notion of productivity and its restrictions in this and the following chapter.

According to a standard dictionary of linguistic terminology, the term productivity is "used in linguistics to refer to the creative capacity of language users to produce and understand an indefinitely large number of sentences." (Crystal 1991:279, see also Chomsky 1957:15). Whereas the role of productivity in syntax is generally not regarded as problematic or is simply ignored[1], there is hardly any work on word-formation where pro-

---

[1] Cf. Aronoff (1980b:71), but see also the critical remarks by Aronoff (1976:35), or Bauer (1983:65-74). In his discussion of syntactic productivity, the latter comes to the conclusion that "syntactic and morphological productivity have more in common than they have to distinguish them" (1983:74). Since we are concerned with morphological productivity here, this point will not be further discussed.

ductivity is not prominently discussed. In most publications, productivity is loosely referred to as the possibility to coin new complex words according to the word formation rules of a given language. Although this definition of productivity seems rather straightforward, we will see in the following sections that numerous problems remain unresolved, and that, inspite of its centrality to the study of word formation, there is still no consensus about the nature of productivity. One is therefore still inclined to agree with Aronoff when he states, "The term productivity is widely used in the studies of derivational morphology, and there is obviously some intuition behind the usage, but most of the discussion is rather vague" (1976:35). Before we try to remove some of this vagueness, some remarks are in order concerning the crucial concepts to which notions of productivity refer. This will be done in the next section.

2.1. Preliminaries:
Possible words, actual words, and the lexicon

A notorious problem in the description of the speakers' morphological competence is that there are quite often unclear restrictions to the possibility of forming (and understanding) new complex words, to the effect that proposed word formation rules may not yield the correct set of complex words.

For instance, word formation rules may predict the existence of forms which are unattested or whose status as well-formed derivatives is more than doubtful. A famous example of this kind is the attachment of the nominalizing suffix *-ity* to adjectival bases ending in *-ous*, which is attested with forms such as *curious - curiosity, capacious - capacity, monstrous - monstrosity*. However, *-ity* cannot be attached to all bases of this type, as evidenced by the impossibility of **gloriosity* or **furiosity*. What is responsible for this limitation on the productivity of *-ity*?

Another typical problem with word formation rules is that they are often formulated in such a way that they prohibit formations that are nevertheless attested. For example, it is generally assumed that person nouns ending in *-ee* (such as *employee*) can only be formed from transitive verbs and, in informal terms, denote the object of the base verb ('someone who is employed'). However, sometimes even intransitive verbs take -*ee* (e.g. *escapee, standee*) or even nouns (*festschriftee*).[2]

Furthermore, some affixes occur with a large number of words, whereas others are only attested with a small number of derivatives. What conditions these differences in proliferance?

Intuitively, the notion of productivity must make reference to the speaker's ability to form new words and to the conditions the language system imposes on new words. This brings us to a central distinction in morphology, the one between 'possible' (or 'potential') and 'actual' words. The separation of actually attested words from non-attested but well-formed words is traditionally recognized[3] and finds a reflection in Coseriu's well-known dichotomy between *system* and *norm* (1952).[4] A possible, or potential, word can be defined as a word, existing or non-existing, whose morphological or phonological structure is in accordance with the rules of the language. It is obvious that before one can assign the status of 'possible word' to a given form, these rules need to be stated as clearly as possible.[5]

The concept of 'actual word', it seems, is harder to define. A loose definition would simply say that actual words are those words that are in use. However, when can we consider a word being 'in use'? Does it mean that some speaker has observed it being used somewhere? Or that the majority of the speech community is familiar with it? Or that it is listed in dictionaries? Rainer defines 'actual word' as a "word that is part of the vocabulary of a specific speaker at a specific point in time" (1987:195f, my translation).[6] The problem with this definition is that it makes reference to the individual speaker's lexicon, whereas morphological theory needs to make reference to the language system. It should be pointed out, however, that this gap between the vocabulary of the individual native speakers of a language and the abstract lexical-morphological language system should not

---

2   See Barker (1995) for discussion.
3   See, for example, van Marle (1985:38-42) for a review of the structuralist literature.
4   See Burgschmidt (1977) for an elaboration of these concepts with respect to word formation processes.
5   It should be noted that there is also a school of thought that completely refuses to consider non-attested language material, but instead exclusively devotes itself to the study and classification of corpora data (e.g. Harris 1960). As noted by many previous authors, such an approach fails to meet a central concern of linguistics, namely the description of the speaker's generative capacity.
6   See Aronoff (1976:19) for a similar view.

be overestimated since a large overlap of lexical knowledge among speakers is necessary for language to work.

However, this and other problems have led some theorists to the complete abandonment of the notion of actual word. Kiparsky, for example, has argued that the whole concept of actual word should be disposed of because "it is ill-defined and of no linguistic interest" (Kiparsky 1982b:26). There are essentially three arguments for this position.

The first argument is that speakers may not know whether a given word has already occurred in the language or not. In support of this claim one could cite Aronoff (1983), who has carried out experiments which indicate that, with highly productive rules, "Speakers tend to judge potential words ... as actual words, though they are not" (1983:166). But what does this result really tell us? First, it simply shows that the speakers' intuitions cannot be used to tap this distinction. This does not at all imply that the distinction is non-existent. Second, it tells us that highly productive processes create words that are so similar to many actual words that the two are no longer distinguishable. Again this is not a good argument against the distinction itself, because no one has ever claimed that actual words and potential words should not have many things in common. What has been claimed is that lexically listed regular complex words form a subclass of actual words (e.g. Jackendoff 1975, Aronoff 1976, see below for further discussion). To put it differently, the class of actual words contains both morphologically regular and morphologically idiosyncratic forms. The crucial difference between actual and possible words now is that only actual words may be idiosyncratic (e.g. semantically or phonologically).

The second argument against the 'possible-actual' dichotomy is that this distinction is not clear-cut. However, the fact that a distinction is not clear-cut does not necessarily mean that it does not exist. For example, we know that the distinction between inflection and derivation is more like a continuum and that a strict boundary between the two can often not be found. However, there is still good evidence that this distinction is theoretically useful and psycholinguistically relevant (see, for example, some of the papers in Booij and van Marle 1996).

Although it may seem that with a given speaker a word is either listed or not, the picture is not clear-cut, because many factors, frequency of occurrence chiefly among them, play a role in memorization and retrieval. For example, the memorizability and later accessibility of a word depends crucially on the word's frequency in the speaker's environment. Hence one could claim that some items are 'more listed' than others, in the sense that they are easier for a speaker to access and retrieve than others.

The third, and perhaps strongest, argument against actual words is that "no rule of grammar even depends on whether a word is 'actual' or not" (Kiparsky 1982b:26). Booij (1987:44-51) presents impressive counterevidence to Kiparsky's claim by showing that certain types of morphological change, and processes of 'paradigmatic' word formation must make reference to the notion of 'existing complex word'[7]. The development of affix clusters and the substitution of morphemes in complex words are cases in point, since both phenomena presuppose the prior existence of a complex model form.

To summarize the discussion of the notions of possible and actual word we can say that the distinction is useful and often necessary for the description of morphological processes. Morphology, as conceived here, concerns the study of both actual and possible words. It is one of the aims of this study to find out more about the kinds of mechanisms that are necessary to define the properties of potential words in English, and this aim will be achieved primarily by studying large amounts of actual words.

The debate on the status of actual words in morphological theory is a direct reflection of the controversy on the nature of the lexicon and its role in the grammar. I will not attempt to review the numerous approaches that can be found in the literature but will only give a very much simplified version of some of the issues pertinent to our discussion.

In syntactic approaches to morphology there is a tendency to see the lexicon "like a prison - it contains only the lawless" (Di Sciullo and Williams 1987:3)[8], i.e. only simplex words, roots and affixes (e.g. Lieber 1981, 1992). What non-syntactic morphological theories have in common is that they assign morphological processes either to a separate component, or see them as part of the lexicon. Their concept of the lexicon may, however, be very similar to the one just mentioned. For example, in a lexicon à la Kiparsky (1982), only simplex words, roots, and affixes have a place, but no regular complex words. Others (e.g. Jackendoff 1975, Aronoff 1976, Booij 1977) assume that both simplex and complex words, regular and idiosyncratic, can be listed in the lexicon together with redundancy rules that relate them to one another.[9]

---

[7]   See also Aronoff (1976:18) for a similar argument, and some of the discussion in chapters 6 and 7 below.

[8]   Note that Di Sciullo and Williams (1987) do not argue for a purely syntactic model of morphology but rather take a special kind of lexicalist position.

[9]   See also Segui and Zubizarreta (1985) for a similar discussion.

But why would so many researchers want to bar complex words from being listed in the lexicon? The main reason for excluding these forms from the lexicon seems to be the widely shared assumption that the lexicon should be "minimally redundant" (Kiparsky 1982:25). As already discussed, there is little independent justification for this assumption. Hence, the major argument for a non-redundant lexicon seems to be the elegance and parsimony of the theory itself which proposes this kind of lexicon. This elegance is, however, achieved at the cost of empirical adequacy and, as we will shortly see, under neglect of psycholinguistic evidence.

Many psycholinguistic studies have demonstrated that the economy of storage, i.e. the elimination of redundancy, must be counter-balanced by the economy of processing, i.e. an increase in storage. Simplifying a bit, there are two conflicting models of the processing and storage of morphologically complex forms, full listing and direct access on the one hand (e.g. Butterworth 1983, Manelis and Tharp 1977), and decomposed lexical storage and morphological parsing on the other (e.g. Taft 1985, Taft and Forster 1975). The full listing model claims that all words, complex and simplex, are stored as single units and accessed via the direct retrieval of the whole word. The decomposition model says that all complex words are obligatorily decomposed into their smallest morphological elements. The full listing model rests on the assumption that direct access involves less cognitive costs than parsing. In contrast to that, the decomposition model assumes that storage is more costly than processing. In short, there seems to be an irresolvable conflict between storage and processing in the sense that less storage involves more processing and vice versa. For example, by increasing the storage costs the processing costs can be minimized, since direct look-up may involve less processing than decomposition or parsing. Among others, Frauenfelder and Schreuder (1992) and, most recently, Baayen, Dijkstra and Schreuder (1997) have argued that the conflict of the two models can be resolved by assuming a morphological race model, in which both ways of accessing a complex form in the lexicon are in competition.[10] The winner of the race is determined mainly by the frequency and the phonological and semantic transparency of the word to be accessed:

---

[10]   The so-called Augmented Addressed Morphology model developed in Laudanna and Burani (1985) and Caramazza et al. (1988) is similar to Frauenfelder and Schreuder's in that it also assumes dual routes of access. It differs from the race model in that the decomposition route is only seen as a back-up procedure. A more detailed discussion of these psycholinguistic works is beyond the scope of this study.

"The probability that the parsing route wins the race is highest for transparent low frequency words. ... The direct route will win the race for high frequency word forms and those word forms that are problematic for the parser, for example, opaque word forms containing unproductive affixes." (Frauenfelder and Schreuder 1992:182). Notably, the dual route mechanism implies that complex words can be stored as a whole and not only in a decomposed fashion.

Additional evidence for this view comes from a series of most recent experimental studies by Schreuder and Baayen (1997), Baayen, Lieber and Schreuder (1997), Baayen, Dijkstra, and Schreuder (1997). These authors demonstrate that the processing of a simplex word depends both on the token frequency of complex words containing the word as a stem and - surprisingly - on the number of different complex words (types) that contain the simplex word as a stem. In other words the size of the so-called morphological family co-determines the processing of the base word. Whatever the explanation for these results is, it must be based on the assumption that a non-negligible amount of regular complex words is stored in the lexicon.

To summarize, both psycholinguistic and structural linguistic arguments support a view of the lexicon, according to which regular complex words can also be stored. Hence the distinction between possible and actual words should be upheld and the notion of a non- or minimally redundant lexicon should be rejected. Having thereby illuminated some of the basic ideas on which notions of productivity are based, we may now turn to the explication of what productivity actually is.

2.2. Defining productivity: Qualitative approaches

The following account of the notion of productivity is partly based on the useful summary presented by Rainer (1987), but also includes more recent approaches such as van Marle (1985, 1986), Corbin (1987), Baayen (1989, 1991, 1992), Baayen and Lieber (1991), Baayen and Renouf (1996).

Two major questions will play a role, the first being whether productivity is a quantitative or a qualitative notion, the second whether productivity is a derived property of morphological rules or not. If productivity is of a qualitative nature, a process or affix could be said to either have this property or not. However, it has frequently been argued that productivity is a gradual phenomenon, which means that morphological processes are either more or less productive than others, and that completely unproductive or fully productive processes only mark the end-points of a scale.[11] In this section I will lay out the qualitative concept of productivity. In section 2.3. we will turn to approaches that have attempted to devise quantitative measures of productivity.

The second important problem is whether productivity is a theoretical primitive, i.e. a non-derivable property of word formation rules, or an epiphenomenon, i.e. a property that results from other mechanisms. It is clear, for example, that the productivity of a rule is never unrestricted in the sense that any given word may serve as its base. In particular, there can be phonological, morphological, syntactic, and semantic conditions on possible bases, or on the derivatives themselves, which limit the productivity of the process. In view of such structural restrictions, Paul (1896:704) already pointed out that it is crucial to determine the limits within which affixes are productive.[12] This type of reasoning has led to the frequently uttered postulate that "The degree of productivity of a WF-rule [word formation rule, I.P.] can be seen as inversely proportional to the amount of competence restrictions on that WF-rule" (Booij 1977:5). According to this position, one would only have to define the word formation rule with its proper restrictions and the degree of productivity would naturally fall out. We will turn to this point in detail in the next chapter.

Definitions of productivity can be found in any standard morphology textbook. Bauer, for example, says that a word formation process is productive "if it can be used synchronically in the production of new forms" (Bauer 1983:18). Spencer considers a rule productive if it is "regularly and actively used in the creation of totally new words" (Spencer 1991:49).[13] These more recent definitions can be regarded as reflections of a more sophisticated one proposed earlier by Schultink (1961). Since Schultink's definition incorporates important aspects of the problem and has become

---

[11]   Botha (1968:138) lists the numerous qualifying terms linguists have used to refer to the different degrees of productivity, such as "quasi-", "marginally", "semi-", "fully", "most", "quite", "immensely", and "very productive". As we will see below, the theoretical status as well as the practical utility of these labels for the linguist is doubtful.

[12]   Speaking about suffixes Paul remarks "Es kommt also darauf an, festzustellen, innerhalb welcher Grenzen das Suffix produktiv ist" (Paul 1896:704).

[13]   See also Adams (1973:197), who uses "the epithet 'productive' to describe a pattern, meaning that when occasion demands, the pattern may be used as a model for new items."

something like the classic definition, it will also be used here as a reference point for our discussion. Schultink writes:

> Onder produktiviteit als morfologisch fenomeen verstaan we dan de voor taalgebruikers bestaande mogelijkheid door middel van het morfologisch procédé dat aan de vorm-betekeniscorrespondentie van sommige hun bekende woorden ten grondslag ligt, onopzettelijk een in principe niet telbaar aantal nieuwe formaties te vormen.
>
> (Schultink 1961:113, footnote omitted)

> [Productivity as morphological phenomenon is the possibility which language users have to form an in principle uncountable number of new words unintentionally, by means of a morphological process which is the basis of the form-meaning correspondence of some words they know.]
>
> (Translation by Booij 1977:4)

Schultink's definition captures the important insight that the vocabulary of a language can be expanded in a regular fashion on the basis of already existing lexical elements, but is problematic in several respects. Since these problems are inherent in many qualitative and quantitative definitions of productivity, it is worthwhile discussing them in more detail.

2.2.1. The problem of unintentionality

The first problem concerns Schultink's notion of unintentionality. He claims that one should distinguish between unintentional expansions of the lexical stock by the unconscious implementation of word formation rules on the one hand, and the intentional creation of new words in order to produce a special effect on the other. The former is often referred to as morphological productivity, the latter as morphological creativity. Creatively-formed neologisms are usually perceived by other speakers as somehow remarkable and have often a humorous or repulsive effect, whereas truly productive neologisms are typically not noticed as such by the speakers. This distinction between intentional and unintentional creations is still considered crucial by more recent authors who claim that coinages on the basis of productive patterns go unnoticed, whereas those on the basis of unproductive patterns always draw attention to themselves (e.g. Baayen and Lieber 1991:808, Lieber 1992:3). Thus, if the unproductive deadjectival nominalizing English suffix -*th* (as in *depth*) were attached to an adjective not belonging to the established set of bases that take this suffix (such as *broad, deep, long* etc.), this would certainly not go unnoticed (cf. *steepth/*stepth), whereas new words in -*ness* are typically not recognized as new formations. These considerations are corroborated by the findings in Aronoff (1983) which we already discussed above: with truly productive formations speakers often cannot tell whether the form is a neologism or not.

There are, however, two serious counterarguments against the necessity of the 'unintentional' criterion. First of all, the notion of unintentionality is notoriously vague. Some speakers have a higher level of awareness of the manipulation of linguistic signs than others, i.e. what goes unnoticed by one speaker may strike the next as unusual. It is hard to see how this criterion could be operationalized.

But, for the sake of the argument, let us leave aside these doubts and take some notion of 'unintentional' as given. Even under this assumption the criterion is not a necessary one, because even productive rules can be applied intentionally. For example, many of the -*ize* neologisms listed in the *OED* and discussed in detail in chapter 6 below can be assumed to be intentional creations, because they are very often coined to designate new concepts in science, which is often done purposefully and with some consideration. Nevertheless, these words should be regarded as productive formations and not incidents of morphological creativity in the above sense because they are in perfect harmony with the semantic and phonological specifications of -*ize* derivatives.[14] The same reasoning would hold for the word *crucialness*, which I consciously and intentionally invented a minute ago, and which is nevertheless undoubtedly a productively formed derivative. Some readers would have noticed the novel character of this word in a text, others would have not.

Given these considerations, I do not take unintentionality to be a necessary characteristic of productive processes, although it may be pertinent in many instances of productive formations.

---

[14]   Neuhaus (1971:158) evokes a similar argument against intentionality with regard to the rise of the suffix -*ite* in the 19th century which "was used systematically in the expansion of scientific terminology, for example in mineralogy and chemistry. Hence, productivity can be the result of planning and need not follow a general tendency in a more or less unconscious fashion." (my translation, I. P.)

2.2.2.   The problem of uncountability

The second problem concerns the criterion of uncountability. Schultink assumes that productive rules give rise to an in principle uncountable number of forms whereas unproductive rules can only yield a fixed, countable, and presumably small number of derivatives (cf. also Lieber 1992:3-4). Again, Schultink's points can be illustrated with the two de-adjectival nominalizing suffixes *-th* and *-ness* in English. The unproductive suffix *-th* only attaches to a limited number of bases,[15] whereas *-ness* can practically occur with any adjective of the English language. Since the number of adjectives is, in principle, infinite, so is the number of possible *-ness* derivatives. With such examples, uncountability seems a clear criterion to distinguish productive and unproductive processes. There are, however, some less clear cases conceivable. Imagine a productive rule that is restricted in such a way that there is a definite limit to the number of potential bases, and therefore to the number of possible derivatives. For example, a suffix may attach productively to words of a certain prosodic make-up, and the number of such words is limited (e.g. because the stress rules of the language no longer permit words of the required make-up). Or, consider the case of *-ment* which is productive with bases that contain the prefixes *en-* or *em-* (henceforth *eN-*).[16] Since this prefix is no longer productive, the number of possible *-ment* forms on the bases of these forms is also limited. If the criterion of uncountabillity is upheld, the attachment of *-ment* to such bases must be considered unproductive. This result is, however, undesired since, in view of the fact that all bases of the pertinent kind can potentially take *-ment*, one would want to classify this process as fully productive.

Scrutinizing the hedge "in principle" in the above definition may shed some more light on this problem. Given a rule like *-ness* suffixation it seems that all adjectives may undergo this rule.[17] Although the number of

---

[15]   See Bauer (1988:59-60) for an exhaustive list of lexemes involving the suffix *-th*.

[16]   See chapter 4.3.1.1. below for a thorough discussion of the interaction of *-ment* and *eN-*.

[17]   To my knowledge, no one has ever proposed a rule-specific restriction on *-ness* that goes beyond the specification that the base words are mostly adjectives. The majority of reseachers stress the fact that, in the words of T. Williams, it "is found in abundance in all linguistic environments" (1965:283).

adjectives an individual speaker knows at a given point in time may be countable, it is in principle unlimited because it is an open class to which new items can easily be added, for example by derivation or borrowing. If the class of possible input words is open, so must be the class of possible derivatives of productive rules. This is the essence of Schultink's reasoning. But what about apparently closed classes of possible bases? According to Schultink, word formation rules making reference to closed classes would be unproductive by definition. Under an alternative view, such a rule would be nevertheless considered productive if all members of the class, and hypothetical new members, could undergo the rule, and provided that the class can be defined intensionally. The latter is possible with the class of *eN-* prefixed verbs, but crucially not with the bases of processes that are lexically governed, such as *-th* nominalization of adjectives.

Let us look again at our example of *eN-* prefixed verbs and *-ment* nominalizations. If the rule were really productive, we would predict that, if there were new possible base verbs in *eN-*, which is of course highly unlikely due to the rule's non-productivity, these base words could take *-ment* as their nominalizing suffix. Fortunately, this prediction can be tested since, in spite of the general non-productivity of *eN-* there are six 20th century neologisms with this prefix attested in the *OED*, all of them apparently creative or analogical formations. For two of these, *endistance* and *embrittle*, nominalizations in *-ment* are also attested, and it seems that the other four derivatives (*encode, envision, emplane, enhat*) could also lend themselves to *-ment* suffixation. What this shows is that the rule of *-ment* attachment is productive with an intensionally defined class of base words inspite of the fact that this class cannot increase indefinitely. However, in principle an uncountable number of productively formed *-ment* derivatives could be created. Seen from this angle, the criterion of uncountability becomes entirely vacuous, because *uncountability in principle* follows automatically from the general potential to create words on the basis of existing patterns. If a rule has this property, the number of possible derivatives is always, *in principle*, uncountable, but crucially only in principle. To summarize, Schultink's criterion of uncountability can be disposed of because this property falls out automatically from other aspects of the definition of productivity.

2.2.3.   *Rules and analogies*

The most problematic point concerning current qualitative definitions of productivity is probably the notion of word formation rule itself, dubbed by Schultink as "a morphological process which is the basis of the form-meaning correspondence of some words they know" (1961:113, see above). The crucial question is on which grounds one can assume the existence of such a morphological process. It seems that Schultink's definition is very liberal because it includes both rule-based and analogical formations, which, in standard generative treatments are considered to be two different things. Thus, form-meaning correspondences of individual items are the basis for all kinds of ad-hoc analogies, although one would not want to consider such processes productive. What Schultink probably means is not just any kind of analogical formation but a regular, predictable process which operates in a non-arbitrary manner on a more or less well-defined set of possible input words.

Let us consider the difference between rules and analogies in more detail, a difference that is not always obvious. For example Becker (1990) has argued for the extension of the notion of analogy even to productive processes by largely equating the notion of rule with the notion of analogy. In my view this has the considerable disadvantage that it is left unexplained why some analogies are never made, but others are frequently observed.[18]

Becker acknowledges the existence of this problem, but claims that the only difference between analogies and rules is their productivity. Having stated that it is generally and correctly assumed that analogy works on the basis of existing words, Becker (1993a:189-191) argues that it cannot be correct that existing words play only a role as a model for analogy when they are few, but play no role at all when they are many, as is the case with highly productive rules. Rules must be acquired on the basis of existing words, and are therefore best seen as the "trivial default case of analogical formations" (1993a:190, my translation). According to this view, the only remaining difference between the traditional generative word formation rule and analogy would then be a quantitative difference: rules yield more forms than analogies. Becker therefore argues for the equation of rules and analogy, which makes the notion of rule redundant because everything can be taken care of by the proportional formula of analogy (see also Becker 1993b).

---

[18]   See also Bauer (1993) for discussion.

Although this argumentation for a purely gradual notion of productivity and the elimination of the concept of rule may be attractive because it would considerably streamline morphological theory, it has a number of pitfalls that lead me to reject a purely analogical model of morphology.

The first pitfall concerns the notion of rule, as used by Becker and by the generative morphologists he attacks. It is crucial to distinguish two entirely different senses of the word *rule*. One is more or less synonymous with *regularity* and expresses a descriptive generalization. The other sense of rule, and this is the sense standardly used in generative studies, is roughly equivalent to a procedural operation, technically known as a re-write rule. With respect to morphology, rule-based models assume that new words are formed by carrying out a certain manipulation on a given input, yielding a certain, more or less well-specified output. It is this concept of 'rule' as a procedural or derivational device Becker's critique aims at.

However, throughout their history, such procedural-derivational models have been criticised on empirical and theoretical grounds, and recent developments in phonology, morphology, and syntax have shown that representational or declarative models have a number of important advantages over traditional derivational ones. Such models do not transform underlying input strings into surface representations by subjecting them to an ordered set of manipulating procedures (as, for example, in *SPE*), but make crucial use of representations and conditions that constrain the form of such representations. Examples of the latter models are Optimality Theory in phonology and morphology (Prince and Smolensky 1993), and unification-based phonological and syntactic theories, such as Declarative Phonology (Coleman 1998), Head-Driven Phrase Structure Grammar (Pollard and Sag 1984, Pollard and Sag 1994), Lexical Functional Grammar (Kaplan and Bresnan 1982). In such frameworks, the idea of rule is that of a regularity, not of an operation. The present book will explore further the capacity of representational models for the description of morphological processes, and substantiate the superiority of output conditions over traditional derivational rules.

Coming back to analogy, I cannot see how such output constraints could be implemented in an analogical model, since they do not work on an item-by-item basis, but entail significant generalizations across large numbers of forms. Once the concept of rule as an operation is abandoned, however,

Becker's arguments have lost their target because the equation of rule and analogy is, if at all, only possible if rules are conceived as operations.[19]

The second serious drawback of the analogical model is that it fails to make strong predictions about possible and impossible forms. Acknowledging this fact, Becker is forced to make this vice into a virtue by claiming that morphologists cannot make correct predictions about the well-formedness of complex words anyway (1993a:190-191). In support of this claim he argues that acceptability judgments are the only way to tap the distinction between possible and impossible words and raises some well-known objections against such judgments as an analytical tool. In particular, he points out that acceptability is a gradual phenomenon, judgments are often variable across subjects, and even individual subjects are not consistent in their rejection or acceptance of forms. Furthermore, judgments are often dependent on the context or can be influenced by repetition. Although these are interesting considerations, recent work on this methodological issue has convincingly shown that these methodological difficulties can be overcome by a careful planning of the experimental design (see, for example, Bard et al. 1996, Schütze 1996, Cowart 1997).[20] Furthermore, predictions about the well-formedness can not only be gleaned from acceptability judgments but also from a careful investigation of the regularities of attested formations, as I will show in great detail in chapters 4, 6, 7 and 8. Thus even without acceptability judgments one can arrive at rather precise predictions about possible and impossible words, provided that one has discovered the correct regularities and restrictions of the process under discussion.

The third problem with Becker's argumentation is that he obviously assumes that his analogical model is incompatible with generative morphology. I don't see why this should be the case. It is of course true that traditional generative approaches have said very little about analogical forma-

---

[19]   Note that throughout this book I use the terms 'word formation rule' or 'morphological process' in a loose sense, i.e. without committing myself to a derivational or a representational interpretation, or to a specific notion of word formation rule (such as, for example, Aronoff's 1976). This is also the reason why lower-case letters are used.

[20]   For example, the fact that acceptability is a gradual phenomenon does not speak against the use of acceptability judgments as such. What is important is not *absolute* acceptance versus *absolute* rejection, but rather *significant differences* in the acceptance of forms. The view that there are no perfect, but only best candidate forms is one of the crucial insights of Optimality Theory. It seems that Becker puts up a strawman to argue against.

tions, but the reason for this lies primarily in the unpredictability of analogy, and not in the denial of their status as morphological formations or in the general impossibility of incorporating analogy into the generative enterprise, as Becker implies. In my view, any competence theory of word formation must certainly include some account of analogical formations, and I don't see any principled argument that would prohibit analyses of the kind Becker proposes for certain paradigmatically motivated processes from being included into such models. This does not mean, however, that the whole model must be analogical in nature.

Finally, there is also psycholinguistic evidence against purely analogical models. Skousen (1989, 1992, 1995), Chandler (1993), and Derwing and Skousen (1989, 1994) have presented an analogical single-system approach to morphology in the same spirit as that of Becker (1990). With respect to regular English past tense formation, for example, they argue that speakers add -ed to nonce words not on the basis of a rule but on the basis of an online analogical mechanism. However, recent psycholinguistic studies of regular and irregular inflection such as Marcus et al. (1995) and Jaeger et al. (1996) have presented strong evidence against "single-system theories [such as Skousen's, I.P.] which hypothesize that both regular and irregular past tense forms are computed by the same mechanism" (Jaeger et al. 1996:488). Although it is not quite clear in detail how these results carry over to derivational formations, they nevertheless seriously weaken the analogical case, especially since the analogical model claims that both derivation and inflection are handled by the same mechanism.[21]

I therefore maintain that analogical formations should be distinguished from instantiations of productive word formation rules. The discussion in chapters 6, 7 and 8 will show that analogical formations nevertheless play a role in certain areas of morphology. Analogical relationships are necessarily paradigmatic in nature, whereas the functioning of word formation rules must often be described as essentially syntagmatic in nature.[22] This will

---

[21]   For a more detailed critique of Skousen's mathematical definition of analogy see Baayen (1995), who compares Skousen's model with general statistical techniques of data classification, thereby showing that purely analogical mechanisms make incorrect predictions.

[22]   Note that I am not making any claim about the psycholinguistic reality of the distinction between rule and analogy. For example, I can in principle imagine a speaker creating a new word in -ize by local analogy with an existing word with that suffix. But this does not imply that there is no word formation rule for -ize words, but only that it was not accessed in this particular instance.

become evident in chapter 6.1., where it is argued that the meaning of the derivative depends on the interaction of the meaning of the base with the templatic meaning of *-ize* derivatives. This interaction is syntagmatic and not paradigmatic in nature.

The postulation of a word formation rule is ultimately an empirical problem which can only be solved by finding evidence for regular form-meaning correspondences across a reasonably large set of complex words. But even if we have found significant generalizations that give evidence of the existence of a word formation rule, this does not yet tell us anything about the possibility to form new words on the basis of this rule or condition. Thus, in the case of the verbalizing suffix *-en* the semantic and phonological regularities among the words with this suffix are certainly sufficient to postulate a word formation rule. The meaning of *-en* derivatives is sufficiently uniform ('make X'), and the morphosyntactic restrictions on possible bases are also quite clear (*-en* attaches to monosyllabic adjectives that end in an obstruent, especially /t/ and /d/, cf. e.g. Marchand 1969:72, Halle 1973:13). However, this rule is generally regarded as unproductive in modern English (see e.g. Szymanek 1980:416, or chapters 5 and 7.3. below). The nominalizing suffix *-th* is also a case in point. Although there are clear correspondences between meaning and form, the rules are unproductive (cf. e.g. *deep - depth*, but *steep - *stepth*). Such generalizations across existing words are generally referred to as 'redundancy rules' (Jackendoff 1975, Aronoff 1976) or 'via rules' (Vennemann 1972), whose function is to relate morphologically complex words in the lexicon to words with a similar morphological/phonological make-up.[23]

Another, more problematic, example of a redundancy rule is the above-mentioned verb-forming prefix *eN-*. It is generally assumed that this prefix is no longer productive in 20th century English, but the *OED* records six

---

[23] Interestingly, in most cases the word will conform to the well-formedness conditions of *-ize* words, so that it is in fact hard to tell whether analogy or some other operation was going on. Only if well-formedness-conditions are violated and strong similarities to particular existing words can be detected is this an indication of the form being created by a psycholinguistic process of analogy. Recent studies of irregular vs. regular inflection (Marcus et al. 1995, Jaeger et al. 1996) have provided new strong evidence for the rule-as-an-operation view for regular inflection. How far these results carry over to productive word formation remains to be seen.

Note that Aronoff (1976:31) reduces the scope of redundancy rules considerably by equating them with his notion of (by definition productive) Word Formation Rule.

new formations in this period. Is there a word formation rule for *eN-* pre-fixation, and is it really unproductive? A reasonable answer to this question would be that there is such a (redundancy) rule, and that the small number of neologisms indicates that these are analogical formations, especially since there seem to be no severe structural restrictions that would limit the number of forms that could undergo *eN-* prefixation, so that one would expect to find many more new derivatives. For instance, the productive verbalizing suffix *-ize* leads to more than 300 20th century neologisms in the *OED*. Discussing such quantitative findings takes us to the second set of major approaches to productivity, probabilistic ones.

Before we turn to a discussion of these let us briefly summarize our remarks on productivity as a qualitative notion. Having scrutinized the different criteria put forward in standard definitions of productivity, it can be stated that this notion boils down to the property of a given word formation process or affix to be used to derive a new word in a systematic fashion. Attempts to further qualify this potential by positing criteria like uncountability or unintentionality have turned out to be misguided. Furthermore, the equation of word formation rules with analogy was rejected and the distinction was introduced between redundancy rules and productive rules.

2.3. Defining productivity: Quantitative approaches

Proposing a dichotomy between quantitative and qualitative notions of productivity may blur the fact that the two are closely related. Thus the idea of potentiality, which is central to qualitative definitions of productivity, can be expressed in the statistical terms of probability. If something *can* happen, it should be possible to quantify the probability of its occurrence. This is the essential insight behind Bolinger's definition of productivity as "the statistical readiness with which an element enters into new combinations" (1948:18). Since the formulation of this insight about half a century ago, a number of productivity measures have been proposed.

There is one quantitative definition that is probably the most widely used and the most widely rejected at the same time. This definition says that the productivity of an affix can be measured by counting the number of attested types with that affix at a given point in time. No linguist would seriously advocate this view of productivity as a single measure because it goes against the crucial idea of productivity as "a design feature of language" (Bauer 1994:3354). Thus there can be many words with a given affix, but nevertheless speakers will not use the suffix very often to make up new words. As mentioned above, language is a system which speakers can use creatively to produce and understand new words and sentences. Reference to existing, lexicalized words cannot shed any light on this central capacity of language. Nevertheless, in many publications 'productivity' is used with reference to the number of existing words, possibly only for lack of a better term. We will shortly see that, together with other measures, the number of attested derivatives can still be of interest to the morphologist.

Lieber (1980:177ff) suggests that the productivity of an affix should be equated with the number of forms that could potentially be derived with that suffix, which in turn is a function of the number of words that can undergo the process. This definition is problematic because in her own theory there is no place for actual words. Consider, for example, the case of nominalizing *-ity*, which is extremely productive with bases in *-able*. In Lieber's framework, however, *-ity* must be considered to be rather unproductive, because the number of potential base words in *-able* does not count for the determination of the productivity of *-ity* because there is only the lexical entry for *-able*, so that the suffix *-able* counts as much for the productivity of *-ity* as any individual base word.

This counterintuitive result is avoided by definitions that make reference to actual words. For example, Aronoff (1976) suggests a productivity index which is the ratio of actual to possible words. The higher this ratio, the higher the productivity of a given rule. Largely ignored by later authors, this measure had already been proposed earlier by Berschin, who labels it "Besetzungsgrad" ('degree of exhaustion', 1971:44-45). Anshen and Aronoff (1981:64) point out the main weakness of this proposal: for extremely productive and for completely unproductive processes it makes wrong predictions. Thus, with highly productive affixes like *-ness* the number of possible words is, in principle, infinite, which necessarily leads to a comparatively low productivity index. With unproductive rules like *-th* nominalization it is unclear how the ratio of actual to possible words should be calculated. If one considers all actual words with this suffix as possible words, the ratio equals 1, which is the highest possible score and therefore counterintuitive. If, however, the number of possible words with this suffix is considered zero, the index cannot be computed at all.

Another, more general problem of Lieber's, Berschin's and Aronoff's proposals is how to actually count the number of possible words, since, as we have discussed above, the number of possible formations on the basis of a productive rule is, in principle, uncountable. How can one quantify something that is, in principle, uncountable?

A partial solution to this problem is provided by Baayen (1989, 1992, 1993), who proposes the reverse of Aronoff's productivity index, and calls this the 'potentiality' of a given rule. This potentiality measure I is the quotient of the number of possible forms S and the number of actual forms V with a given affix in a sufficiently large corpus of text. Using certain statistical models, the number of potential forms with a given affix can be estimated on the basis of the grouped frequency distributions of the forms attested in the corpus.[24]

Although this potentiality measure seems to capture an important property of morphological rules, it has the serious drawback that all truly productive processes should have infinite S. This is, however, not the case. For example, Baayen (1992:121) finds that some productive processes (e.g. agentive *-er* and diminutive *-tje* in Dutch) have infinite values of S, whereas other productive processes (such as the Dutch abstract noun forming suffixes *-sel* or *-heid*) have finite values. From these results Baayen concludes that I should be regarded not as a measure of productivity as such but as a measure of the degree of exhaustion of a productive process and emphasizes the fact that this 'pragmatic potentiality' is codetermined by various pragmatic and conceptual factors.[25]

Strictly speaking, the approaches mentioned so far do not provide probability measures but only quantifications. Let us turn to probabilistic models proper. The crucial problem with probabilistic notions of any kind is to determine an adequate sample on which the computation of probability can be based. Harris rephrases Bolinger's definition by making reference to this notion:

> A question of some interest is that of productivity of some elements: i.e. *given an extremely large sample*, with elements of classes A, B, C, etc., occurring with various members X_1, X_2, etc. of class X, which elements out of A, B, C have a high probability of occurring with any new member X_n, of X, and which elements out of A, B, C, etc. do not?

---

[24]   The relevant statistical models include Zipf's law, and the extended Yule-Simon law. An examination of the intricacies of these models is not necessary for our purposes. The interested reader is referred to Baayen (1989, 1992) for discussion.

[25]   That extra-linguistic factors may influence the degree of exhaustion of a rule has been frequently pointed out in the literature. Adams, for example, includes the phrase "when occasion demands" (1973:197) in her definition of productivity cited in note 13 above. See chapter 3.1. for more discussion.

Those elements which have a high probability of occurring with any new X_n are called productive in respect to X.

(Harris 1960:374f, emphasis added)

The largest sample one can possibly imagine is the entirety of utterances (oral and written) in a language in a given period of time. On the basis of this sample, one could define productivity as the number of new formations in the given period, as done, for example, by Neuhaus (1973:308), who proposes the use of diachronic dictionaries such as the *SOED* or the *OED* for quantification and data collection.[26] Neuhaus does not hesitate to point out that this kind of quantification presupposes the reliability of the dictionaries used, a problematic assumption to begin with. In Neuhaus (1971:140ff) some of the problems in the use of dictionary data are discussed, but the most outspoken criticism of this methodology can be found in Baayen and Renouf (1996), who take objection to dictionary-based approaches to productivity and make a case for the versatility of large text corpora instead. In the following, I will outline this corpus-based approach to productivity in considerable detail and return to the problem of dictionary data in chapter 5, where both dictionary-based and corpus-based approaches will be used and tested in quantifying the productivity of verb-deriving processes in English.

Baayen and some of his co-workers (Baayen 1989, Baayen 1992, Baayen 1993, Chitashvili and Baayen 1993, Baayen and Lieber 1991, Baayen and Renouf 1996) have developed text-corpus-based statistical measures of productivity, which has the advantage that the researcher need not depend on the perhaps insufficient recording of words by dictionary makers. Instead, such measures rely on the existence of more or less representative and sufficiently large samples of computerized texts. What counts as sufficiently large cannot be determined exactly, but it seems that even relatively small corpora like the Dutch Eindhoven Corpus (600,000 words of written text) can yield interesting results (Baayen 1992, 1993). For English, available computerized corpora such as Cobuild (originally c. 18 million words,

---

[26]   Neuhaus (1971:154-156, 1973:309-317) suggests yet another related measure, namely the proportion of new derivatives of a given type among all lexical innovations in the given period. Since the latter number is constant for all derivational patterns of that period this measure is only a notational variant of the number of new types in that period. In a diachronic perspective, the measure is nevertheless interesting because it shows the increase in the use of a certain process in relation to the overall growth of the vocabulary.

now having been turned into the ever-increasing so-called Bank of English), or the British National Corpus (c. 100 million words), can certainly be considered large enough.

Apart from the notion of 'pragmatic potentiality/degree of exhaustion' already discussed above, two central productivity measures are proposed in the said studies, namely 'productivity in the narrow sense (P)', and 'global productivity $(P*)$'.

Given a suitable text corpus, the productivity in the narrow sense P of a morphological process is defined by Baayen and his co-workers as the quotient of the number of hapax legomena n_1 with a given affix and the total number of tokens N of all words with that affix.

(1) $P = n_1 / N$

Baayen and Lieber (1991:809-810) explain the idea behind P as follows. "Broadly speaking, P expresses the rate at which new types are to be expected to appear when N tokens have been sampled. In other words, P estimates the probability of coming across new, unobserved types, given that the size of the sample of relevant observed types equals N."

P makes crucial reference to the notion of 'hapax legomena' (or 'hapaxes' for short), which are words that occur only once in the corpus. But why should hapaxes, i.e. the new, unobserved types, tell us anything about productivity? After all, the new, unobserved types could only be rare words, and not neologisms.

In a sufficiently large corpus, the number of hapaxes in general approximates half the observed vocabulary size (e.g. Zipf 1935). Chitashvili and Baayen (1993:57) call this kind of distribution 'Large Number of Rare Events' distribution. They show that the frequency spectrum of whole texts closely resembles the frequency spectrum of productive morphological categories, and that productive morphological categories play a crucial role in anchoring a text in the Large Number of Rare Events zone (Chitashvili and Baayen 1993:126-132). Unproductive morphological categories show a completely different frequency distribution (cf. Chitashvili and Baayen 1993: 80-86, 125-126 for the difference between productive nominal *-ness* and unproductive verbal *en-*). The crucial assumption now is that the number of hapaxes of a given morphological category correlates with the number of neologisms of that category, so that hapaxes can be seen as some kind of indicator of productivity. Let us look at this assumption in more detail.

Baayen and Renouf (1996) try to illustrate the correlation between the number of neologisms and the number of hapaxes by checking whether the hapaxes are listed in a reasonably large dictionary, choosing *Webster's Third* as a frame of reference. Given the size of their text corpus (c. 80,000,000 words), they expect a large number of words in the corpus not to be listed in this dictionary. Furthermore, they expect that the proportion of non-listed words is highest among the hapaxes, which would substantiate the assumption that the number of hapaxes in a corpus reflects the number of neologisms. These expectations are born out by the facts. With *-ness* and *-ity*, for example, about half of the hapax legomena are not listed in *Webster's Third*, a proportion that significantly decreases with words occurring 2, 3, 4, and 5 times in the corpus (Baayen and Renouf 1996:76). In other words, the fewer tokens of a given type are attested, the more likely it is that the type is a neologism.

The validity of this comparison of hapaxes with *Webster's Third* might, however, be called into question. First of all, it is unclear whether one can rely on a dictionary like *Webster's Third* as a frame of reference for the novelty of a given word. *Webster's Third* does not aim at complete coverage (unlike the *OED*), nor is it clear on which basis items are selected for inclusion into the dictionary. To the contrary, the inclusion of an item into any dictionary must necessarily be arbitrary to a greater or lesser extent, so that the entries in a desk dictionary like *Webster's Third* can hardly be regarded as a representative sample. Combining both dictionary and corpus data in a statistical study is therefore "somewhat unfortunate", as Baayen and Renouf admit themselves (1996:77), especially since there is no common sampling scheme for the dictionary-based and corpus-based counts. Hence, Baayen and Renouf focus on lexical innovation with reference to hapax legomena.

But even if one does not believe in the reliability of these comparisons of hapaxes with dictionary entries, there are strong psycholinguistic arguments for the assumption that the proportion of neologisms among attested types increases with decreasing type frequency. As already mentioned above, high-frequency words are more likely to be stored in the mental lexicon than are low-frequency words (Rubenstein and Pollack 1963, Scarborough et al. 1977, Whaley 1978). Baayen and Renouf write that

If a word-formation pattern is unproductive, no rule is available for the perception and production of novel forms. All existing forms will depend on storage in the mental lexicon. Thus, unproductive morphological categories will be characterized by a preponderance of high-frequency types, by low numbers of low-frequency types, and by very few, if any, hapax legomena, especially as the size of the corpus increases. Conversely the availability of a productive word-formation rule for a given affix in the mental lexicon guarantees that even the lowest frequency complex words with that affix can be produced and understood. Thus large numbers of hapax legomena are a sure sign that an affix is productive.

(Baayen and Renouf 1996:74)

Having established the versatility of the use of hapaxes for productivity studies, let us turn to another problem of P, which lies in the determination of the condition "with a given affix".

For the calculation of P (and the other measures) it is necessary to count all words with a given affix in the corpus. This looks like a rather straight-forward task but in practice this may involve complex decisions, pivoting around two problems. The first is to determine which words can be considered to bear the affix in question, the second is to control for cohort effects in multiple affixation.

Derivatives featuring *-ness*, for example, are relatively easy to sort out because of the low degree of lexicalization. Other affixes, however, have adopted all kinds of idiosyncracies which opacify the relationship between the potential elements. Consider the suffix *-ity* in contrast, which occurs in transparent forms like *opacity* but also in words like *entity, quantity, celebrity*. It is doubtful whether the latter forms should be considered morphologically complex at all (after all, they were most probably borrowed unanalyzed). If not, one should not count them as "words with that affix". However, if one excludes them from the count, one blurs the effect that less transparent processes have more high-frequency types and fewer hapaxes. Thus the exclusion of opaque forms leads to a higher productivity value P than one would probably want to have.

Alternatively, in a very generous count one could define the affix etymologically, so that even the above-mentioned derivatives must be included. In this case it is equally unclear whether this yields a desired effect, since the existence of a potentially large number of old, lexicalized, non-transparent words may blur the productivity of a potential modern process. Of course, it remains to be empirically tested whether the described sampling methods really yield statistically significant differences in their results.

The second problem concerns the sampling of multiply affixed words. Take, for example, the suffix *-ize* in combination with *-able* in a word like *conventionalizable*. Let us suppose this is a hapax legomenon, and let us further suppose that the base verb *conventionalize* is not attested elsewhere in the corpus. Should one count *conventionalizable* also as a hapax belonging to the category of *-ize* derivatives? I am inclined not to do so, since it seems reasonable to partition the lexicon into disjunct classes in order to be able to compare measures across affixes. According to this rationale one should only count the affix that has been attached last, i.e. in the case of our example *conventionalizable* we would assign the word to the class of *-able* only. A minor problem might lurk even here because sometimes it is not clear which affix was 'last' in the case of prefixes and suffixes in one derivative. Leaving this problem aside, a more serious one emerges, that of category-changing inflectional suffixes like *-ing* or *-ed* which can be used to derive adjectives from verbs. It is not clear to me whether these affixes should be ignored, just like other inflectional affixes. Thus a token like 3rd person singular *conventionalizes* certainly counts as a member of the category of *-ize* words. But what about a possible adjective *conventionalized*. Is this a case of a derivational suffix *-ed* or a case of an inflectional (participial) suffix *-ed*? In the first case the token would not be counted under *-ize* but under *-ed*, in the second case the token would be counted under *-ize*, and not under *-ed*.

Unfortunately, these serious methodological problems are nowhere discussed by the above-mentioned authors, so that one does not even get to know on which basis the words were counted and the measures calculated. The reason for this neglect may be partly explained by the authors' potential belief that the affixes dealt with are unproblematic with respect to the questions just raised.[27] Be that as it may, as we will see in more detail in chapter 5, the English verbal suffixes are a case where these methodological problems cannot be neglected.

What this discussion shows is that even 'purely' quantitative approaches cannot do without qualitative decisions. Needless to say, these decisions rest on certain theoretical assumptions that, in turn, presuppose certain concepts of productivity. In particular the decision to exclude opaque forms like *entity* crucially rests on the assumption that it is not a productive formation, but a lexicalized form. Hence by excluding non-productive formations we - to some extent - pre-judge the issue whether *-ity* is productive. The significance of such a pre-judgment may however be reduced

---

[27]   Baayen and Renouf (1996) treat *in-, -ity, -ly, -ness, un-*. Baayen and Lieber (1991) probably largely trusted the parsings done by the CELEX staff.

through the use of complementary measures of productivity. In particular, the exclusion of opaque forms may lead to an increase of productivity in the narrow sense P, but to a decrease of global productivity (see below). In summary, we can say that although the rationale behind P is quite convincing, one has to put up with some methodological problems.

Assuming the versatility of hapaxes for research on productivity, and further assuming that the difficulties of determining relevant tokens and types can be overcome, the productivity of an affix can now be easily calculated and interpreted. A large number of hapaxes leads to a high value of P, thus indicating a productive morphological process. On the other hand, large numbers of high frequency items lead to a high value of N, hence to a decrease of P, indicating low productivity. These results seem to be exactly in accordance with our intuitive notion of productivity, since high frequencies are indicative of the less-productive word-formation processes (Anshen and Aronoff 1988, Baayen and Lieber 1997).

However, van Marle (1992) correctly remarks that sometimes the formula leads counterintuitive results. For example, the productivity measure P for the gender neutral personal noun forming Dutch suffix *-er* ranks 3.5 times higher than that of its marked counterpart of female personal names in *-ster*, a rather unexpected and undesired result.[28] Similarly, the suffix *-erd* receives the highest value of P of all processes investigated (Baayen 1992:123), although its productivity is doubtful. What is most irritable is that the value of P for *-erd* is twice as high as that of nominal compounding (N N), although the latter is normally considered to "exhibit a more or less 'automatic' kind of productivity" (van Marle 1992:154).

In his reaction to van Marle's critique, Baayen (1993) seeks to counterbalance such undesired results by elaborating the second measure of productivity, 'global productivity', which he had originally (Baayen and Lieber 1991, Baayen 1992) introduced as a bi-dimensional measure with the degree of productivity P on the horizontal axis and the extent of use V, i.e. the number of different types with a given affix in the corpus, on the vertical axis. In the case of *-erd* and N-N-compounds, V is extremely low for *-erd* and extremely high for compounds (6 vs. 4277 types in the Dutch Eindhoven Corpus of 600,000 words of written text), which shows that the extent of use is much higher for compounding, which correctly reflects our intuition. For a better illustration of global productivity consider the fol-

---

[28]   See van Marle (1985: chapter 8) for an overview over derived personal nouns in Dutch.

lowing graph for a number of English word-formation processes (see Baayen 1992:124, see also Baayen and Lieber 1991:819). The global productivity is calculated on the basis of the CELEX database.[29] The degree of productivity P is plotted on the abscissa, the extent of use V on the ordinate.

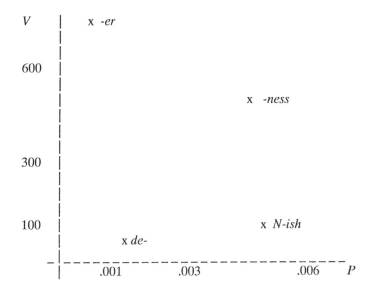

Figure 2.1. Global productivity of some English suffixes (from Baayen 1992:124)

---

[29]   The calculations are not directly based on a text corpus, but on the CELEX lexical data base (Baayen et al. 1993), whose English part is in turn based on the Cobuild corpus. It is important to note that the figures presented in Baayen (1992), and also those in Baayen and Lieber (1991) and Baayen (1993), have turned out to be fundamentally flawed, due to a serious deficiency of the CELEX corpus: many low-frequency items of the Cobuild corpus did not make it into the CELEX data base. Unfortunately, this was unknown to these authors at the time of writing. For some discussion of this, see Baayen and Renouf (1996:92, note 13). Future users of CELEX should be aware that later versions of the CELEX corpus have the same shortcoming. Thus, in my 1994 version of CELEX (version 2.5) I find three hapaxes of *-ize* derivatives, while Baayen and Lieber (1991:822) have only one, I have two *be-* derivatives with verbal bases as against zero in Baayen and Lieber, one *-ify* as against zero, two *de-* as against three, and so forth.
    For simply illustrating the concept of global productivity in figure 2.1. the incorrectness of the CELEX figures can be disregarded.

Figure 2.1. can be interpreted as follows. The suffix *-ness* has a high global productivity whereas *de-* or *-ment* have a rather low global productivity, i.e. *-ness* is both often used and there is a high probability to encounter new formations, whereas *-ment* and *de-* formations are rarely used and less likely to be used to coin a new word. The affix *-er* is often used, but is only rarely employed in new formations, and a suffix like denominal *-ish* is versatile in the creation of new forms but occurs only very rarely in the corpus. But what does this tell us? How can we assess the global productivity of processes when differences between them occur along both dimensions?

Baayen himself points out that global productivity as a bi-dimensional measure has the serious disadvantage that "in general it is unclear how to evaluate the different contributions of *P* and *V* to the global productivity when arbitrary affixes are compared" (1992:123). This has the negative consequence that affixes cannot be ranked on a (mono-dimensional) scale according to their global productivity. In mathematical terms, this deficiency is due to the fact that the function $g(V P)$ is left unspecified, so that *P** cannot be calculated, which makes comparison impossible.

Baayen (1993:192-193) therefore proposes a mathematical function for *P** on the basis of seemingly complicated mathematical operations. The outcome of these operations is, however, not complicated at all. Baayen suggests that the global productivity *P** should be calculated as the quotient of the number of hapaxes with a given affix and the total number of hapaxes of arbitrary constituency in the corpus. Since the latter number is constant for all categorially-determined hapaxes of any kind, the global productivity measure boils down the number of hapaxes with a given affix, already familiar to the reader as an ingredient of our productivity in the narrow sense. Baayen himself seems to be somewhat ashamed of the simplicity of this measure of global productivity, because in his comparative table of *P** for a number of Dutch and English affixes he does not speak of the number of hapaxes with a given affix, although this is what the table shows, but labels the pertinent columns "$P* \cdot h_E$" (Baayen 1993:193), i.e. the product of *P** and the number of all hapaxes in the English corpus. According to his own definition, $P* \cdot h_E$ equals the number of hapaxes with a given affix.

For an evaluation of *P** let us consider some of the figures in more detail. For the English person noun forming suffix *-ee*, for example, the number of hapaxes, and therefore its global productivity *P**, is lowest of all affixes dealt with in Baayen (1993).[30] However, the suffix's productivity in the narrow sense P is rather high, in fact highest of all deverbal noun-forming suffixes in figure one above, since the proportion of hapaxes among all tokens with this suffix is high. How can these contradictory findings be reconciled? Is *-ee* a productive or an unproductive process? Baayen suggests that the two measures should be seen as "complementary measures, the primary use of P being to distinguish between unproductive and productive processes as such, $P*$ being especially suited to ranking productive processes" (1993:194).

The idea that $P*$ should primarily be used for ranking productive suffixes is reasonable since $P*$ can be viewed as a measure for the contribution of a particular morphological category to the expansion of the vocabulary (measured through the number of hapaxes in a corpus). Thus taking all new words, it is certainly interesting to see the extent to which certain processes contribute to the overall vocabulary growth.

The use of P to distinguish between productive and unproductive processes, however, is more problematic since P expresses the probability of encountering new formations of a given type, and as such only provides a continuum of more or less productive processes. Where on this continuum the productive processes end and the unproductive start, remains to be determined (if it can be determined at all).

We are now in a position to summarize and evaluate Baayen's approach to productivity. It should have become clear that, inspite of some remaining methodological problems, the different measures *V, I, P,* and $P*$ have the great advantage that they make certain intuitive aspects of morphological productivity explicit and calculable. In particular, the aspects are

– the number of forms with a given affix ('extent of use' *V* in Baayen's terms),
– the degree of exhaustion ('pragmatic potentiality' *I*),
– the probability of encountering new formations ('productivity in the narrow sense' *P*) and

---

[30]   The affixes mentioned are *-ness* (77 hapaxes), *-ation* (47), *-er* (40), *-ity* (29), *-ment* (9), *-ian* (4), *-ism* (4), *-al* (3), *-ee* (2). Note again, that these figures are flawed to an unknown extent due to the use of CELEX. For the purposes of our discussion the inaccuracy of the figures is not relevant, since the parallel figures for Dutch are correct, and they raise the same questions. This also suggests that the error rate in the CELEX data base is evenly distributed across different affixes.

– the number of new formations in a given corpus or period ('global productivity' $P*$).

The separation and mathematical formalization of these aspects can be
seen as a significant elaboration of Corbin's (1987:177) useful distinction
between three aspects of productivity, namely what she calls profitability,
regularity, and availability.[31]

According to Corbin's definition, a process is 'profitable' if the number of
attested derivatives or potential bases is comparatively high. This is
roughly equivalent to two of Baayen's measures, extent of use and pragmatic potentiality. The advantage of separating these two aspects should
have become obvious during the above discussion.

A process is 'regular' if shape and meaning of the derivatives are highly
predictable. Although the idea of regularity is not directly expressed in
Baayen's mathematical formulae, this property is part of the rationale of the
definition of productivity in the narrow sense. Thus, P allows to register
the effects of (semantic and phonological) transparency, because transparency is negatively correlated with frequency. As discussed in some detail
above, "Categories with less transparent items will, due to this correlation,
show up with more high frequency types" (Baayen 1993:194). Therefore,
less regular processes in Corbin's sense will have more high frequency
types, which in turn lead to a low value of productivity in the narrow sense.

Finally, a process is 'available' if it can be used to create new words. This
notion is encapsulated in Baayen's global productivity and productivity in
the narrow sense.

Although Corbin's trichotomy was a considerable step forward in coming
to grips with the notion of productivity, Corbin did not try to arrive at a
quantitative assessment of productivity in terms of this trichotomy. The
importance of Baayen's work lies in the fact that with his measures the
different aspects of productivity can be brought to light by explicit quantitative operations. Thus, the measures do away with notoriously ill-defined
notions like semi-productivity. Given the advantages of the proposed
measures, it is somewhat surprising that the work of Baayen and his col-
laborators has not yet lead to a proliferation of quantitative studies of productivity, inspite of the easy availability of large text corpora.

---

[31]   The original French terms are "rentabilité", "regularité" and "disponibilité".
The English equivalent terms are taken from Carstairs-McCarthy (1992:37).

In chapter 5 I will implement Baayen's and Neuhaus' productivity measures for a notorious problem of English derivational morphology, viz. verb-deriving processes. Some of the merits and limitations of quantitative approaches to productivity will then become more evident than in this necessarily brief overview.

I will close this chapter with a caveat concerning quantitative approaches to productivity. Although such approaches are useful in many respects, they leave one important question open. Having quantitatively assessed that a process is more productive than another one, the obvious question is, what is the reason for this state of affairs? Which factors are responsible for the relative productivity of a process?

Kastovsky (1986) has argued that there are two aspects of productivity which should be kept apart, the 'scope' and the 'application rate' of a rule. He defines 'scope' as "the degree of semantic specificity of their output and the number and quality of the restrictions that have to be imposed on a given rule" (1986:586), while the 'application rate' is the degree to which speakers make use of a grammatical possibility. Competing terms for this latter notion are 'actuation' (van Marle), or 'probability of application' (Booij 1977:166). It is clear that quantitative measures of productivity can only aim at accurately describing the different aspects of the application rate, and not the scope of a process. Crucially, however, the scope of a rule certainly influences its application rate. The measures are therefore only a more or less accurate statement of the problem and not a solution to it. They constitute the starting point for further, much more interesting investigations into the nature of the mechanisms that restrict morphological processes.

Word formation processes are never totally unrestricted, and even the most productive affixes seem to be subject to certain structural constraints. For example, an affix may only attach to bases of a certain syntactic category or of a specific phonological or morphological make-up. Semantic factors can play a restrictive role, and the fashionableness of an affix is also dependent on extra-linguistic influences. The next chapter will provide a survey of these restrictions and their significance for English derivational morphology.

3. Restrictions on productivity

3.1. Rules and restrictions

One of the central questions concerning productivity is whether the productivity of a given rule can be determined solely on the basis of the properties and restrictions of the rule. In other words, is productivity an epiphenomenon that is the predictable result of other, underlying, phenomena? In this section I will argue that structural restrictions are an important factor influencing productivity, but not the only one.

Let us look again at Booij's justification of the view that productivity is a derived notion, which is repeated here for convenience: "The degree of productivity of a WF-rule [word formation rule, I.P.] can be seen as inversely proportional to the amount of competence restrictions on that WF-rule" (Booij 1977:5). According to this position, one would only have to define the word formation rule with its proper restrictions and the degree of productivity would naturally fall out. Disregarding the non-trivial question how to measure "the amount" of structural restrictions across different derivational processes, it seems that Booij's position is untenable in this strong form.

However, following Booij (1977) and Plank (1981), I maintain that apparent gaps in derivational patterns can in most cases be explained in terms of the structural properties of the process, so that in many cases reference to language use or 'norm' are premature and ill-justified. Therefore, if we talk about the structural properties of a word formation rule, its productivity is crucially dependent on the restrictions imposed on the bases or the derivatives, and therefore an epiphenomenon. This does not mean, though, that one could entirely predict the application rate of a process on the basis of the structural properties. As we will shortly see, the application rate is indeed often governed by extra-linguistic factors. In terms of the individual speaker's behavior, the implementation of a word formation process depends on whether other speakers also use this process to coin new words. In this perspective, the application rate is a property of morphological rules that cannot be derived from linguistic structure, but only from language usage. Hence, we must distinguish between, on the one hand, the *possibility* to apply a process to a given word, which is indeed crucially constrained by structural restrictions and therefore a derived property, and, on the other hand, the use of newly coined derivatives in speech that are licensed as possible words by the restrictions. The following examples illustrate this point.

Let us consider two different cases of unproductive categories, nominal *-th* and verbal *-en*. In principle, only intensionally defined categories can be productive, but not extensionally defined ones. Hence lexically-governed rules like English nominal *-th* (as in *length*) or *-al* (as in *arrival*) suffixation are unproductive. But even intensionally-defined categories may be unproductive, as is the case with English verbal *-en*. Thus, although *-en* suffixation is a well-defined process in terms of its morphological, semantic, and phonological properties, it is practically dead. This example nicely demonstrates that the non-applicability of a process cannot be inferred on the basis of structural knowledge, and that therefore a statement like Booij's needs further qualification.

If the application rate cannot be inferred from the structural properties of the rule, how do speakers (come to) know that some intensionally-defined categories can be used to coin new lexical items whereas others cannot? To my knowledge, this question has not been addressed systematically by anyone working on productivity. I will therefore venture some hypotheses here.

As was pointed out in the previous chapter, productive processes are semantically (and phonologically) transparent and have a high proportion of low frequency types. Psycholinguistic experiments using subjective frequency ratings such as Schreuder and Baayen (1997), Baayen (1997) have shown that, quite surprisingly, speakers have robust knowledge about the frequency of lexical items, which means that speakers are able to glean from their linguistic environment information about the application rate of a given morphological process. If a process does not meet the criteria of transparency and high quantity of low-frequency items, the speaker infers that this process cannot be used to coin new words. This kind of mechanism can also explain the decline of even those morphological categories that are (still) transparent. If, for some reason, the number of transparent low-frequency items in the environment drops, this is an indication for the speaker that the process has become less productive.[1] In this case the speaker may prefer other means of expression, such as rival morphological processes or syntactic constructions.

---

[1]   One reason could be that, for example, the number of possible bases has decreased. In the case of *-en*, for example, the number of monosyllabic adjectives is not infinite, so that, after the majority has undergone the process, new formations are increasingly rare.

In any case, what has been labeled 'application rate' is also an inherent and changeable property of morphological processes, and a property which cannot be completely derived from the structural properties of the processes, but which depends also on pragmatic factors.

Perhaps the most obvious of these factors is fashion.[2] The rise and fall of affixes like *mini-* or *-nik* is an example of the result of extra-linguistic developments in society that make certain words or morphological elements desirable to use, and not the consequence of structural mechanisms (although these are operative in constraining the shape of these words). Ruf (1996), for example, finds a remarkable increase in the use of the German augmentative loan prefixes *Mega-, Giga-* and *Supra-* in a very short time span, a fact that cannot be explained satisfactorily by structural factors, since these affixes seem to be no more structurally constrained than some of their augmentative competitors. But even in these cases structural factors should not be neglected, because on closer inspection the many rival augmentative prefixes are not completely identical in their semantic and phonological properties, which in turn influences their applicability. Thus, the most productive ones seem to be the ones that are also semantically least restricted.

Another general pragmatic constraint is that there must be a need for a new form. This need is a reflection of two main functions new words can have, their capacity of labeling a new concept or referent, and the condensation of information, for example for stylistic purposes or reasons of text cohesion. Kastovsky (1986) calls this latter function 'recategorization' because very often the syntactic recategorization of a word, e.g. the nominalization of an adjective, serves exactly this purpose. The example in (1) is a case in point:

(1)   ... and whether your own conversation doesn't sound a little *potty*. It's the *pottyness*, you know, that's so awful.

(Kastovsky's example 1986:595)

With respect to the relation of these functions to productivity, Kastovsky claims that the recategorization function is the most frequent in speech, so that processes serving this function tend to have a high application rate. Another function (not discussed by Kastovsky) is especially prominent with evaluative affixes, the attitudinal function. By attaching, say, a di-

---

2   Cf. the title of Algeo (1971): "The voguish uses of *non-*".

minutive suffix to a name, the speakers primarily express their attitude, and do not aim at labeling a new concept or making the discourse more coherent (see below for more discussion of diminutives). Interestingly, diminutive affixes are not category-changing, which could be interpreted as the direct consequence of the lack of the other two functions (concept formation and information condensation).

Another pragmatic restriction on productivity is discussed in Lipka (1977), who introduces the concept of hypostatization, which basically says that the existence of a word suggests the existence of an entity to which it refers or which it denotes. Hence, one can only label something that does exist (in a wide sense, allowing also for fictional existence), and any new derivative must have some kind of referent or denotatum. The crucial problem with this constraint is, however, that it does not really constrain anything, since, as Lipka points out, speakers may 'create' a referent by forming a new derivative. This phenomenon is also known as reification and can be observed on a daily basis in political discourse.

Another non-structural requirement new lexemes must meet is that they denote something nameable. Although the nameability requirement is rather ill-defined, it captures a significant insight: the concepts encoded by derivational categories are rather simple and general and may not be highly specific or complex, as illustrated in the famous example of an unlikely denominal verb forming category given by Rose (1973:516): "grasp NOUN in the left hand and shake vigorously while standing on the right foot in a 2.5 gallon galvanized pail of corn-meal-mush". An operationalized definition of the nameability requirement remains to be devised.

Language purists may also show evidence of a pragmatic restriction referred to as neophobia, a notion whose content and theoretical status is utterly obscure. An equally vague notion is euphony, which, as we will see in chapters 6 and 7, should be replaced by explicit accounts of the phonological restrictions at work. In other words, euphony is the result of structural, and not of pragmatic restrictions.

Given the rather unspecific and ill-defined nature of most of the pragmatic restrictions proposed in the literature, it seems that a lot remains to be done to pin down these factors in a more explicit manner. I will, however, not engage in this enterprise, but turn instead to structural restrictions, which are central to the discussion in the rest of this book. The following general considerations are responsible for choosing this focus. No matter which determinants govern the application rate of a rule, it seems that we cannot arrive at significant insights into the role of aspects of language use in morphology without determining which structural constraints operate on that rule. This position is most radically formulated (again) in Booij (1977:6), who states that "we cannot say anything specific about the role of performance factors before we have investigated which competence factors restrict the productivity of a rule". In other words, we should first aim at describing the class of possible derivatives of a given category as precisely as possible in structural terms, and then ask ourselves which pragmatic factors influence its degree of exhaustion.

Let me illustrate this point with an instructive example of the interaction of the two types of restrictions, as provided by K. P. Schneider (1997), who investigates both the structural and pragmatic aspects of diminutives in English.[3] After having outlined the phonological, morphological, semantic and syntactic properties of the different suffixes, he investigates their use in speech, and demonstrates that the application rate of English diminutives is actually constrained by the type of speech act and the kinds of participants involved in the verbal interaction.[4] Crucially, however, the structural restrictions on the affixes he discusses are obeyed no matter how the diminutives are *used*. K. P. Schneider's work demonstrates that when starting out from a clear picture of the structural aspects, researchers do not easily fall victim to the fallacy of explaining certain phenomena as conditioned by language use or by some rather ill-defined notion of norm. As will become clear in the subsequent chapters, even in a well-described language like English a lot of work remains to be done to describe more accurately the structural properties of many derivational categories. This book is an attempt to provide such a description for some of these categories, thereby shedding some new light on two major problems concerning the structural properties of word-formation rules in English, namely the problem of stacking restrictions and the problem of rival derivational processes. Stacking restrictions regulate the combinability of affixes amongst each other, and it is far from clear which mechanisms are responsible for the observable patterns. An equally notorious problem of morphological theory is the nature and distribution of rival morphological processes. Before we turn to the empirical investigation of these problems, I will outline

---

3   K. P. Schneider's investigation shows, among other things, that English has a whole range of productive diminutive suffixes, contrary to the commonly held assumption that this language largely lacks expressive or evaluative word-formation.

4   See Dressler and Barbaresi (1994) for another pragmatically-oriented approach.

some of the theoretical notions and issues that are relevant for an understanding of the kinds of restrictions and mechanisms that we will deal with.

3.2. Structural restrictions: Rule-specific mechanisms

Structural restrictions in word-formation may concern the traditional areas of linguistic research, phonology, morphology, semantics and syntax. A general question that arises from the study of such restrictions is which of these should be considered to be peculiar to the individual rule and which ones are the consequence of a more general mechanism (or restriction) that operates on all (or at least classes of) morphological processes, a question that can only be answered on empirical grounds. The first type of structural restrictions we will discuss here are restrictions that are only operative with a specific process and do not constrain derivational morphology in a principled way. The general constraints will be discussed in section 3.3.

Rule-specific constraints may concern the properties of the base or the derived word (see e. g. Bauer 1982: chapter 4.5., for a summary). Consider, for example, the English personal noun suffix *-ee* and the adjectival suffix *-able*, both of which are often claimed to attach only to transitive verbs.[5] The theoretical status of such syntactic restrictions has, however, been questioned on the grounds that the syntactic specifications are in fact the result of underlying semantic restrictions. In fact, I will argue for this position in chapter 6 (see also the discussion of the unitary base hypothesis below). An example of a semantic restriction proper is the one imposed on *-ee* derivatives, whose denotata must be sentient entities (e.g. Barker 1995).

Rule-specific morphological constraints make reference to the kinds of morphological elements or features (such as [+ Latinate], see below) involved in a process, for example by ruling out certain combinations of affixes, or by making affixation dependent on the presence of a particular affix in the base. The nominalizing suffix *-ity* is a case in point, because it may not be attached to adjectives ending in *-ory* (cf. **satisfactority*). Another affixation process making reference to the non-presence of a particular affix on the base is the German perfect prefix *ge-* which is not attached to stems that feature verbal prefixes such as *be-, er-, ver-* and the

---

5   But see the discussion in Bauer (1983) and Barker (1995) who show that occasionally intransitive verbs occur as bases.

like (cf. **gebesprochen, *geerblindet, *geverarztet*, Carstairs-McCarthy 1993, but see below for an alternative solution).

Phonological constraints may involve segmental and prosodic restrictions. For example, the deverbal nominalization suffix *-al* occurs only on stress-final verbs like *recíte* or *propóse* and verbal *-en* only attaches to monosyllabic bases that end in an obstruent (e.g. Siegel 1971, Gussmann 1987). The full complexity of phonological constraints will become evident in chapters 6 and 7 when we consider the segmental and prosodic restrictions on derived verbs.

A number of interesting empirical and theoretical problems emerge with rule-specific restrictions. As already mentioned above, it is often not clear whether the restriction is indeed rule-specific or the consequence of a more general restriction. A notorious case is haplology, i.e. the avoidance of similar-sounding sequences within and across words. Standardly, cases of haplology have been formulated as constraints on specific rules,[6] but given the proliferance of similar phenomena and the similarities between individual instances of haplology, a more general solution would be desirable.[7]

Another problem is to exactly determine the provenance of the restrictions. Thus it is often uncertain whether one deals with a morphological or with a phonological phenomenon. For example, it has been argued that the apparently morphological restriction on German past participle formation mentioned above is in fact a phonological restriction. Wiese (1996a:89-98) and Neef (1996:233-242) suggest that the distribution of *ge-* can be accounted for by purely phonological mechanisms that make reference to the prosodic structure of the base word or the derivative. Although the two authors differ in their explanation of this particular restriction on German past participles they both observe that past participles must not bear initial primary stress, and that only in cases where this is not the case anyway (as with the prefix-verbs mentioned), *ge-* is prefixed. In this formulation, reference to the morphology of the base is superfluous. German past participles illustrate a more principled theoretical debate about the question

---

[6]   See, for example, Booij (1983:257). A recent rule-specific approach to the well-known problem of haplology with plural *-s* and possessive *-s* in English can be found in Yip (1996).

[7]   Yip (1996), Plag (1998) are attempts in this direction.

whether the morphological structure of a word is "visible" to further morphological operations, a question we will not pursue any further.[8]

The third problem concerns the location of the restrictions. Very often, these have been defined as conditions that affixes impose on possible bases, i.e. as restrictions on the input to morphological rules. The concept of input-oriented constraints implies that it is the affix that selects its base and not vice versa. Although this is a widely-shared assumption, it seems that this is not a logical necessity, so that there appears to be no principled argument against the view that it is the base (with its affixes) that constrains the selection of possible affixes. In the next chapter we will indeed argue that such base-driven mechanisms can have important advantages over affix-driven ones.

The adequacy of input-oriented restrictions has been further questioned on the grounds of examples like the above-mentioned verbal suffix *-en*, whose phonological properties should rather be defined as a restriction on the output, and not, as originally stated, as a restriction on the input of the rule. Siegel (1971) observes that *-en* must be preceded by one and only one obstruent, which may be preceded by an optional sonorant preceded by a vowel (cf. also Gussmann 1987). This generalization runs into difficulties if formulated as a restriction on the input, since derivatives like *soften* and *fasten* would be ill-formed because their base words end in two, and not one, obstruent. However, if formulated as a condition on *-en* derivatives, the derived verbs are well-formed because only one obstruent, and not two, precedes the suffix. I will argue in detail in chapters 6 and 7 that the phonological restrictions on derived verbs are best accounted for in terms of output restrictions.

In summary it is clear that, irrespective of the empirical and theoretical problems in finding the correct generalizations, rule-specific restrictions play a prominent role in word-formation and should be integrated into the formalization of any derivational mechanism (cf. e.g. Anderson 1992: 196).

---

[8]   See for example Kiparsky's 'bracket erasure convention' (1982a), Anderson (1992) for arguments against visibility, Carstairs-McCarthy (1993), Booij (1996) for arguments in favor of visibility.

3.3. Structural restrictions: General mechanisms

As pointed out by Rainer (1993:98), the search for general restrictions is basically a characteristic of generative approaches to morphology, which is a comparatively young discipline. Perhaps due to this fact, many of the hypotheses are doubtful or outright untenable.

In (2) I have compiled the most important general restrictions as they can be found in the pertinent literature. Where appropriate, major proponents of the restrictions are named:

(2)   a. the word base hypothesis (Gauger 1971:9, Aronoff 1976:21)
      b. the compositionality hypothesis
      c. the binary branching hypothesis (Bréal 1904, Scalise 1984)
      d. locality conditions (Siegel 1977)
      e. recursion and repetition constraints
      f. the open-class base hypothesis (N, V, A, Adv)
      g. the unitary base hypothesis (Aronoff 1976:48)
      h. the unitary output hypothesis (Scalise 1984:137, Szymanek 1985:95)
      i. blocking (Paul 1896:27, van Marle 1985, 1986, Rainer 1988)
      j. stratal constraints (Bloomfield 1933)

My comments on the restrictions listed in (2a-2f) will be kept to a minimum, because they are only of secondary relevance for the investigations to follow. A more thorough discussion will be devoted to points (2g-2j), since the morphological processes investigated in the following chapters can be seen as test cases for these restrictions.[9] For a more comprehensive discussion of the hypotheses (2a-2f) the reader is referred to Rainer's (1993:98-117) excellent survey of general restrictions on word-formation.

The word base hypothesis claims that "all regular word-formation is word-based. A new word is formed by applying a regular rule to a single, already existing word" (Aronoff 1976:21). As pointed out by Aronoff (1976:xi), the term 'word' is to be understood in the sense of 'lexeme', not

---

[9]   For example, my analysis of derived verbs casts serious doubts on the unitary base hypothesis (UBH) and certain kinds of blocking, but supports the unitary output hypothesis (UOH).

in the sense of inflected word (see also Aronoff 1994: chapter 1). This position is obviously designed as an alternative to morpheme-based approaches to the structure of words. Later authors have argued that Aronoff's first formulation of the word base hypothesis is too strong because it restricts the application of rules to already existing words. As mentioned by Booij (1977:21-22) and many others, possible words may also serve as bases for derivation or compounding. Taking this objection into account, the hypothesis still makes two predictions, namely that the bases of word-formation are neither smaller nor larger than the word. For the majority of processes this prediction is certainly correct, but many apparent or real counterexamples have been pointed out in the literature. This leads Dressler (1988) to the position that the generalization expressed by the word base hypothesis is a statistical rather than a strict universal, and one which should be explained by a theory of preferences as provided by Natural Morphology.

The compositionality hypothesis states that the meaning of a form derived by a productive rule is a function of the meaning of the rule and the base. This is fairly uncontroversial, although some attempts have been made to argue for a holistic interpretation of derived words, most notably by Plank (1981). However, only clearly analogical formations such as German *Hausfrau - Hausmann* 'housewife (female - male)' constitute unequivocal cases of holistic interpretation, while with truly productive rules the difference between holistic and compositional interpretations is empirically impossible to pin down.

The binary branching hypothesis seems to be untenable with all structures that are semantically coordinate and involve more than two elements. Dvandva compounds as in *a German-French-English corporation* or *a phonological-semantic-syntactic approach* are therefore systematic counterexamples, which indicate that the standard binary branching of non-coordinative structures is best viewed as a consequence of their semantics.

Following syntactic locality constraints like Chomsky's adjacency condition (1973) several locality restrictions on the structure of words have been proposed, such as Siegel's (1977) and Allen's (1979) 'adjacency principle', E. Williams' (1981) 'atom condition', or Kiparsky's (1982a) 'Bracket Erasure Convention' . As shown by Rainer (1993:105-106), the theoretical value and the empirical adequacy of these conditions is questionable.

It has often been noted that, unlike syntactic and compounding structures, derivational structures are not recursive (e.g. Stein 1977:226), or that affixes (e.g. Uhlenbeck 1962:428) or suffixes (Mayerthaler 1977:61, Corbin 1987:596-501) may not be iterated. Chapin (1970) has pointed out that examples like *organizationalization* demonstrate the possibility of recursion even in derivational morphology, though subject to general processing constraints. The iteration of prefixes is certainly possible in English (cf. *anti-anti-abortion*), and the impossibility of iteration of suffixes (**readableable*, **conceptualal*) follows from independently needed properties or constraints, for example of a semantic nature. It could also be argued that the non-iteration of morphological material is caused by (morpho-)phonological mechanisms, i.e. haplology (e.g. Plag 1998).

Another, oft-cited universal constraint on word formation concerns the classes of possible base words. Aronoff (1976:19, 21) states, for example, that both base and derivative must be members of the open class categories noun, verb, adjective and adverb. Although the constraint makes correct predictions (counterexamples are rare, but include, for example phrasal categories[10]), it remains to be shown whether we are really dealing with a formal constraint or whether the constraint follows from independent functional principles (see the discussion in Rainer 1993:109-110).

We may now turn to the restrictions that are more relevant for the investigations to follow, namely the unitary base hypothesis, the unitary output hypothesis, blocking, and stratal constraints.

3.3.1. The unitary base hypothesis

In discussions of word formation it is widely assumed that certain affixes only attach to bases of a certain syntactic category. For example, *-ness* is said to attach only to adjectives to form nouns as in *empty-ness*, *-able* attaches only to verbs to form adjectives as in *breakable*, *-al* is suffixed only to nouns to form adjectives as in *constitutional*. In the generative literature, such facts have led to the formulation of the so-called unitary base hypothesis (UBH), which claims that "The syntacticosemantic specification of the base ... is always unique. A WFR [Word Formation Rule, I. P.] will never operate on this or that" (Aronoff 1976:48, see also Booij 1977:140-141). The UBH is a strong hypothesis that can be refuted by showing that a certain word formation process operates on two distinct classes of bases. According to Aronoff, however, a rule that operates, for example, on nouns and adjectives does not necessarily speak against the UBH because nouns

---

[10]   Baayen and Renouf (1996) list the following attested examples involving *-ness*: *next-to-nothing-ness, thatitness, over-the-topness, olde-worlde-ness*.

and adjectives form a natural class sharing the feature [+ N] to which the rule could refer unitarily. An example of this kind is the adjective-forming suffix -*ly* which attaches to nouns (as in *manly, weekly*), as well as to adjectives (*goodly, northerly*, see e.g. Marchand 1969:329-331).

In those cases where lexical categories do not form a natural class, an entirely different homophonous process must be assumed. Aronoff (1976:48) illustrates the latter point with the English suffix -*able*, which combines with verbal stems, as in *breakable, perishable*, as well as with nouns, as in *serviceable, fashionable*. For Aronoff, there are two -*able* rules, one deverbal with the meaning 'can be VERBed', the other denominal with the meaning 'characterized by NOUN'.[11]

The UBH faces two main problems. The first is that Aronoff's escape hatch, namely the formation of natural classes, makes the UBH practically vacuous. Depending on the system of features and categories selected, even seemingly disjunct classes can be made into natural ones. Thus, in standard generative grammar natural classes can be formed on the basis of the categories [± N] and [± V], which leads to the conclusion that nouns and verbs can never form a natural class. In Jackendoff (1977), however, nouns and verbs form a natural class on the basis of the feature [+ Subj]. In essence, by choosing the appropriate feature system the UBH can be immunized against refutation.

The second problem is of a more empirical nature and is known as affix-generalization. Plank (1981:43-65) discusses a number of affixes (from a number of different languages) that can be found on the basis of more than one category and argues that the meaning of the derivatives is constant across the different categories of the base words. According to Plank, the preponderance of bases of a certain category is therefore best viewed as the consequence of the meaning of the process and not the result of a stipulated general condition on possible bases like the UBH. We will return to this point in chapters 6.1. and 7 of this book.

---

[11]   See Akmajian et al. (1979), Anderson (1992) for similar approaches to -*able*. The reader may have observed that Aronoff's deverbal rule runs into problems with intransitive verbs.

3.3.2. *The unitary output hypothesis*

The unitary output hypothesis (UOH) captures the idea that the derivatives formed on the basis of a certain word formation process can be characterized uniquely in terms of their phonological, semantic, and syntactic properties (cf. Aronoff 1976:22, Scalise 1984:137, 1988:232, Szymanek 1985:95). Two main objections can be raised against the UOH, one phonological and one semantic.

Given the wide-spreadedness of stem and affix allomorphy it can be seriously doubted that affixation indeed produces a phonologically unique output. It has been claimed, however, that processes which involve allomorphy are typically less productive or completely unproductive. For example, Cutler (1981) has argued that phonologically less transparent processes are also less productive. This position is corroborated by the findings in Kettemann (1988), who shows that many of the readjustment rules proposed in *SPE* do not extend to nonce words.

We will see, however, that even productive rules may tolerate a high degree of allomorphy. In particular, many of the derivatives featuring the verbalizing suffix *-ize* display a wide range of different stem alternations (e.g. truncation and stress reduction), which make the class of derivatives look phonologically disparate. It will be demonstrated, however, that these stem alternations can be accounted for in a straightforward unitary manner, thereby lending further support to the UOH.

Modifying his earlier position, Scalise (1988:244f, note 3) claims that the UOH is valid only "for the 'formal' part of a WFR [Word Formation Rule, I.P.], not for the 'semantic' part". To illustrate this point he cites the Italian verb forming suffix *-are* which is phonologically unitary, but, according to the source he cites (Lepschy 1981), semantically diverse.

Scalise's point is unconvincing in several respects. First of all it is uncontroversial that truly homophonous processes should be kept apart. No one would, for example, argue that English deverbal nominalizing *-al* (as in *arrival*) is in any sense semantically related to adjectival *-al* (as in *conventional*). The affixes differ in their meaning but each type of derivative is semantically uniform. Secondly, it is far from clear whether the examples of Italian *-are* derivatives Scalise cites cannot be accounted for in a unitary fashion by a proper semantic analysis (perhaps with certain extension rules that explain the polysemy involved). Interestingly, a similar problem arises for English *-ize* derivatives, whose possible meanings look considerably diverse, but which, at closer inspection, turn out to be a case of polysemy

disposed of as a relevant morphological mechanism. Let us therefore turn to the more fruitful concept of synonymy blocking.

With regard to German nominalization, Paul (1896:704) already noted that "the formation of nouns in *-ung* is blocked by the existence of a simpler formation of the function of a nomen actionis" (my translation, I.P.). Perhaps due to its intuitive appeal, the notion of blocking remained in an imprecise and pre-theoretical state until the 1970s and 1980s, when Aronoff (1976), Kiparsky (1982, 1983), van Marle (1985, 1986) and Rainer (1988) tried to formalize this notion.

Elaborating on van Marle's work, Rainer (1988) lays out the weaknesses of Aronoff's and Kiparsky's notions of blocking and develops the most pronounced theory of blocking to date.[12] He distinguishes between two forms of blocking, type-blocking and token-blocking. Type-blocking concerns the interaction of more or less regular rival morphological processes (for example *decency* vs. ?*decentness*) whereas token-blocking involves the blocking of potential regular forms by already existing synonymous words, an example of which is the blocking of *arrivement* by *arrival* or *stealer* by *thief*. The latter type of blocking is the one envisaged by Paul in the above quote. I will first discuss the relatively uncontroversial notion of token-blocking and then move on to type-blocking.

Token-blocking occurs under three conditions: synonymy, productivity, and frequency. The condition of synonymy says that an existing word can only block a newly derived one if they are synonymous. Thus, many of the doublets that do occur are not synonymous but convey (at least slightly) different meanings.

Another condition on the occurrence of blocking is that the blocked word must be morphologically well-formed, in other words, it must be a potential word, derived on the basis of a productive rule. Although this condition looks rather trivial it serves to exclude cases of blocking that are only apparent. For example, Wellmann (1975:213) attributes the non-existence of German **Schlagung* 'hitting' to the existence of *Schlag* 'hit (noun)'. As argued convincingly by Rainer (1988:162-163) **Schlagung* is ruled out even in contexts where it is not synonymous with *Schlag*, and in which it should therefore not be blocked. In other words, **Schlagung* must be ill-formed due to reasons other than blocking.

---

[12]   For our purposes it is not necessary to repeat here Rainer's (1988) detailed review of Aronoff's and Kiparsky's theories of blocking, in which the serious drawbacks and inconsistencies of these approaches are pointed out. The interested reader is referred to the first section of Rainer's article.

Let us turn to the last condition. The crucial insight provided by Rainer is that, contrary to earlier assumptions, not only idiosyncratic or simplex words (like *thief*) can block productive formations, but stored words in general can do so. As already discussed in the preceding chapter, the storage of words is largely dependent on their frequency. This leads to the postulation of the frequency condition, which says that in order to be able to block a potential synonymous formation, a word must be sufficiently frequent. This hypothesis is corroborated by Rainer's investigation of a number of rival nominalizing suffixes in Italian and German. The higher the frequency, the higher the blocking force of a word with respect to a synonymous derivative. Therefore, both idiosyncratic words and regular complex words can block, provided that they are stored.

This leads us to another aspect of token-blocking, not explicitly discussed in Rainer, namely the problem of really synonymous doublets, which may indeed occasionally occur. Plank (1981:181-182) already notes that blocking of a newly derived form does not occur in those cases where the speaker does not activate the already existing alternative form. This is frequently attested in child language (e.g. Clark 1981), where the lexicalized alternatives are not yet present, and in adult speech errors, i.e. when lexical access fails. For obvious reasons, the likelihood of failing to activate a stored form is negatively correlated to the frequency of the form to be accessed. By making frequency and storage the decisive factor for token-blocking, the theory can naturally account for the occasional occurrence even of synonymous doublets.

In the light of these considerations, token-blocking is not "a prophylactic measure to avoid undesired synonymy", as claimed by Plank (1981:182, my translation, I.P.), but the effect of word storage and word processing mechanisms.

We may now move on to the notion of type-blocking, which is less well understood. According to van Marle's Domain Hypothesis, rival suffixes are organized in such a way that each suffix can be applied to a certain domain. In many cases one can distinguish between affixes with an unrestricted domain, the so-called general case (e.g. *-ness* suffixation, which may apply to practically any adjective), and affixes with restricted domains, the so-called special cases (for example *-ity* suffixation). The latter are characterized by the fact that certain constraints limit the applicability of the suffixes to a lexically, phonologically, morphologically, semantically or otherwise governed set of bases. Van Marle further distinguishes two kinds of special cases, systematic and unsystematic ones. A systematic special case is definable by type, i.e. there is a rule that governs the distribution of the affix in question. The unsystematic special case is characterized by the fact that it is lexically governed, i.e. definable only by token. According to the domain hypothesis, the domains of special cases and general cases interact in ways that allow predictions about possible and impossible derivatives. One such prediction is that there is a tendency for the domain of the general case to be systematically curtailed by the domains of the special cases. The pre-emption of the application of the general case by the systematic special case is labeled type-blocking by Rainer (1988). Rainer also observes that not only the general case may be curtailed by the systematic special case, but that rival systematic special cases may also preclude each other. For instance, it seems that the domain of the German nominal suffix *-heit* is a special case which is curtailed by the more restricted domain of the special case *-ität*, which speaks for the extension of the mechanism of type-blocking even to rival special cases.

Type-blocking may occur under almost the same conditions as token-blocking, except that frequency does not play a role, for the obvious reason that storage of individual words is not crucial here. Thus only the conditions of synonymy and productivity hold for type-blocking.

For an evaluation of the domain hypothesis and Rainer's blocking theory we will consider briefly an example from English derivational morphology, *-ness* suffixation and its rivals. Aronoff (1976:53) regards formations involving nominal *-ness* as ill-formed in all those cases where the base adjective ends in *-ate*, *-ent* or *-ant*, hence the contrast between *decency* and ?*decentness*. This would be a nice case of type-blocking, with the systematic special case *-cy* (*decency*) precluding the general case *-ness*. There are, however, three problems with this kind of analysis. The first one is that, on closer inspection, *-ness* and its putative rivals *-ity* or *-cy* are not really synonymous (cf. Riddle 1985), so that blocking could - if at all - only occur in those cases where the meaning differences would be neutralized. Blocking effects could therefore only be demonstrated in discourse contexts that specify synonymous and non-synonymous interpretations. Riddle's study provides such contexts, thereby showing that rival formations are often possible.

This brings us to the second problem, which concerns the status of forms like ?*decentness*, for which it remains to be shown that they are indeed morphologically ill-formed. The occurrence of many doublets (see Riddle 1985, or many entries in the *OED*) rather indicates that the domain of the general case *-ness* is not systematically curtailed by *-ity* or *-cy*. The final problem with putative cases of type-blocking is to distinguish them from token-blocking. Thus, the avoidance of ?*decentness* could equally well be a case of token-blocking, since one can assume that, for many speakers, the word *decency* is part of their lexicon, and is therefore capable of token-blocking.

Especially in view of the empirical problems, van Marle (1985:238ff) has conceded that the Domain Hypothesis is too strong, and should therefore be used chiefly as a heuristic mechanism, i.e. as a "tool with which we can subject the paradigmatic dimension of morphological structure to a further and more penetrating investigation" (van Marle 1985:239). Rainer comes to a similar conclusion when he states that "The main task for future research in type-blocking will be to try to find out to what extent it is predictable which one of two word-formation rules with rival systematically restricted domains will supersede the other" (1988:179-180).

Chapters 6, 7 and 8 present an in-depth analysis of an interesting test case for van Marle's and Rainer's type-blocking theories, the rival verb-deriving processes in English, i.e. the affixes *-ize, -ate, -ify, -en, eN-, be-* and conversion. It will turn out that the data cannot be adequately handled in terms of type-blocking, and that the distribution of the different processes is not governed by primarily paradigmatic forces, as claimed by van Marle. To the contrary, I will demonstrate that the applicability of a rule to a given base can be most naturally accounted for by referring to the individual syntagmatic properties and restrictions of each process.

3.3.4. *Stratal constraints:*
Level ordering, Lexical Phonology, and the Latinate Constraint

Bloomfield already stated that "Normal roots combine with normal affixes, learned roots with learned affixes" (1933:252). A distinction between two classes of affixes in English has been widely acknowledged and often reformulated since then, finding its way eventually into the theory of Lexical Phonology. The attractiveness and importance of the distinction and the restrictions that go along with it lie in its simplicity: if correct, a whole range of difficult data could naturally be accounted for by positing a single theoretical device. Unfortunately, it is not as simple as that.

The differences between two classes of affixes in English observed by Bloomfield concern not only their etymology but also their phonological and morphological behavior. An example of this is the well-known stress-shift that some affixes impose on their bases, and others do not. In *SPE* this distinction is associated formally with two kinds of boundaries, the word or strong boundary '#' and the morpheme or weak boundary '+'. #-affixes attach to words, i.e. they are outside the domain of cyclic phonological rules like stress assignment, whereas +-affixes do not block the application of such rules. An oft-cited example illustrating this difference is

(3)   a. átom - atóm+ic - àtom+íc+ity
        b. átom - átom#less - átom#less#ness

Siegel (1974) argues that each suffix is associated with one (and only one) boundary and establishes what later became known as the Affix Ordering Generalization (Selkirk 1982a), which says that +-affixes, or 'class I' affixes in Siegel's terminology, are always attached before, and class II affixes (i.e. #-affixes) after stress assignment. This generalization predicts that certain combinations of affixes are ruled out on principled grounds. A derivative like *atom#less+ity* violates the Affix Ordering Generalization and is therefore ungrammatical.

    Later on the ideas of Siegel and other researchers (e.g. Allen 1979, Selkirk 1982a) have led to the development of various more refined stratificational models in the framework of Lexical Phonology (e.g. Kiparsky 1982b, Halle & Mohanan 1985, Mohanan 1986) which distinguish between two levels or strata of affixation in English. In (4), a number of affixes and their stratal affiliation are listed.

(4)   Class I suffixes:
        +ion, +ity, +y, +al, +ic, +ate, +ous, +ive, +able, +ize
        Class I prefixes:
        re+, con+, de+, sub+, pre+, in+, en+, be+
        Class II suffixes:
        #ness, #less, #hood, #ful, #ly, #y, #like, #ist, #able, #ize
        Class II prefixes:
        re#, sub#, un#, non#, de#, semi#, anti#
                            (from Spencer 1991:79)

Note that all stratificational models (except the most recent one by Giegerich 1998) are based on the assumption that the information that crucially decides on class-membership, and thus on the application of phonological and morphological processes, rests exclusively with the individual affix.

    The advantages of a stratal model of morphology are obvious. As mentioned above, only one mechanism is needed to explain a whole range of restrictions on the combinability of stems and affixes or affixes amongst each other. However, there has been abundant criticism of the stratificational model, involving both empirical and theoretical arguments.[13]

The empirical weakness of level-ordered affixation is that the generalizations are both too weak and too strong. Thus it has been pointed out by Strauss (1982) that class I suffixes can be attached outside class II prefixes as in the notorious example *ungrammaticality*. From this and similar facts he concludes that level ordering is not applicable to affixes on opposite sides of the stem, which considerably weakens the power of the generalizations. But even if we limit our attention to only one side of the stem, there appear to be numerous counterexamples to the Affix Ordering Generalization where class II suffixes attach inside class I suffixes. Forms in *-ist-ic* or *-ize-ation* illustrate this phenomenon, since the stress-neutral suffixes *-ist* and *-ize* appear inside the stress-shifting *-ic* and *-ation*, respectively. Such facts suggest that many suffixes seem to behave as if they were associated with both strata. For instance, *-able* is sometimes stress-shifting, sometimes not (*cómpar+able, compár#able*). Although the association of one suffix with more than one level can explain away some undesired facts, this is achieved by further weakening the predictive power of the model considerably. Yet another problem for level-ordered morphology is that sometimes affixes may attach to phrases as in *out-thereness* and *spreadoutness* (see also note 10 above), which is rather unexpected for a well-behaved suffix, since affixes in general should not have access to processes that apply later in the derivation.

The counterexamples mentioned so far reveal that the model rules out many combinations that are actually attested. To make things worse, the model also permits combinations that never occur. Thus, in addition to what stratum-models predict, we need further, perhaps more idiosyncratic, restrictions on stacking. The existing stratum models (again with the notable exception of Giegerich 1998) are not able to account for stacking restrictions or precedence rules within one level. Consider, for example, the failure of *-(u)ous* to be followed by *-ize*, both of them level 1 affixes, as in **sens-uous-ize*. Finally, it is far from clear whether ungrammatical forms like **home-less-ity* are ungrammatical because of a level ordering violation or because of other reasons.

In essence, a level-ordering theory of English affixation is too strong because it rules out attested combinations of affixes, and it is too weak

---

[13]   See, for example, Aronoff and Sridhar (1983, 1987) for a summary of arguments.

because it fails to predict a number of apparent restrictions on affix stacking. The most pronounced systematic attack on level ordering was launched by Fabb (1988) who presents impressive evidence against standard arguments for a stratificational approach to English suffixation. He investigates the combinability of a broad range of English suffixes and comes to the conclusion that the attested and non-attested combinations cannot be explained satisfactorily by level ordering. He therefore claims that English suffixation is constrained only by the selectional restrictions of the suffixes involved. This is not a very attractive solution to begin with, because it assigns all kinds of restrictions to stipulated idiosyncrasies of the suffixes. Although this is a viable solution in principle, one would prefer an account under which at least some of the restrictions observed in the data might be due to more general principles. It is one of the purposes of the next chapter to demonstrate that many of the apparent selectional restrictions proposed by Fabb are the natural consequence of independent morphological mechanisms that have to be stated anyway to account for other phenomena in the realm of English derivational morphology.

The rejection of level ordering is however not equivalent to a complete rejection of Lexical Phonology. Linguists like Booij (1994) have pointed out that the basic insight of Lexical Phonology is that morphological and phonological rules apply in tandem. This assumption is logically independent of level ordering and level ordering can therefore be disposed of without any harm. This is shown by Inkelas and Orgun (1995), who demonstrate that certain (classes of) affixes can trigger certain phonological mechanisms. Although they still call the classes of processes "levels", their notion of level has hardly any resemblance to the one used in earlier models. The standard view of level ordering expressed by Kiparsky (1982b) or Mohanan (1986) is that every form is subject to every level of the phonology. Mohanan conceptualizes Lexical Phonology as a factory with the levels as individual rooms: "There is a conveyor belt that runs from the entry gate to the exit gate passing through each of these rooms. This means that every word that leaves the factory came in through the entry gate and passed through every one of these rooms" (1986:47). Inkelas and Orgun challenge this claim by showing "that in Turkish forms are *not* subject to the phonological levels at which they do not undergo morphology" (1995:764, original emphasis)

An alternative to the idea of level ordering is the (re-)introduction of an etymological-morphological restriction known as the Latinate Constraint (cf. e.g. Aronoff 1976, Booij 1977, 1994, Anshen et al. 1986, Fabb 1988). In general this constraint has taken two forms. Bloomfield (for English) and Booij (for Dutch) postulate a general constraint, whereas the other authors mentioned advance rule-specific restrictions. In the following I will propose an intermediate position.

Refining the aforementioned authors' observations somewhat, it seems necessary to distinguish between three types of suffixes in English. The first type only combines with native stems, the second type only (or primarily) attaches to Latinate stems, and the third type ignores this distinction and combines with both kinds of stems. The only real example of the first type is probably verbal *-en* which almost exclusively attaches to Germanic stems (e.g. Anshen et al. 1986:2, 5), whereas most native affixes are immune to this distinction and attach to any kind of base. Affixes of the second type are all of Latinate etymology themselves, as for example adjectival *-ive* and *-al,* nominal *-ity* and *-cy*, or verbal *-ize*. The third category of affixes consists of the majority of Germanic affixes and some Latinate affixes such as *-ment*, and *-able*.

Affixes and stems can now be characterized as belonging to one of the three categories, expressed by the features [+ Latinate], [− Latinate] or [± Latinate]. The distributional facts mentioned can now be formally accounted for by the following morphological constraint, which operates on stems and affixes:

(5)   **Latinate Constraint**:
       Bases and affixes may combine only if their etymological features
       are compatible.

The constraint in (5) rules out the only possibility that indeed should be ruled out in principle, namely that a [+ Latinate] element combines with a [− Latinate] element. Thus, a [+ Latinate] base may only combine with affixes marked [+ Latinate] or [± Latinate], a base marked [− Latinate] may only combine with affixes that are [− Latinate] or [± Latinate].

Alternative general formulations of the Latinate Constraint have been suggested, but these fail to capture the facts correctly. If Bloomfield's term "normal" in the quotation above is interpreted as being equivalent to our feature [− Latinate], his constraint fails to account for the many attested combinations of [− Latinate] suffixes with [+ Latinate] stems. If the term "normal" is interpreted as equivalent to our feature [± Latinate], Bloomfield's constraint fails to account for the combination of [± Latinate] affixes with [+ Latinate] stems. A stronger version of the constraint would say that [+ Latinate] affixes do not combine with [± Latinate] stems, which is, however, too strong a prediction. Consider, for example, the suffix combination *-able-ity*. *-able* attaches to both [+ Latinate] and [– Latinate] stems and must therefore be characterized as [± Latinate]. The suffix *-ity* on the other hand is, by all accounts, [+ Latinate] because it attaches only to [+ Latinate] adjectives. However, there is one systematic exception, namely adjectives in *-able*, which are [± Latinate]. The only possible generalization is therefore the one suggested in (5), which is in line with the observations made by Plank (1981:132) in regard to Dutch and German. More far-reaching restrictions must therefore be rule-specific.

The crucial question for the researcher, and the native speaker, is of course how the stratal feature of a given suffix can be determined. Unfortunately, one cannot simply consult an etymological dictionary, because even if a certain suffix is borrowed from, say, Old French, this does not entail that it behaves in the expected way. Besides *-able*, an example of such a suffix is *-ment*, which etymologically is Latinate, but morphologically is not, since it attaches equally to native and non-native bases (cf. e.g. Marchand 1969:331-332). Solely relying on the etymology is inadequate in any case, as it presupposes that native speakers need to have etymological knowledge in order to master English derivational morphology. Although etymological knowledge may influence the individual's morphological competence (especially what concerns morphological creativity), it does not make sense to make the native speaker's morphological competence dependent on meta-linguistic knowledge. Thus the Latinate Constraint is, strictly speaking, a morphological constraint, and not an etymological one.[14] The presence of a particular stratal feature may therefore only be detected structurally, by way of observing the combinatorial properties of a given affix. Thus, it is often said (e.g. Burzio 1994:334) that [+ Latinate] affixes attach to bound stems, whereas [– Latinate] only attach to words. As a consequence, [+ Latinate] affixes are always closer to the base than [– Latinate] ones. Another, related difference between Latinate and Germanic affixes is of a phonological nature. The former often affect the phonological make-up of the base through segmental or prosodic changes, while the latter do not. Furthermore, native and latinate words often differ in their phonological structure. Thus it has been frequently pointed out that Latinate stems tend to be polysyllabic with stress patterns different from

---

[14] Consequently, I continue to use square brackets to refer to the morphological property, and no brackets where I refer to the etymological characteristic proper.

that of Germanic stems which tend to be either monosyllabic, or, if poly-syllabic, to bear primary stress on the first syllable.

It seems, however, that none of the criteria can be applied in a strict fashion, since counterexamples can be found quite easily. Furthermore, it is not clear whether phonological properties (instead of a morphological feature related to etymology may be the real cause of the observed combinations of elements. Following suggestions by Inkelas (1989, 1993), Booij (1994:20) has proposed to eliminate the Latinate constraint altogether in favor of a purely phonological distinction between affixes that attach to a phonological stem and those that attach to a phonological word. This appears to be a promising move, since such prosodic constituents are independently needed to account for a number of morphological and morphophonological facts (see e.g. Nespor and Vogel 1986, McCarthy and Prince 1993b). No matter which kinds of features will ultimately turn out to be the most adequate, it seems that affixes form clusters or strata which function as organizational entities in the derivation of complex words.

Before we turn to the more empirical parts of this book let us briefly summarize the discussion of this chapter.

3.4. Productivity: A summary

In this and the previous chapter we have discussed in some detail different notions of productivity and some of the pragmatic and structural mechanisms that are responsible for the systematic limitations on the productivity of a given process. Phonological, morphological, semantic and syntactic properties of the elements involved may constrain the applicability of a process. The productivity measures developed by Baayen and his co-workers allow a more refined, operationalized determination of the different aspects of the applicability of a process in actual speech. These measures are however, only the starting point for investigations that try to explain the observed pattern (at least partially) in terms of linguistic structures.

As already mentioned above, the following parts of this book deal with the question as to which structural restrictions must be incorporated into the derivational morphology of English. I will show that earlier accounts are often empirically inadequate, and that a better empirical description of individual processes provides answers also to some of the theoretical problems discussed in the preceding sections.

The processes to be discussed serve as test cases for the hypotheses given in (2g-2j), and the analysis suggests some interesting, though sometimes tentative, answers to the following questions: Which mechanisms are rule-based, which ones are general, which ones are affix-driven, which ones are base-driven? Do derivational rules necessarily refer to the syntactic category of the base? And should restrictions be formulated as output-oriented or input-oriented? With these questions in mind, we move on to the empirical investigations which deal with two central problems in (English) derivational morphology. The first is the combinability of suffixes (chapter 4), the other is the distribution of rival morphological processes (chapters 5 to 8).

4. The combinability of derivational suffixes

This chapter is an attempt to shed some new light on one of the most intricate problems in English morphology, the combinatorial properties of derivational suffixes.[1] As already briefly mentioned in the previous chapter, Fabb (1988) launches the most pronounced empirical attack on level ordering and claims in the title of his article that "English suffixation is constrained only by selectional restrictions". I will show that Fabb's account, though convincing with respect to the rejection of level ordering, is itself both empirically and theoretically flawed. On the basis of the analysis of a large amount of data from Lehnert (1971), and the *OED on CD*, an alternative account is proposed, which explains the patterning of the data as a result of base-driven (and not exclusively affix-driven, as with Fabb) selectional restrictions, paradigmatic morphological processes, and independent principles and constraints of English derivational morphology.

4.1. Fabb (1988)

Fabb investigates the combinability of 43 English suffixes, restricting himself to suffixes that attach to otherwise free forms (i.e. excluding bound roots). In view of the attested and non-attested combinations he comes to the conclusion that level ordering restrictions and syntactic category restrictions limit the number of a possible 1849 combinations to 459. Fabb, however, finds only 50 combinations attested, which is a strong indication that there must be restrictions operative other than those proposed by level orderists. Although Fabb's arguments against level ordering are substantial, the alternative proposed by Fabb is much less attractive. He posits a model of English derivation that contains four kinds of suffixes, grouped according to the restrictions they show.

---

[1]   An earlier version of this chapter has appeared as Plag (1996). A number of points made in that article have been revised, while others, I hope, have been clarified. The most substantial changes concern my remarks on verbal suffixes.

(1)   Group 1:
       Suffixes that do not attach to already suffixed words (28 out of 43).
       Group 2:
       Suffixes that attach outside one other suffix (6 out of 43).
       Group 3:
       Suffixes that attach freely (3 out of 43).
       Group 4:
       Problematic suffixes (6 out of 43).

Although in principle individual selectional restrictions may constitute a serious alternative to a level-ordered morphology, it seems that Fabb may have thrown out the baby with the bathwater because some interesting generalizations observed by level-orderists are lost under Fabb's approach.

Fabb's model also has consequences for another much debated issue in generative morphology, namely the above-mentioned visibility of word-internal structure to affixation processes. Fabb's model assumes that suffixes are sensitive to whether the base is already suffixed, which contradicts one of the central claims of Anderson's A-morphous Morphology (1992), or Kiparsky's Bracket Erasure Convention (1982a).

The remainder of this chapter will deal mainly with two questions. The first one is whether Fabb's observations are empirically correct, and the second one is to what extent the stacking restrictions of affixes may be explained by independent mechanisms of English morphology instead of idiosyncratic affix-driven selectional restrictions. Especially the second question is extremely difficult to answer and it should be stressed that I will not attempt to provide an all-embracing account. What I rather aim at is to outline which kinds of mechanisms we need to acknowledge and how they may possibly interact. For many of the individual problems to be discussed, only tentative solutions will be offered, which will have to be further refined or backed up by future investigations. For instance, the role of semantic compatibility of suffixes certainly deserves further attention since it seems that in this domain a number of interesting restrictions can be located (see e. g. chapter 7).

It should also be noted that the present treatment is not exclusively meant as a reaction to Fabb's article. My aim is not only to refute some of Fabb's claims, but to come a few steps closer to the solution of some important problems of English morphology, which many linguists have dealt with before. Fabb's study only serves as a reference point because it is justly praised for showing the inadequacy of preceding approaches. Furthermore, Fabb's predictions can be easily tested, which is a virtue that more traditional treatments of English morphology tend to lack (e.g. Marchand 1969, or Jespersen 1942).

4.2. The data

Which data form the basis for the discussion? While Fabb used Walker (1924) and his own collection of items to provide him with examples, I will considerably enlarge the data base with the help of Lehnert (1971) and the *OED on CD*.[2] Due to the nature of the *OED*, the use of examples from this source requires some caution and discussion. The problems concern the lemmata on the one hand, and their treatment by the lexicographers on the other.

The *OED*'s near-comprehensive coverage of the English lexicon from the twelfth century onwards is extremely informative, especially with regard to historical studies, but proves to be problematic for synchronic studies like this one, which try to describe the morphological competence of today's speakers. Thus, many of the attested forms may be no longer in usage, although perhaps no information in the relevant entry indicates this. As a general policy, the *OED* labels these words as 'obsolete' or 'rare', but the decision to classify a word as obsolete is certainly not always easy and the treatment may not be consistent. To illustrate this, it is not immediately clear whether a word with its last citation in, say, 1890, should be considered no longer in usage.

Furthermore, the *OED*'s aiming at comprehensiveness almost necessarily leads to the listing of what one reviewer called 'esoteric words', i.e. attested words that are nevertheless unfamiliar to most native speakers or otherwise somehow strange, and that, consequently, could be argued to constitute doubtful or even irrelevant examples of certain derivational types. While it seems clear that such words should not provide THE crucial evidence for or against certain analyses, it seems unwise to exclude them A PRIORI from one's data base, for the following reasons.

---

[2]   In addition, examples discussed in the pertinent linguistic literature (like Marchand 1969, Jespersen 1942, and many others) have also been included. With regard to Lehnert (1971) and the *OED*, one anonymous reviewer pointed out that there are even larger dictionaries or word-lists available (e.g. Brown 1963). These could of course provide even more counterexamples to Fabb's generalizations than those presented below, but they were not available to me.

First of all, it is not clear where esotericness starts and where it ends. What is esoteric for one speaker, may be rather natural for another. But even if one would overcome this general difficulty (for example through careful experimental studies with native speakers), there is a second problem. Unfamiliarity or uncomfortableness with a certain word is not necessarily an indication of its morphological ill-formedness, but can have a number of causes, with a violation of morphological restrictions being only one of them. Thus, the rejection of esoteric words by a speaker may depend on pragmatic factors, or be the result of prescriptive rules a speaker applies. For example, linguists who work with native speaker informants often experience that words or sentences are first rejected by informants because the speakers fail to make sense of them, and not because the data violate morphological or syntactic rules of their language. Presented with an appropriate context which provides a possible interpretation, the same informants may readily accept the data presented to them. In essence, the claim that a putative word violates a morphological restriction should therefore be based not only on sound morphological arguments but also on the prior exclusion of other possibly intervening factors. Thirdly, and ideally, one would like to have a theory of morphological competence that can account for everyday words as well as for the esoteric ones. If a theory can handle both, it is to be preferred to theories that have to exclude esoteric words from the range of data they want to explain.

Following this line of reasoning we will not exclude esoteric words as evidence, but we will neither use them as *primary* evidence. In the vast majority of the cases presented below, I believe we can make a point on the basis of non-esoteric words, with esoteric words only providing additional evidence in some cases. In any case, the *OED* labels 'obsolete', 'rare', 'rare1' etc. will always be given.

In addition to the attested forms taken from Lehnert, the *OED* and the linguistic literature, we will also occasionally consider potential word forms that are not found in any of the available sources but are made up to test some of the proposed predictions. In such cases, it should be noted that the potential forms are again only used as ADDITIONAL illustration. Even if the reader does not accept these forms as well-formed, the main argument still holds.

4.3. An alternative account

In what follows I will argue that the apparent constraints on the combinability of suffixes are not exclusively or primarily the result of affix-driven selectional restrictions of the kind Fabb (1988) proposes. It will be shown that, instead, the distribution of suffixes is often governed by base-driven selectional restrictions and general factors like blocking. Each group of suffixes as postulated by Fabb will be discussed in turn.

4.3.1. The largest group of suffixes (28 out of 43):
Suffixes that do not attach to already suffixed words

This group of 28 suffixes can be subdivided into the following subgroups (examples are Fabb's):

(2)   a.   abstract-noun-forming suffixes:
           deverbal   *-age (steerage)*
                           -al (betrayal)
                           -ance (annoyance)
                           -ment (containment)
                           -y (assembly)
           denominal *-age (orphanage)*
                           -hood (nationhood)
                           -ism (despotism)
                           -y (robbery)
      b.   person-noun-forming affixes:
           denominal *-an (librarian)*
                           -ist (methodist)
           deverbal   *-ant (defendant)*

    c. relational-adjective-forming suffixes:
         deverbal   *-ful (forgetful)*
                        -ant (defiant)
                        -ory (advisory)
                        -ive (restrictive)
         denominal   *-ful (peaceful)*
                        -ous (spacious)
                        -y (hearty)
                        -ly (ghostly)
                        -ish (boyish)
                        -an (reptilian)
                        -ed (moneyed)
       deadjectival *-ly (deadly)*
    d. verb-forming suffixes:
         denominal   *-ate (originate)*
                        -ify (classify)
                        -ize (symbolize).
       deadjectival *-ify (intensify)*

4.3.1.1. Abstract-noun forming suffixes

Under Fabb's approach the deverbal suffixes *-age* (*steerage*), *-al* (*betrayal*) *-ance* (*annoyance*), *-ment* (*containment*), and *-y* (*assembly*) all share a selectional restriction that does not allow attachment to already suffixed verbs. A closer look at the data reveals, however, that such a selectional restriction is rather ad hoc and conceptually inadequate.

The only verbs that contain a suffix in English are those that end in *-ify*, *-ize*, *-ate*, and *-en*. Thus it is only to one of these verb types that the above mentioned suffixes can potentially attach. Let us look at derivatives in *-ify*, *-ize*, and *-ate* first, because they share certain characteristics that distinguish them from *-en* derivatives with respect to the kinds of derivational processes by which these derived verbs are related to their corresponding abstract nouns.

Standard textbooks or dictionaries, if not the native speaker's intuition, tell us that verbs in *-ify* end up regularly with *-ification* as the nominalizing suffix attached to the root, verbs in *-ize* take *-ation*, and verbs in *-ate* take *-ion*. Following the common assumption that these three suffixes are phonologically conditioned allomorphs of *-ation*, we can simplify our statement and say that verbal derivatives in *-ify*, *-ize*, and *-ate* all take *-ation* as their nominalizing suffix. This is evident if we look at the impossible derivatives given in (3). The suffixes *-age, -al, -ance, -ment*, and *-y* are just as impossible as the inappropriate phonologically conditioned allomorphs:

(3) *magnify-ation   *verbalize-ification   *concentrate-ation
     *magnify-ion   *verbalize-ion   *concentrate-ification
     *magnify-ance   *verbalize-ance   *concentrate-ance
     *magnify-al   *verbalize-al   *concentrate-al
     *magnify-age   *verbalize-age   *concentrate-age
     *magnify-y   *verbalize-y   *concentrate-y
     *magnify-ment   *verbalize-ment   *concentrate-ment

My claim is that the failure of these five nominalizing suffixes to attach to already suffixed verbs is not due to a selectional restriction associated with them, but a natural consequence of the organization of derivational morphology in general, and verb nominalization in particular. I propose that it is the verbal suffix, hence the base, that is responsible for the choice of the nominalizing suffix that can be attached to it. Under this view we are dealing not with selectional restrictions of the nominalizing suffixes (i.e. "affix-driven" restrictions), but with restrictions imposed by the base, in this case the suffix of the base word, on the kind of suffix it can take. Let us call these kinds of restrictions 'base-driven'.

The postulation of base-driven restrictions in this case is conceptually superior to the affix-driven approach, since the possible combinations of suffixes have to be posited anyway. The derivational gaps then follow naturally. If we, however, conceptualize the restrictions as affix-driven, we can only predict the impossible combinations involving *-age, -al, -ance, -ment*, and *-y*, but we fail to predict the possible ones, featuring *-ation*. Let us look at this argumentation in more detail.

Under an affix-driven approach we have to state that *-ion* attaches to, among others, verbs ending in *-ate*, that *-ification* attaches to the stems of verbs in *-ify* and *-ation* attaches to verbs in *-ize*. Such a statement may be adequate to account for existing derivatives involving these suffixes, but there is no way to predict, let alone explain, why the derived verbs do not take *-age, -al, -ance, -ment*, or *-y* as suffixes. In order to save this generalization under an affix-driven approach, one would have to state additional selectional restrictions of just these suffixes. Under a base-driven approach, the fact that *-age, -al, -ance, -ment*, or *-y* do not attach to the derived verbs under discussion can be predicted and need not be stipulated, since the verbal suffixes in question take *only* the competing *-ation* suffix (and the general suffix *-ing* to which no restriction seems to apply).

With regard to verbal bases in *-en* I will argue that all nominalizing suffixes in question can in principle be attached to it, provided that other factors (e.g. of, for example, semantic or phonological provenance) do not intervene. At closer inspection, Fabb's generalization turn out to be not completely accurate. While he seems to be right in his observation that no derivatives in *-enage, -enal, -enance,* and *-eny* can be found in dictionaries or seem possible according to today's native speakers' judgments (cf. for example the unacceptability of **darkenance, *blackenage, *strengthenal, *wideny)*[3], a small number of *-enment* forms is attested (e.g. *enlightenment*). Before we turn to the latter cases we will deal with the question as to how the unacceptable and unattested derivatives can be ruled out without making reference to a selectional restriction of *-en.*

There are in principle two ways to account for the combinatorial properties of *-en* with regard to abstract-noun-forming suffixes, of which one involves an etymological constraint, the other paradigmatic forces.

Turning again to the case of verbal *-en* derivatives, which are [− Latinate] due to the native suffix and its exclusive attachment to native bases, the etymological constraint predicts that they cannot combine with [+ Latinate] suffixes. The Latinate Constraint can therefore nicely account for the fact that *-ation,* for instance, may not attach to *-en.* Deverbal *-ation* almost exclusively occurs with non-native stems, which warrants its characterization as [+ Latinate] (see also, for example, Marchand 1969, Jespersen 1942, Giegerich 1998). Only few counterexamples seem to be attested, of which Marchand (1969:260) gives *flirtation, starvation, botheration, backwardation* (a stock exchange term), *jobation* (colloquial, *OED*), plus a number of jocular or vulgar words. Interestingly, these are all lexically governed, i.e. the fact that *-ation* attaches to these stems has to be listed as a special property of the respective stems[4], whereas Latinate stems may take *-ation* productively, provided that semantic or phonological constraints do not interfere. In fact, this kind of special listing seems to be the only way to circumvent the effect of the Latinate Constraint. The jocular or vulgar

---

3   The only form in the *OED2* which manifests at least one of the combinations of suffixes is *festenance, festynens (fasten + ance,* 'confinement, durance') characterized as obsolete and scientific, with the last citation dating from 1533.

4   This goes hand in hand with idiosyncrasies of various kinds. Thus, for example, *thunderation* or *botheration* are primarily used as exclamations.

words among the counterexamples even support the etymological constraint, because their pragmatic effect originates in the systematic violation
of the constraint. Thus, the use of a learned suffix with non-learned stem
usually has a humorous effect.

   Given the Latinate etymology of the nominalizing suffixes *-ance, -age,
-al, -y*, one may be tempted to ascribe the absence of a preceding suffix *-en*
to the Latinate Constraint. This is, however, not without problems, since
with *-ance, -age* and *-al* the number of derivatives involving native bases
is so large (see Marchand 1969: 248, 234-237, respectively) that these
suffixes may be characterized as [± Latinate], allowing in principle their
combination with *-en*, contrary to the facts. The only suffix that indeed
seems unquestionably [+ Latinate] is *-y* (see, for example, Marchand
1969:285).

   In view of the inability of the Latinate Constraint to explain the selectional restrictions of *-en* with regard to *-ance, -age, -al, -y*, let us examine
an alternative solution. The domains of all four nominalizing suffixes
-ance, -age, -al, -y have in common that they are highly restricted. No
matter, whether one would opt for an analysis that views the domains as
lexically-governed, or as defined by complex rules, it seems that both
-ance and *-al* are restricted to verbal bases that have final stress.[5] This generalization already means that all bases exhibiting non-final (primary)
stress are automatically excluded from this domain. It is exactly this fact
that does not allow *-ance* and *-al* to attach to verbal *-en* derivatives, and not
a putative selectional restriction that forbids their application to suffixed
stems. Again the prosodic restriction on possible bases or derivatives has to
be stated anyway to account for the fact that other (derived or non-derived)
verbs with non-final stress do not take one of these suffixes.

   The distribution of the two remaining suffixes *-age* and *-y* seems to be
entirely lexically governed, i.e. there is no way to predict which verbal
stems they attach to. *Steerage*, for example, is not the result of a synchronically productive or semi-productive morphological rule, but has to

---

5   There is only one counterexample attested for *-al*, namely *burial*, which only
     as the result of a folk etymology of the original form *buriels* became associa-
     ted with deverbal *-al*. There are few counterexamples involving non-final
     stress with *-ance*, cf. *utterance*, but their number is very small. Note that fi-
     nal stress seems not to be a sufficient condition for the application of these
     suffixes (cf. **advance-ance, *advance-al*). This warrants the conclusion that,
     unless other general constraints are detected, we are not dealing with a
     productive rule.

be stored individually.[6] The same is true for words like *assembly, treaty, inquiry*.[7] In any case, a selectional restriction of the form proposed by Fabb is redundant. This leaves us with only one suffix combination that is still problematic, verbal *-en* followed by nominalizing *-ment*, to which we now turn.

A closer investigation of sources like the *OED* and Lehnert (1971) shows that there are some counterexamples to Fabb's claim. The following forms are attested:

(4)   *(re-)awakenment, enlightenment, enlivenment, fastenment* (dialec-
       tal), *disheartenment, dizenment, chastenment* (rare), *lengthenment*
       (rare), *worsenment*

The status of these counterexamples is of course arguable since, firstly, the majority may be considered esoteric in the sense described above. Secondly, one of the bases (*(be-)dizen*) involves a bound root, which casts some doubts on the morphological status of *-en* in this form. Another problem with this derivative is that derivatives of the form [*bound root - suffix - ___*] are not legitimate counterexamples to Fabb's claims, since he explicitly says that his group 1 suffixes "are never found in the environ-ment [*word - suffix - ___*]" (1988:532). We will nevertheless include bases of the form [bound root - suffix] in our data in order to show that the more specific restrictions we are going to propose can account for both types of complex bases, whereas it is unclear how a model like Fabb's would deal with group 1 suffixes that attach to [*bound root - suffix*] combinations. The

---

6   An *OED* search for all twentieth century neologisms with deverbal *-age* only
     yields six forms: *coverage, creepage, frettage, narratage, spillage, stewage*.
     The small number of neologisms is indicative of the non-productivity of the
     process, and the attested neologisms should be analyzed as local analogies.

7   The way the storage of this kind of information is conceptualized depends on
     one's theory of the mental lexicon. Under a base-driven approach, it is part
     of the lexical entry of the verb which kind of nominalizing suffix it may take
     (besides the general suffix *-ing*, which seems to be applicable to practically
     all verbal bases), under an affix-driven approach this information is stored as
     part of the lexical entry of the suffix. In a word-based morphology these
     nouns are simply stored as wholes, possibly with a redundancy rule
     expressing their relatedness with respect to the nominalizing suffix. For the
     purposes of this investigation we need not decide on this issue, because the
     points being made here may be accomodated for under each of the approa-
     ches just mentioned.

rare cases where the second suffix may be considered to be sensitive to the morphological make-up of the base word will be discussed in more detail below (see for example the combination *-ment-al*). Note that with respect to his groups 2 and 4 Fabb does not refer to the word/bound root distinction, which suggests that the suffixes of this group are insensitive to the morphological status of the root even in his approach.[8]

Coming back to the examples in (4), I will show in the following that these derivatives are not isolated, idiosyncratic formations, but that they are systematically derived words. We will see that the small number of attested derivatives in *-enment* results from a number of restrictions on *-ment* that have to be stated anyway in a reasonably adequate description of *-ment*.

In general, the specification of the domain of *-ment* is extremely difficult, and most of the generalizations that have been proposed in the literature are very crude and often accompanied by numerous counterexamples. The following characteristics of *-ment* derivatives have been observed. Jespersen (1942:376) notes that there is a tendency of *-ment* to attach to disyllabic bases with stress on the second syllable. Although this is only a tendency and not an exceptionless generalization, it means that verbs ending in *-en* are not likely candidates for *-ment* suffixation, which correlates with the near-absence of *-enment* derivatives. Another observation with regard to derivatives in *-ment* is that there is a strikingly high number of bases that contain a prefix (like *a-*, *re-*, *dis-*). This may well be related to the tendency mentioned by Jespersen, since prefixed monosyllabic stems will be necessarily disyllabic with ultimate stress. The preference for prefixed stems is especially obvious with stems containing the prefixes *eN-* and *be-*, which seem to take *-ment* obligatorily (cf. also Jespersen 1942:376, Chapin 1967, quoting a paper by Emonds 1966, and the remarks in the *OED*). For our problem this generalization is especially interesting, because it allows the prediction that verbs containing one of these prefixes AND our suffix *-en* will, if anything, take *-ment*.

The number of possible bases of the form *eN/be-X-en* is relatively small. The *OED* lists the following forms:

---

8   For our discussion of groups 2 and 4 this means that also derivatives involving a bound root can count as genuine counterexamples.

(5)   bedarken   bedeafen
       bedizen   benighten (*rare*)
       bemoisten   besweeten
       bethreaten (*obsolete*)   encolden (*obsolete*)
       enchasten (*rare*)   endarken (*obsolete*)
       endizen   enfasten
       engladden   engolden
       engreaten (*obsolete*)   enharden (*obsolete or archaic*)
       enhearten (*now rare*)   enlengthen (*obsolete*)
       enlessen (*obsolete*)   enlighten
       enliven   enmilden (*obsolete*)
       enquicken (*obsolete*)   enripen (*rare*)
       enstraighten (*obsolete rare*)   ensweeten (*obsolete*)
       enweaken (*obsolete*)   enwiden
       enwisen   embolden
       embrighten

Ignoring the fact that the vast majority of these verbs are obsolete or rare, we can say that of the available 31 bases, three (*bedizen, enlighten, enliven*) are attested in combination with *-ment*, and with four derivatives (*enchasten, enfasten, enlengthen, bedizen*) there are attested combinations with *-ment* which, however, lack the prefix *en-/be-*. In all of the latter cases it is striking that the prefix is redundant in the respective base forms, as evidenced by the non-prefixed synonymous (and probably more common) forms *chasten, fasten, lengthen,* and *dizen*. The fact that of 31 possible candidates three to seven forms (depending on the analysist's decision to include or exclude *chasten, fasten, lengthen* and *dizen*) are attested to have actually undergone the proposed word formation process speaks for the regularity of *-enment* derivations.[9] Furthermore, the remaining 'idiosyncratic' examples in (4), namely (*re-)awakenment, disheartenment,* and *worsenment* can be explained on different grounds. Thus, although the bases of (*re-)awakenment* and *disheartenment* do not conform to the disyllabic pattern observed by Jespersen, they both contain prefixes, and, as

---

[9]   We do not discuss here the fact that so many of the base words are obsolete or rare, and the possible consequences this may have had for the diachrony of *-enment* derivatives. In very broad terms, it seems that taking into account the obsoleteness or rarity of the bases would only further reduce the number of available bases, which would add further strength to our argument that the process is regular.

was mentioned above, this property seems to play a role in the domain of -*ment* suffixation. Furthermore, we should not exclude the possibility of analogical formations (cf. *(to) better : betterment = worsen : worsenment*).

From the foregoing discussion we can draw the conclusion that there seems to be a considerable degree of regularity in the apparent irregularity of -*enment* derivatives. They are morphologically possible formations, but are subject to independent systematic restrictions imposed on -*ment* which reduce the number of possible instantiations of -*enment* forms considerably. The proposed restrictions can thus account for both the existence and the scarcity of -*enment* derivatives, whereas under Fabb's approach these forms are entirely idiosyncratic.

To summarize our discussion of deverbal nominalizations, we can state that three of the four suffixed verb types in English, namely -*ize*, -*ify*, and -*ate*, are in domains of nominalization processes different from the domains of the five nominalizing suffixes under discussion. The failure of the nominalizing suffixes in question to attach to the derived verbs is therefore not due to a selectional restriction of these suffixes but a natural consequence of the domain-specificity of the morphological processes under discussion. This is also true for the fourth type, -*en* derivatives, which is systematically excluded from the domains of -*ance*, -*age*, -*al*, and -*y*. With regard to the only remaining possible combination, -*enment*, we saw that although there is only a small number of attested counterexamples to Fabb's claim, these counterexamples are systematic in nature, and that the specific restrictions on -*ment* can account for the combinatorial properties of -*ment* in a more adequate fashion than Fabb's generalization. For all of the deverbal nominalizations discussed above it is therefore unnecessary at best to posit the kinds of selectional restrictions Fabb evokes to account for the data.

Let us turn to the denominal abstract-noun-forming suffixes -*age* (*orphanage*), -*hood* (*nationhood*), -*ism* (*despotism*), -*y* (*robbery*), which are again claimed by Fabb not to attach to already suffixed bases. Empirically, this position is highly questionable. *Absenteeism, expansionism, libertarianism* are only a few of the many documented and not at all strange examples, and if there are *abortionists* (listed in the *OED*) in this world, there seems to be no reason (at least no morphological one) why their frame of mind could not be labeled *abortionism* (not listed in the *OED*). The same holds for -*hood* 'person, personality, sex, condition, quality, rank' (*OED*) as in *creaturehood, farmerhood, beggarhood, loverhood*, to mention only few examples. Documented derivatives of the type N-*age* involving suffixed bases are, among others, *cooperage, lighterage, porterage*.

Looking at the number of forms featuring the suffixes under discussion, one cannot, however, overlook that suffixed bases are clearly in the minority, which calls for some explanation. Apart from extra-linguistic mechanisms at work, which may always influence the productivity of certain word formation patterns, a look at the meaning of the suffixes reveals that the low rate of suffixed bases may be a consequence of the semantics of *-age, -hood*, and *-ism*. Of the nouns that end in a suffix, a large portion are abstract nouns, in which case the stacking of another abstract-noun suffix leads to uninterpretable results. Thus, words like **concentrationhood* or *concentrationage are hard to interpret, to say the least. Hence, the semantics of the bases and suffixes involved rules out a great number of possible derivations.[10] A look at the above mentioned counterexamples to Fabb's claim adds fuel to this argument, since the majority of these nouns involve person- nouns as bases, where the said semantic problems do not arise.

Contrary to what Fabb puts forward, denominal noun-forming *-y* is regularly found with bases ending in the agentive suffix *-er* (*archery, patchery, pottery*),[11] of which, strangely enough, Fabb gives an example himself: *robbery*.

In sum, with respect to the suffixes under discussion, Fabb's claim is empirically wrong, and apparent limitations of productivity can be explained by the semantics of the processes involved.

4.3.1.2. Person-noun-forming suffixes

Let us start with the denominal suffixes *-an* (*librarian*), and *-ist* (*methodist*). The distribution of *-ist* 'adherent of a doctrine/attitude' is identical to that of the corresponding *-ism* derivatives denoting the respective doctrine or attitude.[12] Given our analysis of *-ism* in the preceding section, it does not come as a surprise that we find numerous examples of already

---

[10]   The exact determination of the semantic restrictions involved is a matter of future research.

[11]   This pattern is obviously related to the complex suffix *-ery*.

[12]   There are a number of *-ist* and *-ism* forms that do not have a counterpart in *-ism* and *-ist*, respectively. These cases are, however, confined to semantically distinct forms which simply denote agents (cf. *linguist, theorist*) or (medical) conditions like *mongolism, metabolism* (see Giegerich 1998 for discussion).

suffixed nouns that take *-ist* as a suffix, cf. e.g. *abortionist, expansionist, consumerist, conventionalist.*

The suffix *-an* is more problematic. First of all, it is not quite clear which suffix(es) Fabb means by *-an*. While Marchand (1969), for example, treats *-ian, -an, -oan, -onian* as allomorphs, Fabb does not say anything about *-ian, -onian* or *-oan*. Fabb's example *librarian* itself may be interpreted as involving a bound root *libr-*[13] and two suffixes, namely *-ary* ('a place for', *OED*) and *-an*. Under the assumption that *library* is morphologically complex Fabb's claim is empirically inadequate.

There are, however, three possible counterarguments that might be adduced in order to save the generalization that *-an* does not attach to already suffixed nouns. First, one may assume that words like *library* are not morphologically complex, i.e. they do not end in a suffix, and therefore allow the attachment of *-an*. While for *library* this may still be a plausible analysis, for words like *salutatorian* it is definitely not. Second, one might say that the example *librarian* is badly chosen and that we are in fact not dealing with the suffix *-an*, but with a compound affix *-arian*. If we follow this argument (which is itself shaky, given the compositional meaning), we have to turn to those cases of *-an* suffixation which definitely do not involve preceding *-ary*. Such cases seem to be restricted to either proper nouns and place names (*Pennsylvanian, Chomskyan, Andersonian*, sometimes accompanied by phonological adaptation) or nouns ending in *-ia* or *-y* (*academian*). Items in the first group, proper names and place names, usually do not involve any suffixes. It is this morphological property of the members of the - probably most productive - *semantically* defined domain of *-(i)an* suffixation that is responsible for the impression that *-(i)an* does not attach to suffixed stems. The second group of stems, those ending in *-y*, can indeed be argued to be morphologically complex, refuting the claim that *-an* does not attach to already suffixed nouns. The paradigm *barbaric, barbarous, barbarian, barbary* for example, strongly suggests that *barbary* consists of a stem *barbar-* and an affix *-y*.

In summary, no matter how we analyze denominal *-an* derivatives, it is unnecessary to posit an idiosyncratic selectional restriction which forbids the suffix to attach to already suffixed bases.

Let us turn to the deverbal person noun forming affix *-ant* (*defendant*), which denotes a personal or material agent. Again, possible verbal bases

---

[13]   Support for the existence of this bound root may come from the analogical coining *libricide* 'book slaughter' (rare1).

involve those ending in *-ify*, *-ize*, *-ate*, and *-en*. A look at Lehnert (1971) and the *OED* shows that, almost without exception (see below), these verbs are subject to the domain of agentive noun forming *-er/-or*.[14] The rival suffix *-ant* has a somewhat peculiar distribution, since its attachment is partly lexically governed (i.e. unproductive) and partly rule-governed and productive. In the semantically distinguishable domains of medical/pharmaceutic/chemo-technical and legal/corporate jargon, *-ant* can be used productively to form words denoting substances and persons, respectively, as evidenced by the following examples *disinfectant, repellent, consultant, accountant, defendant*, to mention only a few.

The two rival domains of agent nominalizations *-er* and *-ant* are potentially in conflict, whenever base forms may conform to both domains. This is necessarily the case where the semantic specification (which is part of the definition of the domain of *-ant* nominalizations) clashes with the general applicability *-er*. For instance, verbs ending in *-ize* denoting an event of the, say chemical or medical realm, are potentially subject to two nominalization rules. Hence it does not come as a surprise that we find *tetanizant* 'an agent or substance that causes tetanus' (*OED*), where *-ant* supersedes *-er*.

These facts could possibly be interpreted as supporting van Marle's Domain Hypothesis. Since *-er* is the general case, its domain of application may be systematically curtailed by the domains of the special cases, e.g. *-ant*. This means that all verbs form agent nouns by default through *-er/-or* attachment, unless otherwise specified. Thus, apart from lexically marked verbs such as *defend*, only verbal stems denoting concepts of the chemotechnical and legal/corporate fields may take *-ant*. The fact that derived verbs generally form agent nouns with *-er* indicates that they do not carry the diacritic marking for *-ant*. It is only by way of their belonging to the semantically defined domain of this suffix that derived verbs may become subject to *-ant* agentive nominalizations. However, contrary to the prediction of the domain hypothesis, they do not do so obligatorily, but rather tend to choose the general case *-er/-or*. Thus, for the combination *-ize-ant*, the above-cited *tetanizant* seems to be the only unquestionable example, whereas a much larger number of derivatives are attested with *-er* even in the semantic domain of the special case (e.g. *atomizer, carbonizer, crystallizer*). The same holds for the combination *-ate-ant*, which is attested only once (*inflatant*, rare1), while *ate-or* is rather common (e.g. *calibrator*,

---

[14]   I consider *-er* and *-or* allographs of one suffix.

chlorinator, defibrillator). In essence, the special case does not pre-empt the general case, hence type-blocking cannot explain the distribution of *-ant* and *-er/-or*.

4.3.1.3. Relational-adjective forming suffixes

Of the deverbal suffixes *-ful* (*forgetful*), *-ant* (*defiant*), *-ory* (*advisory*), *-ive* (*restrictive*), *-ful* only attaches to monosyllabic verbs or disyllabic verbs with ultimate stress, which automatically rules out all suffixed verbs, since they are either trisyllabic (*-ify*) or do not have final (primary) stress (*-en, -ize, -ate*).[15]

A similar situation we encounter with *-ant*, which attaches regularly to verbs with ultimate (primary) stress, especially to Latinate verbs. Suffixed verbs fall out of this domain. There are, however, some counterexamples, which show that sometimes semantic considerations may overrule conflicting morphophonological constraints. That this is only rarely the case, can be seen from the fact that the *OED* lists only chemical *acidifiant,* physical *calorifiant, ossifiant, personifiant* (of which the last two are marked as rare), and *cognizant* (also with three prefixes), obsolete *agonizant,* medical obsolete *apophlegmatizant,* mathematical *canonizant,* medical *cicatrizant,* and obsolete *symbolizant.*

With derivatives of the form V-*ory* we find lots of counterexamples to Fabb's generalization that deverbal *-ory* does not attach to already suffixed verbs. In fact, verbs ending in *-ate* may take *-ory* as an adjectival suffix productively, cf. *acceleratory, calculatory, stipulatory.* In addition, there seems to be a phonological constraint at work that only verbs ending in a consonant may take *-ory.* Hence verbs ending in *-ify* are not possible input to *-ory* suffixation. Neither do verbs in *-ize* take *-ory* as a suffix.[16] This leaves us with verbs in *-en*, which are equally never followed by *-ory*. Although this failure may be due to undesired effects of a semantic or prag-

---

[15]   There are also good reasons to say that V-*ful* is lexically governed, which excludes all verbs, derived or not, that are not especially marked for this process. In view of the phonological restrictions we need not decide on this issue.

[16]   This is not a purely phonological constraint since words like *revise, advise* take *-ory* as a suffix.

matic nature[17], the Latinate Constraint introduced above can nicely account for this. For *-ory*, a [+ Latinate] suffix, the constraint demands that it cannot attach to the native suffix *-en*.

Yet another example of the operation of the Latinate Constraint is the behavior of *-ive*. This suffix, of which Fabb says that it does not attach to suffixed verbs, only occurs with [+ Latinate] bases, which, furthermore, must feature /d/, /t/, or /s/ as their final consonant. Together, these constraints bring down the number of possible suffixed bases to one, namely those ending in *-ate*. And, as already mentioned above, these take *-ive* quite productively, often alongside the rival *-ory*: *accelerative, complicative* etc.

In conclusion, we can state that it is primarily the phonological, morphological or semantic properties of the base plus independent constraints on the morphological processes involved that decide on the attachability of any of the adjectival suffixes discussed here. The fact that these adjectival suffixes do not attach to suffixed verbal bases is merely the consequence of the described mechanisms and not a significant structural generalization, the latter being empirically unjustified anyway.

We may now move on to the selectional restrictions of the denominal adjectival suffixes *-ful* (*peaceful*), *-ous* (*spacious*), *-y* (*hearty*), *-ly* (*ghostly*), *-ish* (*boyish*), *-an* (*reptilian*), *-ed* (*moneyed*). In general, of the possible suffixed nouns which adjectival forms may be derived from, quite a number take suffixes that are conditioned by base-driven selectional restrictions. Thus *-ion* takes *-al*, *-ment* takes *-al/-ary*[18], *-ing* and *-ant* are also

---

[17]   It is not clear to me what the meaning of a relational adjective relating to a causative event should be. Incidentally, this semantic argument equally holds for *-ize*. Note also that for quite a number of (derived and non-derived) verbs no derived adjectives are attested (*go, sleep, buy*, etc.), which calls for an explanation independent of the morphological make-up of the base verbs.

[18]   It has been argued by Aronoff (1976:53-54) that the attachment of *-al* to *-ment* is subject to the negative restriction that the base of the *-ment* form may not be a word. Although this restriction could be formulated in a positive way, i.e. the base must be a bound root, there are still some counterexamples (Aronoff himself discusses *governmental* and *departmental*, the latter of which is not a real counterexample because it is no longer related to the base verb *depart*). In view of these counterexamples, Giegerich (1998) suggests that *-al* attaches only to semantically non-transparent *-ment* forms such as *fragment, ornament, department, pigment, experiment, government, compartment* but not to transparent forms like *deployment, enrollment* (Giegerich 1998). Raffelsiefen (1996:205) proposes that the fused suffix *-mental* only attaches to bases with non-final stress, which correctly rules out *employmental, *deploymental, *enrollmental,* but unfortunately incorrectly

used as adjectival endings, *-ism* nouns convert into adjectives by replacement of *-ism* by *-ist* or *-istic*, *-ist* nouns are homophonous to their corresponding adjectives, or take *-ic*. In sum, all of the complex nouns just mentioned are more or less systematically excluded from the domains of the adjectival suffixes under discussion, which considerably reduces the number of possible types of bases. Furthermore, a number of nominal suffixes do not seem to lend themselves easily to adjectival derivations, consider *-ette-?, -let-?, -ling-?, -ship-?, -ee-?, -hood-?, -ure-?*, most probably for semantic reasons.[19]

In any case, there are numerous counterexamples to Fabb's claim that the adjectival suffixes under discussion do not attach to already suffixed bases. For N-*ful* there is *healthful, meaningful*, for N-*ous* we find *treacherous, traitorous, harmonious* (the number of free forms as bases of *-ous* is very small anyway, the majority being bound roots). The suffix *-y* occurs in the following multiply suffixed nouns: *Japanesy, healthy, wealthy, ancestory* (and many more in *-OR*$_{AGENT}$-*y*), *layery* (rare), *physicky, strengthy* (rare/dialectal), *weighty*.[20] The most important constraint on *-y* is perhaps that mostly mono- and disyllabic words take *-y* (bases in *-ese* and *-or* are systematic exceptions), which considerably reduces the number of potential suffixed noun types.

Contrary to Fabb's analysis, denominal *-ly* seems to attach quite easily to nouns denoting human beings, be they simplex or derived, as exemplified by *christianly, teacherly*. The same holds for N-*ish* (*Romanish, toadyish, undergraduateish*). It should also be noted that there is a rival morphological process which is extremely productive and which may hinder the proliferance of synonymous affixed forms, namely *-like* attachment.

With N-*ed* we also find a number of counterexamples like *kingdomed, qualitied, conditioned*, whereas for adjectival denominal *-an* (*reptilian*) the same arguments hold as with nominal denominal *-an* (see the discussion above). There is however one set of bases for *-an* not mentioned so far,

---

*employmental, *deploymental, *enrollmental*, but unfortunately incorrectly predicts the non-existence of attested forms like *fragmental, pigmental*. This phenomenon certainly merits further investigation.

[19] Person nouns in *-ee, -let* should be semantically, if not phonologically, compatible with *-ish* and *-y*, and *-ful* with abstract nouns in *-ship*.

[20] Some of the bases of the derivatives mentioned may not be considered morphologically complex, such as *healthy, wealthy, weighty*. However, even if the relationship to the related free form is opaque to most native speakers, and the nominal suffixes *-th* and *-t* are not productive any more, they can paradigmatically be identified as suffixes.

namely a semantically and phonologically conditioned set of Latinate animal names (see Marchand 1969:247 for details). Such names are in general not suffixed, at least not according to English morphological processes.

With respect to deadjectival *-ly* (*deadly*) Fabb's observation is correct, there are indeed no suffixed bases attested. Does that mean we need a selectional restriction on *-ly*? Certainly not, because the suffix is completely unproductive in the modern language, which means that the forms involving deadjectival *-ly* have to be stored individually anyway. This makes a special restriction of the type suggested by Fabb superfluous.

To summarize we have to state that again we have found that numerous counterexamples considerably weaken Fabb's claim, and that, furthermore, base-driven and domain-specific constraints can account for the existing stacking restrictions in a more systematic fashion. Similar arguments apply to the last group of suffixes that supposedly do not attach to suffixed bases.

4.3.1.4. Verb-forming suffixes

For the type N-*ate* some marginal counterexamples are attested in the *OED*, (*affectionate* (obsolete), *compassionate, divisionate*), thereby contradicting Fabb's claim. What is more important, though, is the fact that the productive rule of N-*ate* formation is semantically restricted to chemical substances, whose names, similar to Latinate animal names mentioned above, usually do not involve suffixes. Hence no suffix combinations with *-ate* can arise. Fabb's example *originate* and a few others are not productive formations but must be individually listed. In other words, Fabb's observation follows from independently needed mechanisms, namely the listedness of unproductive formations and the semantic restriction imposed on productively formed derivatives.[21]

The domain of *-ify* derivatives (denominal and deadjectival alike) is restricted by the fact that bases must have either ultimate primary stress or must end in [ɪ] (see chapter 7.1.2. for details). Given that only very few nominal or adjectival suffixes in English have primary stress (*-ee, -eer, -esque*, and *-ese*), or end in [ɪ] (*-ly* and *-y*), possible suffix combinations with *-ify* boil down to *-ee-ify, -eer-ify, -esque-ify, -ese-ify*, and *-ly-ify*,

---

[21]   In Plag (1996:787) it was still claimed that the whole domain of denominal *-ate* was lexically governed. Since then, a more thorough investigation into the nature of *-ate* derivatives has convinced me that this is not the case. For details, see chapter 7.2.

-y-ify. All other combinations (e.g. with nominal *-er*, adjectival *-al, -ous*) are a priori excluded. No examples exist of combinations with primarily stressed suffixes, but it is unclear whether the non-existence of such verbs is really indicative of any structural constraint on *-ify*, or rather the consequence of pragmatic factors or of some prosodic mechanism affecting primarily stressed monosyllabic suffixes. Thus, it seems that these suffixes are subject to their own peculiar restrictions, perhaps guided by phonological principles.[22] Further research is called for to explain the behavior of the three primarily stressed suffixes.

Let us turn to the other combination involving *-ify*. Examples of *-ly* preceding *-ify* are attested (*lovelify, sicklify*, both rare, *wordlify*), and cases of words in *-y-ify* are equivocal because only one [ɪ] surfaces in the derived verb. Therefore, a derivative like *artify* could in principle be derived from *art* as well as from *arty*. The paraphrases given in the *OED* ("To bring art into; to make 'arty' ") suggest that both possibilities occur. In sum, from the phonological constraints on *-ify* derivatives one can largely predict the possible combinations of *-ify* with adjectival suffixes.

The denominal suffix *-ize* seems to attach quite often, and naturally, to suffixed nouns of various types. Consider for example *computerize, christianize, preacherize, protestantize* (if one assumes that the stem is a noun and not an adjective). It is interesting to note that, according to Fabb, deadjectival *-ize* belongs to a different group of suffixes, i.e. the 'problematic' group 4, which contains suffixes that attach to several preceding suffixes. This has the theoretical consequence that one must assume the existence of two distinct homophonous *-ize* suffixes, one denominal, the other deadjectival. In chapter 6 we will see, however, that both in terms of meaning and in terms of phonology, denominal and deadjectival can be unified and that therefore the homophony account must be rejected. Under the assumption of a unitary suffix *-ize* it does not come as a surprise that Fabb's generalization concerning denominal *-ize* turns out to be wrong.

---

22 Derivatives in *-esque* and *-ese* seem to take only *-ness*, and *-ee* is only attested with following *-ism*. Both *-ness* and *-ism* seem to be phonologically peculiar in the sense that they allow certain structures that are otherwise uncommon with suffixes. For example, *-ism* may follow words ending in schwa without truncation of schwa (as in *Indianaism*, example from Goldsmith (1990:261), but cf. *propagandism*, where schwa is deleted), and *-ness* seems to tolerate deletion in coordination (cf. *happy- and sadness*). It is not clear how these facts can be explained, although making reference to notions like the phonological word seems promising (see, for example, Wiese's remarks on a similar case, German diminutive *-chen* (1996a:69-70).

In sum, our discussion of verbal suffixes has shown, that many of the observations by Fabb do not hold up against a larger data base and that existing restrictions on the combinability of verbal suffixes with other suffixes are primarily the result of prosodic constraints.

To conclude our review of Fabb's group 1 suffixes we can state that many of Fabb's empirical claims are wrong and that the proposed base-driven selectional restrictions, semantic and phonological constraints are conceptually and empirically superior to Fabb's selectional restrictions.

4.3.2. Group 2: Suffixes that attach outside one other suffix (6 of 43)

Fabb claims that the following six suffixes only attach to one other suffix, noun-forming *-ary* (attaches to *-ion*, as in *revolutionary*), adjective-forming *-ary* (with the same property, cf. *revolutionary*), denominal *-er* (attaches again only to *-ion*, as in *vacationer*), *-ic* (only occurs after *-ist*, as in *modernistic*), *-(at)ory* (only after *-ify*, as in *modificatory*), and deadjectival *-y* (only after *-ent*, as in *residency*).

As was the case with group 1 suffixes, Fabb's observations are empirically and theoretically flawed. With *-ary*, combinations involving *-ate* and *-ment* are also attested, as in *commendatary, complementary, sacramentary, sedimentary, supplementary*, which enlarges the number of possible suffixes preceding *-ary* to at least three. The same is true for adjective-forming *-ary*, since most of the above forms are also used as adjectives.

Denominal *-er* (*vacationer*) attaches to quite a number of suffixes as the following examples show: *adventurer, allegorister* (rare), *annoyancer, conveyancer, aphorismer* (obsolete), *assurancer, astromancer, astrologer*[23], *baggager, bondager* (Scottish), *complimenter*[24], *concordancer, conjecturer*. Thus, *-er* may also be preceded at least by *-ure, -ist, -ance, -ment, -age*, and *-ar*.

Concerning *-ic*, Fabb's observation is empirically correct, counterexamples are extremely rare (although geological *agglomeratic* may be one). The question, however, remains whether we are faced with a base-driven or with an affix-driven restriction. It seems that the constraint should be

---

23   The forms attested in the *OED* suggest that the the combination *-log-er* has competed with *-log-ist* for quite some time, with the latter having now superseded the former in most of the cases.

24   The primary stress on the first syllable suggests a denominal origin since *-er* is a stress-neutral suffix.

formulated as a base-driven requirement, i.e. as a property of *-ist* rather than as a property of *-ic*. If we say that *-ist* takes only *-ic* as an adjectival suffix, we explain the occurrence of not only *-ist-ic,* but also the obvious ungrammaticality of **-ist-al, *-ist-ive, *-ist-ent* and the like. Again we see the empirical and theoretical advantage of a base-driven restriction over a suffix-driven one, since both legal and illegal combinations can be predicted.

Strangely enough, *-(at)ory,* Fabb's suffix [38], is also mentioned as a member of the group of suffixes that Fabb claims does not appear outside any suffixes. In the relevant section above, I have already pointed out that verbs in *-ate* productively take *-ory* as an adjectival suffix, and have argued for a base-driven constraint. On the same grounds we can state another base-driven restriction, namely that verbs in *-ify* regularly take *-atory* as an adjectival suffix (accompanied by an alternation of *-ify* into *-ific,* which is already familiar from *-ion* suffixation).

Fabb's claim that deadjectival abstract noun-forming *-y* only attaches to one adjectival suffix is not quite correct, since at least adjectives in *-ate* also take *-y* productively as the noun-forming suffix (accompanied by a change of the final plosive into a homorganic fricative). Consider *intimacy, privacy, literacy, degeneracy, (con)federacy, accuracy, adequacy.* Hence, a base-driven constraint is to be favored along the same lines as argued repetitively above.

To summarize our review of the suffixes that are claimed to attach only outside one other suffix, we can say that, with the exception of *-ic,* all of them attach to at least two other suffixes. Furthermore, the base-driven selectional restrictions suggested here to replace Fabb's restrictions have been shown to be superior in their predictive power. This group of suffixes does not form a homogeneous class at all. In fact, it seems strange to posit a class of suffixes on the basis of the number of suffixes to which they attach. Since very specific idiosyncratic selectional restrictions have to be posited anyway, nothing is gained for a theory of derivational morphology by generalizing over the number of such idiosyncrasies.

4.3.3. Group 3: Suffixes that attach freely outside other suffixes (3 of 43)

According to Fabb, *-able,* deverbal *-er* and deadjectival *-ness* are subject to no selectional restrictions other than those involving part of speech. While at first glance this analysis seems valid, Fabb's conclusion that "About these, nothing need be said" (1988: 535), is premature. Since none of these suffixes can be blindly attached to all verbs or all adjectives, it is necessary to posit additional restrictions in order to rule out apparently impossible derivatives. With *-er* impossible formations like *resembler come to mind, *-able* does not attach to verbs ending in a postconsonantal liquid (e.g. *doublable, *saddlable, *wriggleable, Szymanek 1985:102), and even *-ness* is subject to complex phonological constraints that trigger schwa epenthesis in certain cases (e.g. *mark*[ə]*dness*, *well-form*[ə]*dness*, see Wiese 1996b for a detailed analysis).

Fabb adds deadjectival *-en* to his list of freely attaching suffixes, since it may appear outside *-th* (*lengthen*). He concludes that *-en* is subject to two selectional restrictions, one involving part of speech, the other involving only monosyllables. Unfortunately, Fabb does not discuss *-en* in more detail, because the former constraint is problematic. In section 1.1 of Fabb's article *-en* is introduced as a suffix taking adjectives as a base, whereas undoubtedly bases ending in *-th* are nouns. This would call for a constraint of the kind that *-en* attaches to monosyllabic adjectives and nouns, which is, however, much too weak in view of the fact that the vast majority of monosyllabic nouns do not take *-en* as a suffix. In fact, *only* those nouns that end in the nominalizing suffix *-th* (and nominalizing *-t*, as in *height*) take *-en* (almost) regularly as a verbal suffix (but note that the forms *breadthen*, *depthen* (rare) are marginal at best), whereas other denominal forms are entirely lexically governed (*threaten*, *earthen*, *frighten*, *hasten*, *hearten* (obsolete), *heaten*, *kidden* (obsolete/rare), *nighten* (obsolete/rare), *shapen* (rare), *soapen*, *waxen* (obsolete/rare)).

In sum, there are indeed some restrictions operating on the would-be freely attaching suffixes, and these restrictions are much more complex than Fabb would have it. Furthermore they do not differ in kind from the ones observed in the preceding sections, in that they involve morphological, semantic and phonological properties of the base or the derivative.

4.3.4.   Group 4: "Problematic suffixes" (6 of 43)

We may now turn to the last group of suffixes, which Fabb labels "problematic" (1988:536), because they do not display the kind of clear-cut restrictions Fabb posits for the suffixes discussed so far, namely that they either attach only to non-complex bases, to one other suffix, or with no restriction at all. However, as we have learned from our close inspection, the stacking restrictions of the suffixes dealt with so far are much more intricate than Fabb conceived. We will see that his "problematic" suffixes are no more (and no less) problematic than the ones discussed in the above sections.

The six suffixes of this group are denominal -*al* (which, according to Fabb, attaches to -*ion*, -*ment*, and -*or*), the nominalizing suffix -*ion* (which attaches to -*ize*, -*ify*, and -*ate*), the nominalizing suffix -*ity* (which attaches to -*ive*, -*ic*, -*al*, -*an*, -*ous*, and -*able*), and the three deadjectival suffixes -*ism*, -*ist*, -*ize*, which may all be preceded by -*ive*, -*ic*, -*al*, and -*an*. Fabb speculates about possible explanations, like blocking effects, etymological restrictions, and affix-driven restrictions, but does not arrive at a satisfactory solution to the - in his framework - somewhat strange behavior of the six suffixes. Under the alternative approach sketched in this chapter, the facts can be accounted for in a more elegant fashion. Let us look at the details.

Contrary to Fabb's claim, denominal -*al* attaches not only to -*ion*, -*ment*, and -*or*, but also to derivatives involving nominal bases in -*ure* (*apertural, cultural*), -*ent*/-*ant* (*presidential, componential, consonantal*), -*ance*/-*ence* (*concordantial, conferential*), -*cide* (*insecticidal, suicidal*), -*ory* (*laboratorial*), -*ary* (*secretarial*), -*ive* (*relatival, substantival*). Most of these nominal suffixes take the adjectival suffix -*al* regularly, but rival processes, especially -*ous*, may intervene.[25] The data clearly speak against the first of the two possible solutions Fabb discusses, namely that "-*al* belongs with affixes like -*ism* in that it attaches to underived words and to three specified suffixes" (1988:536). The - equally unsatisfactory - alternative Fabb proposes is that "-*al* is in principle free to attach, but there are other (unknown) selectional restrictions involved which prevent it attaching to these suffixes" (1988:536). As will become clear shortly, the Latinate Constraint, in conjunction with individual base-driven selectional restrictions can nicely account for the attested combinations.

With reference to Anshen et al. (1986), Fabb discusses briefly the role of the feature [+ Latinate] as a possible solution of the combinatorial properties of -*al*. He comes to the conclusion that positing an etymological constraint of the kind that -*al* attaches to (all) Latinate suffixes cannot be correct, since there are no attested combinations of -*al* preceded by the Lati-

---

[25]   Sometimes the form involving -*ous* is lexicalized (cf. *adventurous*), sometimes doublets exist (*medicamental* (rare)/*medicamentous/medicamentary*), and quite often the -*ous* form has become obsolete in favor of the -*al* derivative (e.g. *matrimonious*).

nate nominal base suffixes *-ity* and *-ism*[26]. In our view, this fact does not necessarily speak against the operation of the Latinate Constraint, since the Latinate Constraint does not preclude the operation of additional restrictions of a different kind. Thus the absence of *-ity-al* and *-ism-al* can be straightforwardly explained by base-driven selectional restrictions and semantic constraints of these nominal suffixes, which have to be stated anyway. As was mentioned above, *-ism* only allows adjectivization through *-ist(ic)*, which automatically rules out *-ism-al*, and there seems to be a general semantic constraint that does not allow the formation of relational adjectives by suffixation to quality nouns that are derived from adjectives (cf. *-ity-al, *-ity-ary, *-ness-y*), which probably has something to do with the fact that such forms would be synonymous with the root.

We have already argued in section 4.3.1.1. that there is a base-driven restriction with respect to the Latinate suffixes *-ize, -ify*, and *-ate*, namely that they all take *-ation* (i.e. the respective allomorph) as an abstract-noun-forming suffix. The "problematic" distribution of *-ion* is therefore only apparent. In the base-driven model presented here the behavior of *-ion* is the natural consequence of the properties of the Latinate verbal suffixes.

With respect to *-ity*, Fabb offers a more promising account. He observes that *-ity* attaches to Latinate bases in general, which rules out all combinations with Germanic suffixes. Furthermore he posits that *-ity* only attaches to non-glide consonants, which rules out the supposedly non-occurring combinations involving *-ory* and *-ary*[27]. However, at least with adjectives in *-ary*, the nominalizing suffix *-ity* is possible, if not necessary; consider *complementarity, supplementarity* (rare). Selectional restrictions seem to be responsible for the apparent lack of forms in *-ority*. All derivatives ending in *-ority* given by the *OED* are nominalizations of bases ending in the string *-or* (like *minority*), not in the string *-ory*. With adjectives in *-ory*, standard nominalization involves either replacement of *-ory* by *-ion* (*satisfactory/satisfaction*), or suffixation by *-ness*. In any case, adjectival derivatives in *-ory*, but not those in *-ary*, are outside the domain of *-ity*.

There are, however, more adjectival suffixes that can be followed by *-ity*, namely *-ar*, (as in *polarity, peculiarity, scalarity*), and *-ile* (*infantility*). These are both [+ Latinate] suffixes and, pending other constraints, the

---

[26]   Furthermore, Fabb assumes that *-ance* may not precede *-al*, which, as we have just seen, is incorrect.

[27]   Fabb also mentions *-y* here, but adjectival *-y* is ruled out by the Latinate Constraint anyway.

Latinate Constraint predicts their existence. One other mechanism, blocking, is responsible for the only remaining possible combination Fabb considers, *-ant-ity*, which is blocked by *-ance*. Under a base-driven approach, all of the suffixes that can be followed by *-ity* need to be marked for this property. Since *-ory* is not marked for any specific abstract noun suffix, it undergoes the most general process, *-ness* suffixation, whereas *-ant* is marked for *-ce* or *-cy*. Alternatively, and probably more elegantly, one may conceive the domain of *-ity* as comprising potentially all Latinate stems (including derived stems with a Latinate suffix, of course), unless otherwise specified.[28]

In sum, the distribution of *-ity* can be tentatively explained by a careful definition of its domain, the Latinate constraint, and blocking effects due to base-driven selectional restrictions of potential bases. Such base-driven selectional restrictions are needed in any case to rule out forms like *notorious-ity*, or *adventurosity*.

The deadjectival suffixes *-ism* and *-ist* seem to attach freely to all kinds of adjectives, provided that the combination is licensed semantically. Thus, in addition to the four suffixes Fabb finds, the adjectival suffixes *-ile*, *-able*, and *-ar* are also attested to precede *-ism* (as in *infantilism, probabilism, particularism*), and it seems that only semantic-pragmatic factors speak against forms involving other more picturesque adjectival suffixes like *-esque* preceding *-ism/-ist*. Consider the putative *kafkaesquism*, which could certainly denote a theoretical framework developed by a circle of literary critics who try to find kafkaesque traits in any piece of fictional writing (with a *kafkaesquist* being a member of this circle). It is the oddness of the denotation and not of the morphological form that makes *kafkaesquism* a presumably unacceptable derivative. Parallel arguments hold for putative derivatives involving other adjectival suffixes, consider *?girlishism, ?peacefulism, ?wholesomeism*. Factors like blocking may additionally be involved (as always), as can be seen with *?helpfulism* which is probably blocked by *altruism*.

The last "problematic" suffix is *-ize* to which roughly the same arguments apply as to *-ism/-ist*, namely that a whole range of additional adjectival suffixes may precede *-ize*. Consider *redundantize, privatize, probabi-*

---

[28]   The interaction of the domains of *-ity* and its rival systematic domains remains to be determined in a more exact fashion. The problem of *-ity* illustrates the above-mentioned general difficulty to account for the blocking effects between two word-formation rules with rival systematically restricted domains.

lize, permeabilize, respectablize, terriblize, particularize, familiarize, seniorize, exteriorize. The fact that certain combinations (like e.g. *-able-ize*) are not often attested seems to be not due to a morphological constraint but rather due to phonological or pragmatic factors and token-blocking. For example *visualize* 'make visible' blocks *visibilize* (rare). The Latinate Constraint seems again operative to exclude bases with Germanic suffixes. Derivatives on the basis of adjectives in *-ory* and *-ary* are not attested at all, which is most probably due to the prosodic shape of such adjectives. Featuring a disyllabic unstressed suffix, they exhibit a three-syllable stress lapse (e.g. *órdinary, mándatory*), which is strictly prohibited with *-ize* verbs.[29] The intricacies of the phonological constraints are laid out in detail in chapters 6 and 7 and the reader is referred to that discussion for more detailed information.[30]

To summarize, the discussion of the last group of suffixes has shown that these suffixes are not more problematic than any others, since they are subject to the same kind of idiosyncratic, paradigmatic, and semantic-pragmatic constraints as are all supposedly non-problematic ones.

4.4. Conclusion

In this chapter it has been argued that Fabb's generalization concerning English suffixation, expressed in the title of his article, is substantially flawed, both empirically and theoretically.

The analysis of a large amount of data has demonstrated that there is an abundance of counterexamples to many of Fabb's claims. Although it is a well-known fact that lexical rules are often subject to exceptions, this point cannot be evoked to explain away the numerous and often systematically occurring patterns since in Fabb's framework we are not dealing with rules, but with selectional restrictions, i.e. idiosyncratic information of individual lexical items (in this case: suffixes). Thus, even if we accept Fabb's analy-

---

[29]   Deletion of the base-final vowel (as in forms such as *summary - summarize*) could reduce the stress lapse by one syllable. However, it seems that only vowel-final dactyls are truncated (cf. again *súmmary - súmmarìze*). See chapter 6.2. for a detailed discussion of stem allormphy effects observable with *-ize* derivatives.

[30]   The in-depth phonological analysis of verbal derivatives as presented in chapters 6 and 7 has led to a thorough revision of my earlier explanations for the apparent stacking restrictions involving *-ize* as given in Plag (1996:793).

sis, the counterexamples are not exceptions to proposed rules but violations of lexical requirements as stated in the individual suffix's lexical entry. And systematic violations of such requirements are a rather unexpected phenomenon, to say the least.

In my view, however, the most important arguments against Fabb's proposed selectional restrictions are of a conceptual nature. Thus, even if we did not count the numerous "exceptions", many, if not all failures of suffixes to attach to already suffixed forms are the natural consequence of phonological, morphological, semantic, and pragmatic constraints that have to be stated anyway in a reasonably adequate description of English suffixation. These constraints, in particular base-driven selectional restrictions and general morphological constraints like the Latinate Constraint and blocking, regulate the applicability of derivational processes to given domains, ruling out a great many logically possible combinations of stems and affixes. The kinds of selectional restrictions proposed by Fabb have been shown to be either empirically and theoretically inadequate or simply superfluous.

From the discussion of Fabb's last group of suffixes one can conclude that generalizations like "affixes that do not attach outside any affix/that attach outside one other affix" are of no theoretical significance. The fact that there are suffixes which share the property that they only attach to one or to two other suffixes does not make them a natural class, nor a morphologically relevant one. In fact, according to the restrictions that apply across the board, we would have to posit groups of suffixes that attach outside three, four, five, six, seven, and so forth, suffixes. In the present account the number of possible preceding suffixes is a mere artefact of the phonological, morphological, and semantic-pragmatic constraints at work, and thus theoretically insignificant.

The rejection of Fabb's proposal has wider theoretical implications. One of these implications concerns the problem whether word-internal structure is accessible to morphological processes. As was mentioned in section 4.1. above, Fabb's model rests crucially on the assumption that suffixes are sensitive to the morphological make-up of potential bases. The rejection of Fabb's selectional restrictions does, however, not entail that we argue against the accessibility of word-internal structure to morphological processes. The approach taken here is rather neutral with regard to this controversy, although some of the processes discussed (e.g. *-ment* suffixation to prefixed bases) seem to involve access to the morphological make-up of the base word. At least some morphological processes are best explained by assuming access to word-internal structure (Carstairs-McCarthy 1993).

Future research will have to determine when word-internal structure is crucially visible and when it is not.

Finally, we have made some potentially controversial claims in this chapter concerning the nature of selectional restrictions in morphology. For many of the suffixes it was shown that the incapability of a given suffix to attach to a certain class of stems was not due to some assumed property of the suffix, but rather due to a crucial property of the putative base. Taking this point seriously means to question any strictly affix-driven approach as put forward by standard lexical morphology or other stratum-oriented approaches. Most recently, Giegerich (1998) has proposed a base-driven stratificational model of English morphology, in which he argues against affix-driven morphology on different grounds. His idea of the base-drivenness of morphological processes is independently supported by our findings. It seems, however, that we do not need a stratum model to account for the intriguing phenomena discussed in this chapter.

The foregoing presentation was designed as a tour d'horizon through English suffixation, giving an outline of what I consider the most important structural mechanisms that restrict the productivity of derivational processes. The following chapters will offer a more microscopic view of the matter through an in-depth analysis of verb-deriving processes in English.

5. Rival morphological processes 1:
The productivity of verb-deriving processes

5.1. Introduction

In English there are a number of morphological processes by which verbs can be derived from items of a different syntactic category (mostly adjectives and nouns). Disregarding the affixes that add a negative, privative, or reversative element of meaning (*de-, un-*), the following category-changing verb-forming affixes are attested: the prefixes *en-, em-* and *be-* (sometimes accompanied by the suffixation of *-en*), the suffixes *-en, -ize, -ate,* and *-ify*, and a process of conversion. (In what follows I will refer to the latter process also as a kind of affixation or 'zero-derivation', but only as a matter of terminological convenience and not out of theoretical conviction. See section 7.4. for more discussion of this point). It is this group of processes which we will deal with in the remainder of this book.

The verb-deriving processes in English have been the topic of many studies, but three major problems are still unresolved: the problem of meaning, the problem of rivalry and the problem of productivity. There is only one study to date which has tried to tackle these questions in a systematic fashion across affixes, E. Schneider (1987). In that paper, a number of interesting observations are made, but many questions remain unanswered. Thus, Schneider only investigates the suffixes *-en, -ize,* and *-ify*, but not their other potential rivals, *eN-, -ate* or conversion. Furthermore, Schneider's generalizations (and the numerous exceptions he mentions) remain unexplained. The present investigation is an attempt to provide more satisfactory solutions to the three above-mentioned problems, which will be discussed in the following paragraphs.

The first of these problems is how many rules or processes we are actually confronted with. Are the suffixes allomorphs of one or two underlying morphemes, or are we confronted with a variety of rather independent processes? A crucial point in this discussion is of course the meaning of derived verbs, which are remarkably diverse not only across affixes, but also concerning one single affix, for which often more than half a dozen meanings have been postulated. Derivatives involving the suffix *-ize*, for example, seem to be quite heterogeneous in their semantics and in the kinds of bases they attach to. Thus, *-ize* can attach to adjectives and nouns, the resulting derivatives may be transitive or intransitive and they may have one or more of the following meanings (cf. e.g. Marchand 1969:320; X stands for the base word): 'render X, make X, convert into X, put into the form of X, give the character or shape of X, subject to the action, treatment or process of X, subject to a process connected with X, impregnate, treat, combine with X, act in a way characterized by X, imitate the manner of X'. Given a somewhat similar situation with the other affixes, how many processes should we distinguish, in view of the abundance of different affixes, different bases, different meanings and different syntax of the derivatives?

So far, no convincing account of the polysemy or homonymy of the affixes has been proposed, although individual affixes have been studied extensively. Two diverging approaches can be found in the literature. Some studies take the supposedly central meaning as their starting point and investigate the range of affixes that may express this meaning and discuss their formal properties. The problem with such approaches is that the polysemy of the affixes is not taken into account, in spite of the fact that this may influence the behavior of the affixes. Furthermore, the status of such a general rule may be questionable. Gussmann, for example, assumes that there is a so-called rule of derivation, i.e. a "uniform semanto-syntactic formula whereby adjectives become verbalised" (1987:82) with the meaning 'make (more) X'. While the postulated meaning is intuitively plausible, the rule fails to explain why so many of the verbalizing suffixes also take nouns and bound roots as their bases. In such a framework we would have to posit yet other rules, an approach that suspiciously calls for Occam's Razor.

In a more general perspective, Gussmann's analysis represents an approach to morphology that separates the meaning of affixes from their phonological spell-out. The most pronounced theory of this kind is the so-called 'lexeme-morpheme base morphology', developed by Robert Beard over the last two decades (e.g. 1981, 1987a 1987b, 1988, 1990a, 1990b, 1994), slightly modified versions of which have been proposed by Szymanek (1985, 1988), and Don (1993). The central claim of these authors is that the frequent mismatches of form and meaning in morphology arc best accounted for if both aspects are strictly separated. This has been come to know as the 'separation hypothesis', which claims that word formation rules split into two different kinds of rules: the categorial and semantic operation is done by so-called lexical (or derivational) rules, whereas the phonological operation is performed by a morphological rule which simply adds the appropriate phonetic material or manipulates the base form in some other phonetically relevant way (e.g. by ablaut). By separating the meaning from the phonetic realization the theory can elegantly account for the synonymy of different affixes and for the polyfunctionality of individual affixes. In the case of derived verbs, there would, for example, be a lexical rule (or 'derivational category' in the terminology of Gussmann or Szymanek) CAUSATIVE which is paired with a number of morphological, or 'affixation', rules, i.e. [aɪz], [ɪfaɪ], [eɪt], [ən] (Gussmann 1987, Don 1993:66). The crucial assumption of the theory is however the absolute synonymy of the processes (e.g. Beard 1990b:162). As we will see, this assumption is most problematic.

Non-separationist accounts, called 'direct articulation models' by Beard, maintain the idea that there is a direct link between the form and the meaning of affixes but often fail to present an account of whether or how these meanings are related (cf. e.g. Lieber's (1996) study of -*ize*).

In what follows, the meaning of each affix will be investigated on the basis of a large collection of forms, and an explicit account of their polysemy will be proposed.[1] The comparison of the semantics of the individual affixes will reveal that the affixes are only partially synonymous and that there are compelling arguments for the postulation of a number of different affixation rules for verb-forming affixes.

The second problem is the problem of rivalry. Assuming that at least some of the processes can be shown to be semantically overlapping, the question arises how the affixes select their bases (or the bases select their affixes). The data in (1) illustrate that there must be certain restrictions at work:

(1)	academicize	*academicify	*academic-Ø$_v$
	computerize	*computerate	*computeren
	artify	*artate	*art-Ø$_v$
	Nazify	*ennazi	*Naziate
	passivate	passivize	passivify

Basically, two different kinds of mechanisms are conceivable, syntagmatic and paradigmatic. We will see that it is primarily the properties of the individual processes in combination with the properties of their base words, that are responsible for the distribution of the different affixes. Paradigmatic mechanisms are of less relevance, in fact type-blocking will be dem-

---

[1] An earlier version of my account of the polysemy of -*ize* derivatives (section 6.1 below) has appeared as Plag (1997).

onstrated to play no role at all, which seriously questions its usefulness as a theoretical notion and descriptive tool.

This brings us to the third of the above-mentioned problems, namely productivity, which is of course closely related to the second. Which of the processes are (still) productive, and which factors are responsible for the differences in productivity among those affixes that are still used to coin new words? While it seems clear that some of the processes are more productive than others, a clear assessment of their productivity is still lacking. On the basis of dictionary data and text corpus data we will close this gap in the description of these affixes.

Starting out from these three central problems I will proceed as follows. In the remainder of this chapter the productivity of the different processes will be measured, making use of the Cobuild corpus and the *OED*. In chapters 6 and 7 we will then scrutinize very closely the structural properties of the individual processes, which will finally lead to a solution of the two remaining problems, meaning and rivalry.

As outlined in chapter 2, there are a whole range of measures available to the researcher, of which Baayen's corpus-based measures and Neuhaus's dictionary-based counts seem to be the most promising. These two methods will be employed below. In the earlier discussion of the different productivity measures I already briefly hinted at the methodological problems inherent to Baayen's and Neuhaus's measures, and much of the examination to follow will further illustrate these points. Hence, this chapter does not only provide the first explicit quantitative account of the productivity of verbal derivation in English, but also contains a detailed discussion of hitherto unmentioned methodological problems involved in the application of productivity measures.

We will start with the dictionary-data, then move on to the text corpus data, and finally compare the results of the two analyses.

5.2. A dictionary-based account

5.2.1. *The use of dictionaries in productivity studies: A controversy*

Neuhaus (1971, 1973) proposes that the degree of productivity of a rule should be measured by counting the number of derivatives in a given period, which is most conveniently done by checking historical dictionaries like the *OED*. The use of dictionaries in the determination of the productivity of a process is, however, problematic.

For example, Baayen and Renouf (1996:69) object to the use of dictionaries in productivity studies and claim, "Dictionaries, unfortunately, are not a reliable source for studying morphological productivity". They back up this position by some general considerations on the nature of dictionaries and by pointing out the obvious failure of some dictionary-based studies to provide correct results. In particular, they cite the findings presented by Cannon (1987), and contrast them with their own corpus-derived results. Through this comparison it becomes obvious that Cannon's dictionary-based account is thoroughly inadequate. The question remains, however, whether the refutation of Cannon's analysis can be used as an argument against the use of dictionaries as such. Let us dwell on this question a bit.

Three main arguments against dictionaries as data bases for productivity studies can be put forward. First, for commercial and practical reasons, dictionaries usually do not aim at the comprehensive documentation of productively-formed, transparent words, but rather cover the more frequent and idiosyncratic items. This is quite sensible since dictionary-users need not check those words whose meaning is entirely predictable from its elements, which by definition is the case with productive formations. However, this argument against dictionaries may hold for learner dictionaries or even large desk dictionaries (such as *RHCD, Webster's Third*, or *SOED*), but certainly not for dictionaries like the *OED,* which aims at complete coverage (e.g. Berg 1991:4), and whose virtues and versatility lie exactly in this fact. The *OED* (at least before its release on compact disc) is not meant to provide quick and easy reference, but thorough and complete information on individual words and the development of the English vocabulary.

Hence, it is not surprising that in comparison to the amount of data provided by current innovational dictionaries, the *OED* coverage is better. For example, according to Cannon (1987) *The Barnhart Dictionary of New English since 1963, The Second Barnhart Dictionary of New English*, and Merriam's Addenda Section to *Webster's Third New International Dictionary of the English Language* contain only 19, 12, and 15 *-ize* neologisms, respectively, whereas the *OED* lists 284[2] for the period from 1900 to 1985,[3] including almost all of the derivatives listed in the three other dictionaries.

But, and this is the second argument against dictionaries, even if lexicographers aim at complete coverage, this intention does possibly not prevent them from overlooking new, regular formations just because they are regular. We already saw in chapter 2 that productive formations tend to go unnoticed by language users (e.g. Schultink 1961). Therefore, even the *OED* lexicographers fall victim to the unavoidable tendency to include the more salient idiosyncratic forms and neglect the listing of regular derivatives. That this is not pure speculation can be illustrated by the almost equal numbers of 20th century neologisms listed for nominal *-ness* and verbal *-ize* (279 vs. 284, respectively), although no one would seriously doubt that *-ness* is far more productive (in respect to *P*, *P**, and *V*) than *-ize*. It seems that *-ness* forms do not strike the lexicographers' eyes to the same degree as do *-ize* words, for whatever reason. As we will see in the next chapter, the vast majority of *-ize* neologisms are completely regular, and therefore reasons other than idiosyncrasy must be responsible for the saliency of *-ize* verbs. One might venture the hypothesis that, other things being equal, new verbs tend to be more salient than new nouns. For example, the number of nouns in English is extremely large whereas the number of verbs is comparatively small, which makes new verbs potentially more noticeable as such than new nouns. For example, the CELEX lexical data base (Baayen et al. 1993), which is based on the Cobuild corpus, lists 6582 simplex nouns and 2727 complex nouns involving the most common noun-deriving suffixes (*-ee, -er, -ation, -ment, -al, -ness, -ian, -ity, -ism*), but only 2581 simplex verbs and 400 complex verbs involving not only the suffixes *-ize* and *-ify,* but also the prefixes *de-, re-, be-* and *en-*. But even if there are discrepancies in the comprehensiveness of the *OED*'s listing of different types of derivatives, this fact does not make the *OED*-based measure useless. In the case of *-ize* and *-ness*, the number of neologisms is so high that it is uncontroversial to state that both suffixes have been productive in the twentieth century. In contrast, the verbal suffix *-en*, for example, is only listed with two neologisms in this century, which is in line with the opinion unanimously expressed in the literature that *-en* is dead.

---

[2]   This figure excludes the 62 neologisms in *-ize* that are only listed as participles (*-izing/-ized*). See the discussion below for details.

[3]   Even if the period of sampling is perhaps longest for the *OED*, this does not suffice as an explanation of these discrepancies.

From all this one can conclude that the number of neologisms in the *OED* can reliably be used to tell productive processes from unproductive ones, but that the measure is less reliable in ranking productive processes, i.e. in determining their respective degrees of productivity. Interestingly, the *OED*-based measure shares this property with Baayen's measure *P*, the 'productivity in the narrow sense', about which Baayen says that its "primary use ... [is] to distinguish between unproductive and productive processes as such", whereas the global productivity *P** is "especially suited to ranking productive processes" (1993:194).

The third argument against dictionaries is that they drag along a whole range of old complex forms that may distort the analysis because they are residues of morphological processes that have long ceased to be productive or because they are unanalyzed or reanalyzed borrowings.[4] Again this argument is not valid for a historical dictionary like the *OED*, because the search can be restricted to a given period, so that only the neologisms of that stretch of time enter the analysis.

To summarize, the main disadvantage of a dictionary like the *OED* is that the sample from which the dictionary entries are collected is left unspecified and that there is some inconsistency in the sampling of individual forms. However, these shortcomings do not make the *OED* unsuitable for productivity studies. As we have seen, if very few neologisms are attested in a rather long period of time, this is a strong indication of unproductivity. Hence, the dictionary-based measure is a reliable instrument for distinguishing between productive and unproductive processes. In conclusion, comprehensive historical dictionaries like the *OED* should be able to yield significant results in productivity studies, contrary to the claims by Baayen and Renouf (1996). The comparison of dictionary-based and text-based measures below will substantiate this claim.

After the review of arguments against dictionary-based productivity accounts, we may now briefly examine three points where a dictionary-based measure appears superior to text-based measures. First, lexicographers of extremely large dictionaries like the *OED* scrutinize larger quantities of texts than hitherto available electronic corpora can provide, which may lead to a more comprehensive picture of the derivational patterns. For ex-

---

[4]   Note that this is also a serious problem for text-based approaches, as will become clear below.

ample, the number of Cobuild hapaxes involving verbal affixes is much smaller than the number of neologisms in the *OED*.[5]

Another advantage of the use of a dictionary lies in the circumvention of complex statistical calculations. The problem is of course not the calculation of the different measures itself, which is a fairly easy task if one has a modern calculator at hand, but lies in the determination of the tokens and types upon which the calculation should be based. Whereas with the dictionary data, the decision to count a form as belonging to the given derivational category only means the addition of one item, a few types more or less in the text-based calculation may result in significant changes in the overall number of tokens of a category.

Perhaps the most important positive trait of the *OED*-based measure is that the productivity of zero-derived items can be determined, which is impossible to do with the computer-programs used for the analysis of the text-corpora. Thus, under a strict text-based approach the degree of productivity of conversion cannot be calculated at all. In view of the importance of conversion as a verb-deriving process, this is the most serious drawback of the text-based measures.

5.2.2.   Employing the OED on CD: Practical problems

Having established the versatility of the *OED* for productivity studies, we may now turn to the investigation itself. The relevant data have been extracted from the *OED on CD* with the help of the query language that comes with it, which enables the user to carry out complex search routines across the different sections of the dictionary (e.g. headwords, part of speech, etymology, definitions, quotation date, author of quotation, etc.).[6] For the purposes of this study the software was programmed to search for the relevant strings of letters in combination with the first dates of attestation.[7] The twentieth century (i.e. 1900 to 1985, where the *OED* coverage

---

[5]   The hapaxes are significant, because the proportion of neologisms is highest among the types with the lowest frequency, especially hapaxes (see chapter 2 and below for discussion).

[6]   The possibility of combining different search criteria makes the *OED* a powerful electronic data base for all kinds of lexicological studies. See, for example, Jucker (1994) for an overview.

[7]   The dates of first attestation given in the *OED* are of course only the first attestations in written documents as they were detected by the lexicographers or

ends) was chosen as the relevant period because it is large enough to yield a sufficient number of neologisms if a rule is to some extent productive, and small enough to exclude major diachronic developments within that period. The resulting files of raw data had to be thoroughly scrutinized for forms that did not belong to the derivational category in question. The remaining words, which are given in appendix 1, formed the basis of the productivity counts and of the structural analysis to follow in chapters 7 and 8. For the measure of productivity presented below, the affixes were not distinguished by the category of the base word. Overall, there is a clear dominance of denominal formations over deadjectival ones with practically all processes. The nature of the base-words undergoing the individual processes will be discussed more thoroughly in the next chapter.

Let me illustrate the sampling procedure with the suffix *-ize*. The compact disc version of the *OED* was searched for all forms ending in the strings <ize> or <ise> with the first citation dating from 1900 to 1985. The resulting list of words contained a considerable amount of forms that, by all accounts, did not feature the suffix *-ize* (such as compounds involving the second element *-wise*, or borrowings like *decatise*), and which needed to be excluded.

Furthermore, all forms were removed from the lists of raw data that were derived by the prefixation of already existing words, and all forms derived by parasynthesis. A form was classified as prefixed if the stem was an existing complex verb of the relevant category, and if the derivative was also semantically and phonologically transparent as a prefixed complex verb (e.g. *repolarize*). A form was classified as parasynthetic if the stem was attested earlier than the derivative, the derivative was semantically transparent and was not a prefixed verbal derivative. An example of such a parasynthetic form is *decaffeinate*.

Under the strict application of the criteria just mentioned, the determination of relevant forms proved fairly unproblematic with *-ize, -ify, eN-, be-* and *-en,* but the processes of *-ate* suffixation and conversion turned out to be more difficult.

---

other people studying the phenomena. Thus, a word may have been in usage before the first documentation, or, conversely, it may not have gained any currency after its first documentation. It is unlikely that these unavoidable problems cause any serious defects in our investigation since all processes under discussion should be affected to the same degree.

As I will show in section 7.1. below, especially the processes by which -*ate* verbs are derived are rather diverse and include many cases of back-formation, conversion (with or without reassigning stress), and local analogies. In fact, suffixation is not even the most frequent of the processes which give rise to -*ate* verbs. In the count given below, the derivatives were counted by only analyzing the derivative (i.e. the output), disregarding its particular derivational history. Thus, if a form contained, for example, the morph -*ate* and a discernible stem, it was included in the count. The resulting figure is therefore much larger than the number of forms that were presumably coined by the suffixation of -*ate* to a given stem. This effect is much less significant with the other overt suffixes.

Equally problematic were the zero-affixed verbs, which were extracted from the *OED* by searching for all verbs with their first attestation between 1900 and 1985 that do not contain any of our verbal affixes. The result file of raw data contained more than one thousand verbs, of which 488 made it into the final list. I excluded all forms derived by the truncation of a suffix or other material (e.g. *to bibliograph* < *bibliography, to bolsh* < *Bolshevik*), by prefixation (e.g. *defocus*) or compounding (e.g. *pistol-whip*), and those that could be determined as loan words. All unclear cases were included.

A few remarks are in order concerning the accuracy of the search procedure. In principle, we can expect the software to find all neologisms of the pertinent kind that are listed in the *OED*, if the query language is used properly. However, the use of the *OED* for the purposes of chapter 4 revealed that, due to occasional inconsistencies in the programming of the entries, this is not the case (see also Plag 1996). There are sometimes words that do not make it into the appropriate result file, inspite of the fact that they correctly match the search string.[8] Their number seems to be negligible, though. In the case of -*ize*, for example, I have detected only one form, *scenarioize*, that should have been retrieved by the query software, but was not.[9]

Another problem emerging from the *OED* as a data base is the fact that some of the derivatives involving overt suffixes are only listed as participles, i.e. with the inflectional endings -*ing* and -*ed*, which are used as ad-

---

[8]   These bugs in the program are officially acknowledged by the *OED* staff, and will possibly be eliminated in the next edition.

[9]   For the investigation of the phonological properties of -*ize* derivatives I carried out all kinds of searches with more specified search strings and compared the results with my original files. Of all the neologisms I found, only *scenarioize* had escaped the original search.

jectives or nouns in the quotations given in the *OED*. Whatever the reason for this peculiarity may be, these words were excluded from the structural investigation of chapters 6 and 7. The reason for this decision was that this is a study of derived verbs, and not of deverbal nouns and adjectives, even if the latter might have a lot in common with their base verbs. However, for the present purpose of determining the productivity of the verb-forming affixes, the numbers of new participles are included in the frequency tables given below. This decision had to be taken in order to insure that the dictionary-based figures are comparable to the text-based ones, since, for reasons to be discussed in section 5.3., the Cobuild count had to include participial forms. The *OED* participles can be found in separate sections in appendix 1.

5.2.3. Results

Of all affixes searched for (*eN-*, *be-*, *-en*, *-ize*, *-ate*, *-ify*, and Ø), only *be-* was totally unproductive in the relevant period,[10] whereas all other processes yielded between two and 488 neologisms.

In order to assess and compare the productivity of the processes under discussion, the number of types as attested in the *OED* have been summarized in table 5.1.:

---

[10] Note again that parasynthetic formations were eliminated from the data, which excludes productive formations where *be-* occurs in combination with the ornative denominal suffix *-ed*. This parasynthetic *be-* is described by the *OED* as follows (prefix *be-* 7):

"Forming participial adjectives, which unite the preceding senses, esp. 6 and 2, in the notion of 'covered or furnished with,' usually in a conspicuous, ostentatious, unnecessary, or overdone way. In modern use (e.g. with Carlyle) the force of the *be-* is often merely rhetorical, expressing depreciation, ridicule, or raillery, on the part of the speaker, towards the appendage or ornamentation in question; cf. *booted* and *bebooted*, *gartered begartered*, *wigged bewigged*. Some of these words have no form without *be-*, and closely approach the verbs in 5, e.g. *bedaughtered*, *bepilgrimed* 'overrun with pilgrims.' This is now the most frequent use of *be-*, and the formations of this kind are endless". See Marchand (1969:148) for a similar statement.

Table 5.1. Number of attested 20th century neologisms in the OED

affix	N (number of types)	N$_{PART}$ (number of neologisms only attested as participles)	N$_{TOTAL}$ (total)
-ize	284	62	346
-ate	72	15	87
-ify	23	7	30
eN-	7	0	7
-en	2	0	2
be-	0	0	0
Ø	488	0	488

The figures in table 5.1. allow the following generalizations. Of all *overt* verbalizing affixes, *-ize* is by far the most productive. Novel formations in *-ate* are much less frequent, followed by those in *-ify*. The affixes *eN-* and *-en* are attested only in very few isolated coinages and can therefore be considered unproductive. The same conclusion holds for the prefix *be-*, which is not attested at all in formations of the twentieth century (except in the parasynthetic formation of ornative participles, see note 10 above).

These results are roughly in line with the existing literature, which can be summarized as in Marchand's statement that the "only derivative mor-phemes Present-day English has for denominal verbs are *-ate, -ify, -ize*." (1969:364). A more detailed picture is given by Gussmann (1987), who does not only hold *-ize* to be the only truly productive affix, but also states a sharp contrast between *-ate* and *-ify* on the one hand, and *-en, eN* and *be-* on the other. Of the latter three affixes he says that they are "completely unproductive" (p.96, see also Marchand 1969:164, 148), which is corrobo-rated by our findings. According to Bauer (1983:223) *-en* "is only margin-ally productive, if at all", which seems too conservative a statement, since two new formations in 86 years make an affix clearly belong to the cate-gory 'not at all productive'. The two suffixes *-ify* and *-ate* are set apart from the unproductive ones by Gussmann not only because of "the greater num-ber of derivatives [...] but primarily because non-accidental redundancies can be stated here." (1987:96-97). According to his analysis, *-ify* and *-ate* appear to be semi-productive, which is in line with the results in table 5.1. Bauer comes to a similar conclusion when he states that *-ize* is the most productive overt affix, followed by *-ify* (1983:222-223). Unfortunately, he does not say anything about *-ate*, but Marchand (1969:258) and Plank (1981:214) point out that a certain type of denominal *-ate* is productive, a claim that is not refuted by the above figures and will be further substantiated in chapter 7.

The high number of converted verbs in Table 5.1. is not surprising at all, since it has long been observed that in Modern English conversion is the most productive verb-deriving process (e.g. Jespersen 1942:112f, Bauer 1983:226-227). We will see in chapter 8 that the observed differences in the productivity between *-ify, -ate, -ize* and Ø correspond nicely with the structural restrictions imposed on these processes, which lends further support to the validity of the *OED*-based count. Notice, however, that the quantitative difference between *-ize* derivatives and converted verbs is perhaps not as big as one might have expected, given the general unrestrictedness of conversion. A possible explanation for this result could lie in the greater saliency of overt morphological marking.

Overall, the observed quantitative differences between the processes under discussion corroborate existing accounts of their productivity. It should not be overlooked, though, that the above-cited claims by other linguists are founded to a large extent on dictionary-based investigations themselves. Therefore, it could be argued that my own count is a mere replication of earlier studies. However, to my knowledge, no explicit comparative dictionary-based account of the productivity of these processes has ever been proposed before.[11]

Having established a reasonable dictionary-based analysis, we may now move on to a text-based account of the productivity of the processes under discussion.

---

[11] Mahn (1971) provides a comprehensive count of one type of derivatives, those in *-ify*, but does not include counts of its rival affixes. Based on earlier editions of the *OED*, data from other dictionaries, and on his own collection of words, Mahn arrives at 29 putative 20th century neologisms, of which only 16 he found documented with their first attestation, whereas the others are assumed to be neologisms on the grounds that they are not listed in historical dictionaries (1971:186). At least three of his putative neologisms are already attested earlier (e.g. *bronzify* 1855, *complexify* 1839, *tourify* 1820, see *OED*), so that his list boils down to 26 as against my 23.

5.3. A text-based account

For computing the productivity measures proposed by Baayen I chose the Cobuild corpus, which has been developed and used extensively for a number of dictionary projects (e.g. the *COBUILD* dictionary 1987, see Sinclair 1987 for an account of the development and use of the corpus). The Cobuild corpus is an on-line available sample of a much larger corpus, the so-called Bank of English. Both the full and the sample corpus are constantly enlarged and updated, so that, unfortunately, it is impossible to make reference to a particular version of the Cobuild corpus. I have mainly worked with the complete tagged[12] word list that I extracted in July 1995, when the Cobuild corpus had reached the size of c. 20 million words. The tagged word list contains all word forms (tokens) and their frequencies as they are found in the July 1995 corpus. This particular version of the corpus is archived with CobuildDirect and was re-accessed in September/October 1996 for the checking of problematic items.[13] By that time, the regular Cobuild corpus had already increased in size to c. 50 million words.

In view of the uncontroversial unproductivity of *eN-*, *-en*, and *be-*, and the impossibility to search for zero-derived verbs, I limited my attention to the only three productive ones, *-ize*, *-ate* and *-ify*.

From the complete Cobuild word list all forms were extracted that contained the strings of letters that may represent the three suffixes *-ize*, *-ate*, and *-ify*. To extract all *-ize* formations, for example, I searched the complete word list for words ending in the strings <ize, izes, ized, izing, ise, ises, ised, ising>, using the TACT® text retrieval program. The resulting lists still contained a large amount of data that were either irrelevant or problematic. Whereas obviously useless data (such as *bodywise* or *Dianagate*) were fairly easily eliminated, the treatment of the problematic forms proved extremely difficult. This brings us to the methodological problems already mentioned in chapter 2.

---

[12] The following tags from the word list are relevant here: NN (common singular noun), NNS (common plural noun), JJ (adjective), VB (verb base form), VBD (verb past tense form), VBN (verb participle form), VBZ (verb 3rd person singular), VBG (verb -ING form).

[13] I would like to thank the CobuildDirect staff, especially Jeremy Clear, for their assistance.

For the calculation of P (and the other measures) it is necessary to count all words with a given affix in the corpus. The problematic task is now to decide which words can be considered to bear the affix in question, i.e. to determine which strings of letters represent the relevant verbal suffix. What looks like a straightforward procedure with an affix like *-ness* proved to be extremely difficult with words in *-ate* and, to a much lesser extent, *-ize* and *-ify*. The problems include the following.

The verbal suffixes under discussion appear to be semantically diverse and many of their derivatives are semantically or phonologically opaque. The semantically diverse affixes pose the question as to whether they really represent a single morpheme or a number of different, homophonous ones. Furthermore, there are derivatives that are not based on existing words but on bound roots. Thus it could be argued that forms like *baptize* or *propagate* are morphologically simplex, since they are not derived by the suffixation of *-ize* or *-ate* to an already existing base word. However, independent of the theoretical approach taken, there is an undeniable non-arbitrary connection of these two derivatives to other words featuring *-ize* and *-ate*, in that the two strings at least indicate the verbal status of the word. Thus, even in opaque formations one could argue for the presence of a suffix which indicates the verbal category of the word, if nothing else. This problem becomes even more complicated when we take into consideration that many *-ate* verbs that look perfectly transparent are actually analogical formations or back-formations, and not derived by the suffixation of *-ate* to a given word (see section 7.1. for details).

Even if it were possible to neatly separate transparent from opaque formations, the exclusion of non-transparent forms from the sampling would possibly lead to an overly high productivity measure, obliterating the effect that non-transparent items have on the overall productivity of a process. As discussed in chapter 2, a high proportion of many non-transparent types (with usually higher token-frequency) are indicative of less productive processes. Hence, the exclusion of opaque forms would lead to a higher productivity value P than one would probably want to have. From a structural viewpoint the semantic opacity and diversity of a large number of derivatives is also indicative of less productive processes (cf. van Marle 1988). The exclusion of opaque formations would therefore artificially clean up the messy state the process is actually in.

It was therefore decided to leave all opaque words in the list, as long as a suffix could be identified that indicated the verbal status of the word. On the basis of this criterion, *baptize* and *propagate* were included, because of the existence of, for example, *baptism* and *propaganda*. However, one has to be aware that, on this policy, the existence of a potentially large number of old, lexicalized, non-transparent words may negatively influence the productivity measure.[14]

Another important problem concerning the sampling of derived verbs lies in multiple affixation. Coming back to the example from chapter 2, in combinations of *-ize* with *-able* (as in *conventionalizable*) the question arises whether such words should be counted as *-able* derivatives, or as *-ize* derivatives, or both? For the researcher, it seems reasonable to partition the lexicon into disjunct classes in order to be able to compare measures across affixes. According to this rationale, only the affix that has been attached last is counted, i.e. in the case of our example *conventionalizable* we would assign the word exclusively to the category of *-able* derivatives. Although not mentioned in his publications, this policy has been confirmed by Baayen (personal communication, October 1996).

However, psycholinguistically this partitioning of the lexicon does not seem to be completely adequate because speakers do not only parse the outmost suffix. A speaker who has never come across *conventionalize* will probably still note that this (potential) word is contained in the new word *conventionalizable*, and this information will somehow add to the speaker's knowledge of possible *-ize* formations. Baayen's measures therefore cannot reflect the influence multiply affixed words may have on the representation of the inner affixes occurring in such derivatives. In essence, the decision to exclude tokens with inner affixes of the relevant category from the count is largely dictated by practical considerations at the cost of the psycholinguistic value of the measures. This somewhat weakens Baayen's claim that his measures are psycholinguistically well-founded.

The treatment of multiple affixation is especially problematic with the verbal suffixes under discussion because they are often followed by inflectional elements. The most obvious treatment would be to ignore inflectional endings altogether because they have no bearing on the issue of derivational productivity. However, the participial suffixes *-ing* and *-ed* could be argued to derive adjectives or nouns from the verbal stem. It is therefore not obvious whether a participle like *conventionalizing*, which

---

[14]   Note again that this kind of problem practically does not occur with processes like *-ness* suffixation, which is indeed one of the reasons why Baayen and Renouf (1996) chose this suffix for investigation, among others (Baayen, personal communication, July 1997). Unfortunately they do not reveal their policy concerning the sampling of *-ity* words, which, similar to the verbal suffixes, is also often found in lexicalized forms.

can surface as an adjective or as a noun, should in this case be counted as an instance of a derivational suffix *-ing* or of a derivational suffix *-ize*. The problem of the syntactic category of participial forms is notorious and will not be discussed in detail here.[15] I have settled for a count that treats the participial endings as purely inflectional, hence treating the relevant forms as verbs inspite of their possible occurrence in the syntactic positions of nouns or adjectives.

This problem is further complicated by the fact that the tagging in the Cobuild corpus is often incorrect, with the consequence that many of the nominally and adjectivally tagged words in question are in fact clearly verbs (the reverse seems to be less frequent).[16] According to a rough estimate, about ten percent of all relevant tokens are adjectivally or nominally tagged.

In sum, I decided to ignore all inflectional endings and count not only the verbally tagged tokens but also the nominally and adjectivally tagged ones. Unfortunately, some more problems emerged with *-ate*. While it was still relatively easy to deal with verbs such as *create* and *debate*, which were eliminated on the basis that they have primary stress on <ate>, a major problem occurred with forms that have adjectival or nominal homographs. For instance, *discriminate* can be a verb or an adjective, *estimate* can be a verb or a noun. The only way to overcome, if not solve, this dilemma was to use the tagging, in spite of its potential error-proneness.[17] Hence, of all types in *-ate* on the list that were ambiguous between the adjectival, nominal and verbal interpretation only those tokens were counted that were tagged as verbs. Thus, all homographs tagged as adjectives or nouns were excluded from the calculation. For illustration, consider *alternate*, which entered the list of *-ate* derivatives with an overall number of 89 verbally tagged tokens, whereas the 70 adjectivally and nominally tagged tokens were erased from the list.

---

[15]   See, for example, Haspelmath (1996) for a recent account of category-changing inflection.

[16]   The high error rate in the tagging, acknowledged by CobuildDirect, is due to the fact that the tagging is done automatically by a computer program.

[17]   The other possible alternative would have been to double-check all pertinent tokens with their context on-line in the corpus, which was decided against for practical reasons. Presumably, the distorting effect by wrongly tagged items is not significant, so that the probably slightly more accurate result would not have justified the enormous costs (in terms of money and effort) of the investigation.

Note that by excluding the nominally and adjectivally tagged tokens of ambiguous -*ate* words I treated -*ate* derivatives in a manner slightly different from -*ize* and -*ify* words. Thus the exclusion of the adjectivally and nominally tagged tokens that are homophonous with -*ate* verbs may have led to the exclusion of some tokens of participles of -*ate* verbs which the tagging program has tagged as adjectival or nominal. This distortion seemed negligible in comparison to the alternative, namely counting only the verbally tagged items for all suffixes, which would have been theoretically less preferable and practically would have meant an even greater reliance on possibly wrong taggings.

Another alternative option would have been to include even the homographic adjectival and nominal -*ate* forms. As shown in table 5.2. below, -*ate* is the least productive suffix (in terms of P), even under the exclusion of the homographic adjectival and nominal forms. The inclusion of these forms would only have increased the overall number of -*ate* tokens, without significantly raising the number of hapaxes. In other words, the inclusion of the homographic adjectival and nominal forms would have only led to a further decrease in P. In view of these considerations the policy chosen seemed to be the best of all available ones.

Before we turn to the results of our investigation, a note of caution is in order. The foregoing discussion of the intricacies of the sampling method has made clear that the procedure adopted here is only one out of a whole range of possible others. Different methodological decisions could be justified, leading perhaps to different results. Possible effects of the sampling method on the results are occasionally mentioned below, but a more systematic investigation of such effects is certainly called for. This will be left to future studies, however, since this book is more concerned with the structural than with the quantitative aspects of productivity. In view of the methodological problems, the importance of the results given below should not be overestimated.

Performing the procedures just outlined, I arrived at the following figures:

Table 5.2. Types, hapaxes, tokens, and productivity P of derived verbs in the Co-
build corpus

suffix	types (V)	hapaxes (n_1)[18]	tokens (N)	productivity P $(P=n_1/N)$
-ate	481	69	41561	0.0017
-ify	88	18	7236	0.0025
-ize	347	80	20865	0.0038

We will discuss the three central productivity measures, namely the number of forms with a given affix ('extent of use' V), the probability of encountering new formations ('productivity in the narrow sense' P), and the
number of new formations in a given corpus or period ('global productivity'
P^*), which is indicated by the number of hapaxes (n_1, see chapter 2 for
discussion). We will not discuss the degree of exhaustion ('pragmatic potentiality' I), since its value is rather questionable (see chapter 2).

The following picture emerges from table 5.2. The suffix *-ate* has the
highest extent of use V, followed closely by *-ize*, whereas *-ify* occurs in
much fewer types. However, *-ate* is clearly the least productive in the narrow sense, since in relation to its extremely high number of tokens
(N=41561) there are very few hapaxes, i.e. new types. The suffix *-ate* can
therefore be characterized as a suffix that occurs in many different existing
words, but which is not used very often to coin new verbs.

By far the most productive process in the narrow sense is *-ize*, which
occurs in almost as many different types as *-ate*, but gives rise to many
more new words in relation to the overall number of tokens. Thus the
probability of encountering a neologism among all *-ize* derivatives is much
greater than with *-ate* verbs. The suffix *-ify* occupies the medial position in
terms of P, although only few existing verbs contain this suffix, i.e. V and
n_1 are low.

A qualitative look at the hapaxes corroborates these results. Most of the
hapaxes featuring *-ify* and *-ize* are phonologically and semantically transparent, which indicates their status as productive formations. The majority
of them are either not listed at all in the *OED* or are listed there as twentieth century innovations, which results in a considerable overlap of forms in

---

[18] The hapaxes are listed in appendix 2. All hapaxes were checked against the
original corpus. On the basis of this check, a number of hapaxes as they occur
in the Cobuild word list had to be eliminated as incorrect spellings.

the list of *OED* neologisms and the list of Cobuild hapaxes (see appendices 1 and 2). Hence the qualitative analysis of the *-ize* and *-ify* hapaxes gives evidence for the productivity of these suffixes. The hapaxes involving *-ate*, however, are in their majority words that are not transparent neologisms, but simply rare words or rather strange innovations, a fact that is indicative of the low productivity of the process. Let us pick out randomly the alphabetically first 10 *-ate* hapaxes for illustration. Of these, seven are rather old words (*acidulate* 1732, *agglomerate* 1684, *agglutinate* 1586, *annuate* 1623, *apostemate* 1582, *contemplate* 1605, *concatenate* 1598[19]), only two forms seem to be genuine productive formations (*caffeinate, cavitate*), and one has remained opaque even after the consultation of a number of different dictionaries (*calvulate*). This qualitative look at the data reveals that the use of hapaxes as indicators of productivity is not generally justified. Whereas with more productive suffixes like *-ness*, *-ize* and *-ify* the proportion of real neologisms among the hapaxes is rather high, this is not the case with *-ate*.[20] This casts a shadow over the rationale of Baayen's productivity measures P and P^*, for it seems that the proportion of neologisms among the hapaxes can vary a great deal between different word formation rules. Hence, the *-ate* derivatives in the Cobuild corpus run counter to the general trend that low-frequency items are semantically transparent, as argued, for example, by Baayen and Lieber (1997).

The low productivity P of *-ate* could, however, also be seen as an artefact of our sampling procedure because all opaque formations were included, which has increased the number of all tokens, leading to a low measure P. However, the exclusion of opaque formations would have resulted in a rather drastic decline of the number of hapaxes and the number of different types, thereby negatively influencing these productivity measures. Thus it seems that including only the transparent formations would at best upgrade P, but further downgrade P^* and V.

---

[19]   The dates given are early attestations as given by the *OED*.

[20]   Interestingly, Baayen and Renouf (1996:86) mention the same unexpected behavior with the negative prefix *in-*. Thus, many hapaxes in *in-* are well-established technical terms like *incompetence* that just "happen not to enjoy a high frequency in the *Times*". They try to make a virtue out of the vice of their methodology by claiming that the small number of overall hapaxes and the fact that less than half of the hapaxes are innovations indicates that *in-* is hardly productive. However, they do not discuss the fact that such ill-behaved affixes are problematic with regard to quantitative measurements.

It is interesting to briefly compare the results for derived verbs with those obtained by Baayen and Renouf (1996) concerning other derivational affixes (they consider *-ity, -ness, -ly*[21], *un-, in-*). The figures for types (*V*) and hapaxes (*n₁*) of these affixes can be taken from Baayen and Renouf (1996:74), but the numbers of tokens are not given in this article. However, Harald Baayen kindly provided me with the relevant figures (personal communication, July 1997). Consider the following table:

Table 5.3.   The productivity of affixes

affixes	types (V)	hapaxes (n_1)[22]	tokens (N)	productivity P $(P=n_1/N)$
-ness	2027	793	42858	0.0185
-ity	1020	280	206287	0.0013
un-	1672	659	80130	0.0082
in-	243	48	41048	0.0012
-ly	4900	1098	990502	0.0011
-ate	481	69	41561	0.0017
-ify	88	18	7236	0.0025
-ize	347	80	20865	0.0038

Types, hapaxes, tokens, and productivity P of different affixes in the Times corpus (Baayen and Renouf 1996, Baayen p.c., July 1997), compared with verbal suffixes in the Cobuild corpus

Let us start with a comparison of global productivity. The number of hapaxes observed for the derived verbs are much smaller than those of extremely productive affixes like *-ness* and *un-*, let alone *-ly*. For example, in the 80 million word *Times* corpus Baayen and Renouf find 739 and 659 hapaxes for *-ness* and *un-*. Assuming an equal distribution of the hapaxes

---

[21]   The status of adverbial *-ly* as a derivational suffix is controversial. Whereas Bauer (1983:225) treats it as derivational, Marchand (1969) obviously takes a different position, since he only describes adjectival *-ly* and does not mention adverbial *-ly* at all. I am also inclined to classify *-ly* as an inflectional suffix. For our discussion this issue is irrelevant.

[22]   The hapaxes are listed in appendix 2. All hapaxes were checked against the original corpus. On the basis of this check, a number of hapaxes as they occur in the Cobuild word list had to be eliminated as incorrect spellings.

across the corpus, which seems justified for the purposes of a rough comparison (cf. figure 3 in Baayen and Renouf 1996:77), we can divide these figures by 4 in order to arrive at comparable numbers of hapaxes (recall that the Cobuild corpus was 20 million words). Thus we end up with calculated 180 and 165 hapaxes of *-ness* and *un-*, respectively, as against 80, 69, and 18 for *-ize, -ate,* and *-ify.* Although there is still a big difference between the two sets, we have to keep in mind that the overall productivity of verbs is very low in comparison to adjectives and, especially, nouns (e.g. Baayen and Lieber 1991). What emerges from this comparison of hapaxes is that at least *-ize* and *-ate* reach a reasonable degree of global productivity, whereas the global productivity of *-ify* is indeed low.

A comparison of the productivity in the narrow sense reveals that the verbal suffixes lie between the comparatively unproductive *-ity* and *in-* on the one hand, and the highly productive affixes *-ness* and *un-*. What is perhaps more surprising is the fact that the value of P for adjectival and adverbial *-ly* is lower than that of any of the verbal suffixes. This low value of P is not mentioned in Baayen and Renouf but certainly needs some explanation in view of the high global productivity of this suffix. This discrepancy between the different measures shows that one should not rely on one measure alone, because each measure highlights different aspects of productivity. The number of hapaxes for *-ly* indicates that there is a high probability to encounter new *-ly* forms as the corpus increases.[23] The productivity in the narrow sense for *-ly,* however, is very low because there are so many tokens of this category that there is a small chance to encounter new formations among them. Ignoring possible differences concerning the text types exemplified in the two corpora, we can summarize this brief comparison by saying that the verbal suffixes under discussion are reasonably productive, but certainly not as productive as affixes like *un-* or *-ness* which seem to be subject to little restrictions.

Before we finally compare the dictionary-based analysis with the text-corpus analysis, a word is in order concerning earlier calculations on the basis of the CELEX corpus. As already discussed in some detail in chapter 2, the CELEX corpus is based on the original Cobuild corpus (c. 18 million words) but is inaccurate in representing low-frequency items, which in turn negatively influences the calculation of the productivity measures. The figures in table 5.2. now enable us to show the extent to which the

---

[23]   For instance, in the last month of sampling, Baayen and Renouf find 40 new words in *-ly*, 29 in *-ness*, 25 in *un-*, 11 in *-ity*, and none in *in-*.

CELEX-based figures given by Baayen and Lieber (1991) are false. These authors arrive at only 102 overall types (*V*) for -*ize* and 50 types for -*ify*, with *P*=0.0000 for -*ify*, and *P*=0.0001 and *P*=0.0002 for deadjectival and denominal -*ize*, respectively (-*ate* is not considered). Even if we take into consideration that the July 1995 Cobuild corpus is roughly 10% larger than the Cobuild corpus used for the CELEX database, the huge discrepancies are still obvious. In view of the differences between the original Cobuild figures and the distorted CELEX figures all conclusions on the basis of the CELEX figures are disposable.

5.4. Productivity measures compared: *OED* vs. Cobuild

Let us compare the Cobuild and *OED* figures. For convenience the measures are put together in table 5.4.:

Table 5.4.   Comparison of OED and Cobuild productivity measures

suffix	#*OED* neologisms (N_{TOTAL})	# types (*V*)	# hapaxes (n_1)	# tokens (*N*)	productivity *P* (P=n_1/N)
-ate	87	481	69	41561	0.0017
-ify	30	88	18	7236	0.0025
-ize	346	347	80	20865	0.0038

Both the *OED* measure and the Cobuild *P* measure show -*ize* as the by far most productive overt verbalizing affix. Both analyses are also in accordance with regard to the question whether -*ate* and -*ify* are productive (they both are), but differ partly in the ranking of the two latter suffixes. How can this discrepancy be reconciled?

Interestingly, the difference only occurs with respect to productivity in the narrow sense. In respect to *V* and *P** the ranking is the same, which is easily understood: the *OED* is ignorant of token frequencies and only lists new types as they occur, which is basically the same procedure as listing the hapaxes in a text-corpus. Therefore, both data-bases should yield similar results (if the corpus is representative and the *OED* coverage is good).

In the *OED* data, the ratio of -*ify* neologisms to -*ate* neologisms is somewhat higher than the ratio of the respective Cobuild hapaxes (0.34 vs. 0.26), which is explained by the fact that the number of -*ate* hapaxes includes fewer neologisms. The almost identical ranking of *-ify* and *-ate* in the dictionary-based count on the one hand, and in terms of *V* and *P** on the other is therefore strong evidence for the accuracy and versatility of the *OED* data.

One difference between the two data sets should not go unnoticed. In the *OED*, *-ize* neologisms are much more frequent than *-ate* neologisms, whereas in terms of Cobuild hapaxes the difference is small. As already mentioned above, the number of *-ate* hapaxes does not reflect the proportion of neologisms as accurately as assumed. The proportion of neologisms is high among the *-ize* hapaxes, but low among the *-ate* hapaxes. The calculation of *P* corrects the wrong impression of *-ate* as gained on the basis of *P** alone. The text-based analysis brings out this double-faced character of *-ate* (high global productivity, low productivity in the narrow sense) quite clearly, whereas the *OED* figures cannot bear witness to it.

But why is *-ate* significantly more productive than *-ify* according to the *OED* measure? It seems that two factors may be responsible for the good result of *-ate* in the *OED*. For one, it could be an artefact of the sampling method. By not excluding *a priori* certain kinds of *-ate* formations I ended up with more derivatives than actually belong into this category. As will be shown in detail in chapter 7, only 25 of the 72 derivatives (i.e. N in table 5.1.) are actual exponents of the productive rule of *-ate* formation, which would set *-ate* on a par with *-ify*.

The second factor influencing the high number of *-ate* neologisms in the *OED* can be found in the nature of the data base itself. A look at the productive *-ate* formations in the *OED* reveals that the majority of them are highly technical terms cited mostly from scientific texts. The Cobuild corpus, however, represents a very broad range of text types (see Renouf 1987), so that the chance of encountering new terms from a highly specialized domain is relatively small. On the other hand, in a comprehensive dictionary like the *OED* marginal text-types with a high rate of innovational terms, such as scientific writing, must necessarily be overrepresented with their neologisms. This explanation is in line with earlier observations in corpus-based studies that there are significant differences in word-formation patterns across different text-types and styles (Baayen 1994, Baayen and Renouf 1996).

To close our discussion of table 5.4., let us consider why *-ify* fares much better than *-ate* in terms of *P* in the Cobuild corpus, which seems to contradict the *OED* measure. This contradiction is, however, only apparent, since *P* is of course also dependent on text types, so that parallel arguments hold for *P* as for *P**. Furthermore, the *OED* measure cannot reflect accurately the probability measure P, because token frequencies do not play a role in its calculation. Thus the *OED* measure reflects at best the probability of encountering a new derivative in a given period, whereas P reflects the probability of encountering a new derivative among other derivatives of the same type. Strictly speaking, these are two related, though inherently different things, as became clear in our above discussion of adverbial *-ly* in the *Times* corpus.

5.5. Conclusion

In this chapter it was shown that both the OED-based and the corpus-based productivity measures have turned out to be useful analytical tools, contrary to earlier claims in the literature. In general, the nature and results of the *OED* measure are similar to those of global productivity P^* but also incorporate an element of probability by counting the number of neologisms for a given period. In the text-based measure P, this aspect is expressed by dividing the number of new types by the number of all tokens of the relevant category. In the light of these considerations, the *OED* measure combines aspects of Baayen's P^* and P without being exactly equivalent to either one of them.

Although the quantitative results are useful and important, the methodological problems involved with both types of data-bases are enormous, and no single measure should be overinterpreted in its estimation of the productivity of a process. In fact, the above account can be seen as a case for the combination of both types of measures, since a careful comparison of different data bases can help to detect and balance the bias necessarily involved with each individual measure. It seems, however, that the text-based measures are much better suited for affixation processes which are both semantically more clearly defined and phonologically more transparent. Especially with the verbal suffix *-ate*, the methodological problems abound because of its high degree of semantic, phonological and morphological opacity.

The quantitative assessment of the productivity of the verb-deriving processes can be summarized as follows. The most productive one is conversion, followed by *-ize*, the most productive overt suffix by far, and the suffixes *-ify* and *-ate*. All other processes examined are practically dead. In comparison to *-ize*, the suffixes *-ify* and *-ate* seem to be more severely restricted, in that *-ate* has a high global productivity, but the probability of encountering new forms is rather low. Conversely, *-ify* has a higher chance of occurring in new formations, but the sheer number of these instances is rather low.

Where do these differences among the suffixes come from? As already pointed out in chapter 2, the productivity measures are only the first step in our analysis. They state the problem, but do not solve it. In chapters 7 and 8 we will see that the observable differences in productivity between the verb-deriving processes are largely a reflection of the structural restrictions imposed on these processes.

6. Rival morphological processes 2: The structural properties of *-ize* derivatives

This and the remaining chapters of this book will shed some new light on the phonological, morphological and semantic properties of verb-deriving processes in English. The main purpose of the investigation is to discover the structural restrictions that may be responsible for the observed differences in their productivity. As was pointed out earlier, restrictions are an integral part of a word formation rule. In other words, an adequate description of a rule entails the determination of its restrictions. It will become clear, however, that existing descriptions of derived verbs are often unsatisfactory, in spite of the extensive treatment in numerous publications. One prominent reason for this state of affairs is that the enormous semantic diversity and heterogeneity of these formations is paired with a rich polyfunctionality of the elements that are used for deriving the verbs, making the analysis of these processes a very difficult task.[1]

The primary data for this investigation are the *OED* neologisms already introduced in the preceding chapter, complemented by further data as they were found in other sources. The advantage of dealing primarily with neologisms is that by largely excluding lexicalized formations one has a better chance to detect the properties of possible words rather than of actual words, which may eventually lead to the correct formulation of the productive word formation rule instead of merely stating redundancies among institutionalized words.

I will start the discussion with the semantic and phonological properties of *-ize* (sections 6.1. and 6.2.), then move on to *-ate*, *-ify* and conversion in chapter 7. A few remarks on the unproductive affixes *eN-* and *-en* can also be found in that chapter. The findings presented in chapters 6 and 7 prepare the ground for the investigation of the distribution and interaction of the rival suffixes in chapter 8.

---

[1] Cf. similar remarks by Laskowski (1981:19) on derived verbs in the Slavonic languages, or by Rainer (1993:237ff) on their Spanish equivalents.

6.1. The meaning of *-ize* derivatives

6.1.1.   *The theoretical framework: Lexical conceptual semantics*

For the semantic analysis of derived verbs in this and the following chapter I will use the theory of lexical conceptual semantics developed by Jackendoff (1983, 1990, 1991). The reason for adopting this framework is that it is particularly useful for the description of the semantics of verbs in general and the analysis of verbal derivation in particular (e.g. Lieber and Baayen 1993, Lieber 1996). For readers unfamiliar with this theory, this section provides a short introduction to the main concepts and technology of lexical conceptual semantics relevant for the investigation to follow.[2] Some problematic or controversial aspects of the theory are ignored in this necessarily rough overview but will be taken up later, as our investigation proceeds.

The theory of lexical conceptual structure as developed by Jackendoff assumes that there is a form of mental representation, so-called 'conceptual structures', that is common to all languages and that serves as the 'syntax of thought' (Jackendoff 1991:10). These conceptual structures can be described in terms of semantic primitives on the one hand and principles according to which these primitives can be combined on the other. The primitives of the theory are at least major conceptual categories such as Thing, Event, State, Property, Path, or Place, which are combined by functions that operate on these primitives. Verbal meanings, for example, can be represented by hierarchically organized structures containing semantic functions like GO, CAUSE, TO, and arguments on which these functions operate, namely the major conceptual categories just mentioned. Let us see how this works. Consider the sentence in (1), which corresponds to the conceptual structure in (2) (see Jackendoff 1991:13):

(1)   Bill went into the house

(2)   [$_{\text{Event}}$ GO ([$_{\text{Thing}}$ BILL], [$_{\text{Path}}$ TO ([$_{\text{Place}}$ IN ([$_{\text{Thing}}$ HOUSE])])])]

---

2   For a short first-hand introduction to the basic concepts and functions used in lexical conceptual semantics, see Jackendoff (1991:10-15).

GO is a two-place function that maps a Thing (here: 'Bill') and a Path (here: 'to the interior of the house') into an Event consisting of the Thing traversing the Path (the expressions BILL and HOUSE are not decomposed for the present purposes). The entire expression in (2) can be read as "Bill traverses a path that terminates at the interior of the house". The lexical entry of the verb *go* can (roughly) be represented in this theory as in (3):

(3)   *go*   (phonological structure)
       V   (syntactic strucure)
       [$_{Event}$ GO ([$_{Thing}$]$_A$, [$_{Path}$]$_A$)]   (conceptual strucure)

The subscript A indicates the argument status of Thing and Path for the function GO. Such arguments must be expressed by a syntactic argument, with the linking of conceptual arguments to syntactic arguments being done by general principles of linking, which need not concern us here any further (see Jackendoff 1990: chapter 11 for discussion). Thus, in a sentence like (1) the empty argument slots in the lexical conceptual structure (LCS) of *go* are filled by the appropriate arguments [*Bill*] and [*into the house*]. The preposition *into* (with its complement [*the house*]) provides an appropriate Path argument for the function GO because the LCS of this preposition is a Path, and [*the house*] is an appropriate argument for the function IN, which is also part of the LCS of *into*. Consider (4):

(4)   LCS of *into*
       [$_{Path}$ TO ([$_{Place}$ IN ([$_{Thing}$]$_A$)])]

As we will see, the LCSs of *-ize* verbs can be represented in a similar fashion. In essence, the theory of lexical conceptual structure is a theory of semantic decomposition, a fact that is particularly useful for the description of derived verbs, because it allows the teasing apart of the respective contributions to the meaning of the derivative by the different morphological elements that are combined to derive a complex form. I believe that the main insights of the analysis to follow do not hinge on the formalism of this particular decompositional theory, but that they could equally well be expressed in the terminology of other existing frameworks.

We are now in a position to turn to the problem at hand, the meaning of *-ize* derivatives.

6.1.2.   The problem

It has often been noted that derivatives involving the suffix -*ize* in English are extremely heterogeneous in terms of their semantics, syntax and the types of bases the suffix attaches to. Thus adjectives and nouns may be verbalized by -*ize*, the resulting derivatives are transitive or intransitive, and they may have a whole range of different meanings, often paraphrased as 'render X, make X, convert into X, put into the form of X, give the character or shape of X, subject to the action, treatment or process of X, subject to a process connected with X, impregnate, treat, combine with X, act in a way characterized by X, imitate the manner of X' (cf., e.g., Jespersen (1942:319), Marchand (1969:320); X stands for the concept of the base word). Although this particular affix is generally regarded as the most productive overt verb-forming suffix in English (see the discussion in the preceding chapter), there is only one more detailed study of the semantic heterogeneity of -*ize* to date. In this study, Lieber (1996) proposes four different semantic structures for -*ize*, which are partly considered polysemous, and partly homophonous.

I will argue that all of the meanings suggested in previous studies are derived from one single semantic representation, which is claimed to be the underspecified Lexical Conceptual Structure (LCS) of possible -*ize* derivatives. It is shown that this LCS can not only account for almost every single -*ize* formation in the neologism corpus, but that it can also explain their relatedness in meaning in an explicit and straightforward manner. Furthermore, the polysemies of existing and possible derivatives can be predicted, which makes the claims easily testable against further data.

The case of -*ize* derivatives has implications for morphological theory, in particular the status of affixes and word formation rules in the lexicon, and the role of semantic and pragmatic information in word formation. The results of this study can be interpreted as evidence for an output-oriented model of the formation of -*ize* derivatives, in which the meaning of the derivative results from the interaction of the meaning of the stem with the semantic structure of possible -*ize* derivatives. An important consequence of the present analysis is that the syntactic category of the base is underspecified. This finding challenges the standard practice (generative and non-generative alike) of treating the information about the syntactic category of the base word as crucial for derivational processes.

Before turning to the analysis of the neologisms let us consider some of the earlier approaches. As mentioned above, standard sources like Jespersen (1942) and Marchand (1969) give a whole range of meanings for -*ize* derivatives, but do not try to explain the semantic relation between these meanings. The paraphrases they give often appear to be imprecise, or different paraphrases seem to encode rather identical concepts. Thus the two categories 'render, make X' (Marchand's example: *legalize*), and 'convert into, put into the form of, give the character or shape of X' (*itemize*) could easily be unified as change-of-states. Similarly, it is left unclear, what exactly the difference is between the paraphrase 'subject to the action, treatment or process of X' (*propagandize*), the paraphrase 'subject to a special (technical) process connected with X' (*winterize*), and the paraphrase 'impregnate, treat, combine with X' (*alcoholize*). A third group of paraphrases seem to be derivatives whose meaning is given as 'do as, act in a way characterized by X' (*astronomize*), or 'imitate the manner or style of X' (*Petrarchize*).

In a recent attempt to clarify this picture, Lieber (1996) proposes four different LCSs, which are given in (5):

(5) a. $[_{Event} \text{ACT} ([_{Thing} \quad], [_{Event} \text{INCH} ([_{State} \text{BE} ([_{Thing} \quad], [_{Place} \text{AT}$
$([_{Thing,Property} \text{ base N, A }])])])])]$
(unionize, civilianize, epitomize, velarize)

b. $[_{Event} \text{ACT} ([_{Thing} \quad], [_{Event} \text{GO} ([_{Thing} \text{ base N}],$
$[_{Path} \text{TO/ON/IN} ([_{Thing} \quad])])])]$
(carbonize, texturize, apologize)

c. $[_{Event} \text{ACT} ([_{Thing} \quad], [_{Event} \text{GO} ([_{Thing} \quad], [_{Path} \text{TO}$
$([_{Thing} \text{ base N }])])])]$
(summarize, hospitalize)

d. $[_{Event} \text{ACT} ([_{Thing} \quad], [_{Manner} \text{LIKE} ([_{Thing, Property} \text{ base N }])])]$
(cannibalize, economize)

These structures show that "all *-ize* verbs are action verbs of some sort" (p. 8), i.e. they all share the first semantic function ACT, which Lieber borrows from Pinker (1989). In addition to this rather distant semantic relationship between all four types of derivatives, Lieber claims that at least the first three categories constitute a case of polysemy, because they have causative meanings. The exact nature of this polysemy is not further discussed. On the basis of the four LCSs, Lieber argues that the LCS of *-ize* derivatives is only partially determinate.

Lieber's account suffers from a number of weaknesses. First of all, it is unclear on which data she bases her claims. She mentions only 15 different derivatives altogether, of which very few are discussed in some detail. Furthermore, the status of these examples as productive derivatives is not discussed. Thus, it is difficult to assess the empirical adequacy of her claims. Second, the problem of polysemy is not solved by simply stating that different types of *-ize* derivatives share certain functions. How are these functions related? And why do *-ize* derivatives share just these functions and not others? Third, it is not clear why certain forms are cited as examples of certain LCSs. For example, why is *unionize* a case of (5a) and not of (5c), why is *summarize* a case of (5c) and not of (5a)? It seems that both analyses are possible, but if so, why should this be the case? And why is one structure, (5a), possible with verbal and nominal bases, whereas others are reserved for nominal bases? In addition, it is not obvious how some of her examples can be subsumed under the LCSs they are supposed to illustrate. For example, according to Lieber's 'Manner' structure (5d), *economize* would paraphrase roughly as something like 'act like (the) economy', which seems rather strange. Finally, it is unclear how a verb having a LCS as in (5d) can be used as a transitive verb, since there is no possible way to introduce a Theme argument into the LCS. Crucially, however, verbs of this kind are often, if not regularly used transitively, so that there should be an argument slot available for the object in the LCS.

In sum, the previous accounts of *-ize* are unsatisfactory in many respects. The following section presents an attempt to develop an empirically and theoretically more adequate solution to the problems of *-ize* verbs.

6.1.3. The polysemy of -ize derivatives

As a first step in the analysis, the data in the corpus were classified according to the set of semantic categories given in (6), which more or less include all of the paraphrases and meanings mentioned so far.[3] The left column gives the name of the category, the second contains a paraphrase, and the third provides an example from the corpus. In the remainder of this book I will use the names of the categories as convenient mnemonic terms for some of the semantic representations to be introduced.

---

[3]   Lieber's representations, for example, roughly correspond to the categories locative, ornative, causative, resultative, inchoative, and similative. See Rainer (1993:235-241) for a similar classification of Spanish derived verbs.

(6)   locative   'put (in)to X'   *hospitalize*
       ornative   'provide with X'   *patinize*
       causative[4]   'make (more) X'   *randomize*
       resultative   'make into X'   *peasantize*
       inchoative   'become X'   *aerosolize*
       performative   'perform X'   *anthropologize*
       similative   'act like X'   *powellize*

As mentioned already in the introduction, explicit accounts of the relationship between these categories are non-existent. I will show that each of the seven categories can be subsumed under a single LCS, which the reader can find in (24) below. For expository purposes, however, I will go through the different meanings successively and develop the unitary LCS step by step.

Let us first look at locative uses of *-ize*, for which I propose the following LCS:

(7)   LCS of locative *-ize* verbs
       $[[\quad]_{\text{BASE}}\ \text{-}ize]_{\text{V}}$
       $\text{NP}_i \underline{\quad} \text{NP}_{\text{Theme}}$
       $\text{CAUSE} ([\quad]_i, [\text{GO} ([\quad]_{\text{Theme}}; [\text{TO} [\quad]_{\text{Base}}])])$
       (e.g. *channelize, cinematize, computerize, containerize*[5])

In non-technical terms the structure in (7) reads as follows. Locative verbs involving the base $[\quad]_{\text{Base}}$ and the suffix *-ize* are transitive and denote an Event in which the subject causes the transfer of what is denoted by the object NP to the entity that is denoted by the base. An example from the corpus is *containerize* 'pack into containers' which, according to (7), must

---

4   Traditionally, 'factitive' is used to refer to the induction of a property or properties in an object, whereas 'causative' is used for the incitement of an event. Hence Rainer (1993: 235, 238) employs the term 'factitive' for deadjectival formations, and the term 'causative' for denominal ones. In the morphological literature, these two concepts are often not distinguished. For reasons that will become clear below, the necessity of such a distinction for the description of derived verbs is indeed doubtful, and we will therefore use 'causative' as the cover term. Note, however, that nothing hinges on this decision since the terms used in (6) do not have any independent theoretical status in our model.

5   Note that some of these forms are polysemous themselves, i.e. they also have other, non-locative, interpretations. We will return to this issue below.

be interpreted as in (8), given a sentence like *The men containerized the cargo.*

(8)   CAUSE ([*The men*]$_i$, [GO ([*the cargo*]$_{Theme}$; [TO [*container*] $_{Base}$])])

(8) could be read as "the men caused a transfer of the cargo into a container or containers".

This example possibly raises the question whether the locative function TO should not be represented by a more specific function, e.g. IN. From a lexicographic point of view, this would certainly yield a more adequate interpretation of *containerize*. However, we are not primarily concerned here with the accurate lexicographic representation of individual lexemes, but with the fundamental morphological problem how complex words are semantically related to other complex words, and how stems and affixes in complex words interact with one another. In other words, no semantic description of a morphological process can even hope to give a *lexicographically* precise description of all possible or attested derivatives, but can only aim at capturing regularities that predict the *range* of possible meanings of possible derivatives. This means that we are dealing with semantic structures that are necessarily underspecified.

Coming back to the derivative *containerize*, the LCS in (7) can therefore only tell us that, in informal terms, someone puts something somewhere, and that, in the case of *containerize*, 'somewhere' is denoted by the base *container*. With *containerize*, speakers will interpret TO as 'into', in other cases other interpretations are possible. In the notation used here, TO is thus considered an underspecified locative function.

Having illustrated the LCS of locatives, we may turn to ornatives like *patinize*[6], for which I propose the following LCS (given a sentence like *They patinized the zinc articles*, a modified version of the original *OED* quotation):

(9)   CAUSE ([*They*]$_i$, [GO ([*patina*] $_{Base}$; [TO [*zinc articles*]$_{Theme}$])])

---

[6]   *Patinize* is the first derivative from the corpus which involves stem allomorphy. In general, stem allomorphy is rather common with *-ize*. However, as shown in section 6.2., cases of allomorphy can be straightforwardly accounted for by a number of morpho-phonological constraints without making reference to semantic properties of the base or the derivative. For the purposes of the semantic analysis, we can therefore ignore stem allomorphy.

Thus ornatives denote the transfer of the referent of the base word to the referent of the object NP, which is exactly the reverse of what we observed with locatives.[7] The LCS of ornatives may be represented as in (10):

(10)   LCS of ornative -ize verbs
[[   ]$_{BASE}$ -*ize*]$_V$
NP$_i$ ___ NP $_{Theme}$
CAUSE ([   ]$_i$, [GO ([   ]$_{Base}$; [TO [   ]$_{Theme}$])])
(e.g. *acidize, chemicalize, patinize*)

A comparison of the LCSs of locatives and ornatives brings to the fore the close semantic relationship between the two categories: only the arguments of the GO function are exchanged in (7) and (10). In other words, it is the occurrence of the arguments in the different slots which makes the verb ornative or locative, respectively. The two LCSs can therefore be united in a - now polysemous - LCS, given in (11):

(11)   LCS of locative/ornative -ize verbs
[[   ]$_{BASE}$ -*ize*]$_V$
NP$_i$ ___ NP $_{Theme}$
CAUSE ([   ]$_i$, [GO ([   ]$_{Theme / Base}$; [TO [   ]$_{Base / Theme}$])])

(11) expresses the fact that it is either the referent of the base that is transferred to the referent of the object or the other way round. How do speakers know which argument goes into which slot? In the default case, one of the two interpretations will be ruled out on the basis of our encyclopaedic knowledge. Thus one knows that it is usually the patients that are transferred to the hospital and not the hospital brought to the patients. If we imagine a world where the latter would be the case, this event could be easily referred to by the verb *hospitalize*. Thus, the LCS in (11) is in principle ambiguous between an ornative and a locative meaning. One can therefore suspect that there be cases where it is impossible to assign a clearly locative or clearly ornative meaning. And this is exactly what we find in the corpus.

---

7   Note that in Jackendoff's (1990) system, verbs of attachment and covering would require a structure involving the functions INCH and BE (AT). For the present problem this difference can be ignored, since both locative and ornative meanings could equally well be formulated using these functions. We will return to this issue below.

Consider, for example, *channelize*, which can mean 'put into a channel or channels', which is the locative interpretation. *Channelize* can, however, also mean 'to provide with channels' as illustrated by the quotation given in the *OED*, in which *channelize* is paraphrased as 'to control traffic by curbs and dividers'. Another example is *computerize* which cannot only mean 'put (data) into the computer', which is locative, but also 'to install a computer or computers in (an office, etc.)' (*OED*), which is ornative.

Coming back to the initial examples *containerize* and *patinize*, let us briefly consider the alternative interpretations, given in (12a) and (12b):

(12)   a.   CAUSE ([*They*]$_i$, [GO ([*the zinc articles*]$_{Theme}$; [TO
                                                            [*patina*]$_{Base}$])])

        b.   CAUSE ([*The men*]$_i$, [GO ([*container*]$_{Base}$; [TO
                                                            [*the cargo*]$_{Base/Theme}$])])

These interpretations, though structurally possible, are again ruled out on the basis of the meaning of the base word and world knowledge. A patina is a 'A film or incrustation ... on the surface of old bronze ... or other substances' (*OED*). A patina is therefore something that cannot exist without the object whose surface it covers. Hence, it must be the patina that is brought onto the object's surface and not the object that is attached to the patina. Similarly, it is the cargo which is placed inside the container and not the container which is placed around the cargo. The examples illustrate that it is unnecessary to provide a more restrictive LCS since unwarranted interpretations are ruled out on the basis of independent semantic or conceptual knowledge.

The underspecified LCS structure does therefore not only account for the differences in interpretation between different derivatives, but can also explain putative and actual polysemies of individual derivatives. This is an important point because in earlier approaches the polysemy of individual derivatives is mostly ignored. Previous authors seem to have tacitly assumed that each derivative can only express one of the many possible meanings *-ize* words can express.

Let us turn to the causative meaning, which is closely related to the locative/ornative case. The crucial difference between these two categories is that the transfer denoted by the function GO is not of a physical nature with causatives. Whether we are dealing with a physical or a non-physical transfer depends on the semantic interpretation of the arguments of the GO function. While with spatial locatives/ornatives the arguments [   ]$_{Base}$ and [   ]$_{Theme}$ belong to the semantic category Thing, the respective arguments in the LCS of causatives are Properties. This is expressed in (13) below by the subscript "Thing, Property" in the empty argument slots of the GO and TO functions. In more traditional terms locatives/ornatives can be characterized as change-of-place verbs, whereas causatives are change-of-state verbs. In the unified LCS, the nature of the arguments is not fixed, but is projected by the arguments themselves. I therefore propose to extend the LCS for locatives/ornatives, given in (7) above, to causatives:

(13)   LCS of locative/ornative/causative *-ize* verbs
   [[   ]$_{BASE}$ *-ize*]$_V$
   NP$_i$ ___ NP$_{Theme}$
   CAUSE ([   ]$_i$, [GO ([$_{Thing, Property}$]$_{Theme / Base}$,
                       [TO [$_{Thing, Property}$]$_{Base / Theme}$])])

It could be argued that Jackendoff's functions INCH and BE (AT) (roughly 'become') are better suited for the expression of change-of-states than GO. As already mentioned in note 10 above, this option would also be available for the locative and ornative meanings. Jackendoff argues for INCH, and against GO, with verbs of touching and attachment (a class that roughly corresponds to my locatives and ornatives) because "there are no alternative paths available for verbs of attachment [and touching, I.P.], nor can anything be said about intermediate steps in the process of attachment [or touching, I.P.]" (1990:114). Especially the argument concerning intermediate steps is compelling with the simplex verbs Jackendoff discusses, but in the case of *-ize* derivatives it loses its force, because these words often make reference to intermediate steps. It is a well-known fact that causatives (and inchoatives, discussed below) often do not mean 'make something X' but 'make something *more* X'. A nice example of this kind is the linguistic term *grammaticalize*, which is standardly used in the sense of 'make or become more grammatical'. Under the INCH analysis, such an interpretation would be impossible because we cannot refer to intermediate steps. Jackendoff discusses this problem with respect to the two causative verbs *yellow* and *cool*. While he finds the case of *yellow* equivocal, he prefers the function GO for the semantic description of *cool* because only GO can express a change over time without necessarily achieving a certain state. Hence, he paraphrases *cool* as 'continuously change temperature towards the direction of coolness' (1990:95).

Returning to the discussion of *-ize* derivatives, parallel arguments apply. GO is superior in expressing the semantics of these derivatives because it allows both readings, the 'contact' reading with ornatives, locatives, and many causatives ('achievement' in Jackendoff's terms), as well as the 'intermediate step' reading with certain causatives ('change over time in a certain direction' in Jackendoff's terms). The same holds for inchoatives.

Let us now illustrate the workings of (13) with the derivative *masculinize* 'render (more) masculine' in a sentence like *They masculinized her name* (again modeled on the *OED* quotation):

(14)   a.   CAUSE ([*They*]$_i$, [GO ([*her name*]$_{Theme}$; [TO [*masculine*]$_{Base}$])])
       b.   CAUSE ([*They*]$_i$, [GO ([*masculine*]$_{Base}$; [TO [*her name*]$_{Theme}$])])

In (14a) GO is the function expressing the change-of-state of the argument [*her name*]$_{Theme}$, which can be paraphrased as something like 'They rendered her name (more) masculine'. (14b) is also permitted by the given LCS, and differs from (14a) in that [*masculine*]$_{Base}$ is imposed on the argument [*her name*]$_{Theme}$. Hence, (13) predicts that there are two possible, slightly differing interpretations of the verb *masculinize*, formally expressed as (14a) and (14b), respectively. This prediction is borne out by the facts, since, in addition to the meaning (14a) 'render masculine', the interpretation (14b) is also listed in the *OED* ('*Biol.* To induce male sexual characteristics in'). In other words, the LCS in (13) does not only predict the canonical meaning of causative derivatives standardly cited as 'make, render X', but also the less prominent, but equally possible, meaning 'induce X in'.

But not only the causative meaning itself is ambiguous, one also finds some derivatives in the corpus that can be interpreted both in the locative/ornative and in the causative sense. Take, for example, *nuclearize*, which is attested with the meanings 'To supply or equip (a nation) with nuclear weapons' (*OED*) and 'To render (a family, etc.) nuclear in character' (*OED*). In the first case the base word is interpreted as a Property 'Of, pertaining to, possessing, or employing nuclear weapons' (one of the meanings of *nuclear* in the *OED*). With the second meaning of *nuclearize* the base is interpreted as the Property 'Having the character or position of a nucleus; like a nucleus; constituting or forming a nucleus', which is another meaning of *nuclear* given by the *OED*. Spelling out the semantic categories of the relevant arguments of GO, the LCS looks as follows:

(15)   a.   CAUSE ([   ]$_i$, [GO ([   ]$_{Theme}$; [TO [$_{Property}$ *nuclear*]$_{Base}$])])
       b.   CAUSE ([   ]$_i$, [GO ([$_{Property}$ *nuclear*]$_{Base}$; [TO [   ]$_{Theme}$])])

Another example of this kind of ambiguity is *publicize* whose LCS predicts again two interpretations:

(16)   a.   CAUSE ([   ]$_i$, [GO ([   ]$_{Theme}$; [TO [$_{Property/Thing}$*public*]$_{Base}$])])
       b.   CAUSE ([   ]$_i$, [GO ([$_{Property/Thing}$*public*]$_{Base}$; [TO [   ]$_{Theme}$])])

(16a) either denotes that something is made public (the Property reading), or the transfer to the public (the Thing reading). Both interpretations of (16a) are given by the *OED* ('to make generally known', '[t]o bring to the notice of the public'). In the first case traditional analyses would claim that the base is adjectival, in the second case nominal. The analysis along the lines of (13) and (16a) makes reference to the syntactic category of the base unnecessary, and arguments about whether a derivative is deadjectival or denominal appear futile. (16b) illustrates the ornative variant, of which only the first alternative (inducing a Property) is in accordance with the extra-linguistic world, i.e. it is the news that is brought to the public rather than the public to the news.

The derivative *publicize* thus illustrates two important points. First, arguments about the exact categorization of the semantic nature of the derivative (locative, ornative or causative?) are fruitless, if they fail to recognize the identical structures that unite locative, ornative and causative *-ize* verbs. Second, we have seen that the syntactic category of the base is irrelevant. In standard treatments locative and ornative *-ize* derivatives are regarded as denominal, while causatives have adjectival bases. Based on these generalizations, different denominal and deadjectival word formation rules have been proposed. While the observations concerning the syntactic category of the bases are not entirely wrong, it seems that the specification of the syntactic category of the base is an unnecessary complication which leads to empirical and theoretical   problems. In a purely semantic approach, the syntactic category of the base can be disregarded because the only restriction necessary is that the base can succesfully be interpreted as an appropriate argument in the LCS.

However, if the syntactic category of the base is not specified, why can only adjectives and nouns, and not verbs, serve as bases of *-ize* derivatives? As was just mentioned, possible bases must be able to be interpreted as appropriate arguments in the LCS. In the above LCSs possible arguments of GO and TO in the LCS of *-ize* verbs are restricted to Things and Properties. Arguments as projected by verbs, i.e. Events, Actions or States, are therefore excluded. Note that this restriction is also expressed in Lieber's LCSs, where the open argument slots are equally reserved for Things and

Properties. Given that this argument specification is independently needed, our analysis has the advantage that the restriction to nominal and adjectival bases falls out automatically, making the specification of the syntactic category of the base redundant.

Let us turn to the category 'resultative', which is usually depicted as the denominal counterpart of the deadjectival causative (cf. e.g. the treatment in Rainer 1993:238-239). However, the distinction between 'make X' and 'make into X' seems to be conceptually unmotivated and can be characterized as an artefact of an inappropriate meta-language that treats paraphrases as if they were direct representations of meaning. In our framework, the resultative and the causative collapse into one category. Take, for example, the meaning of *peasantize* 'to make (oneself) into a peasant' (*OED*), where the base is interpreted either as a Property induced in the object NP$_{Theme}$, or as a kind of person into which NP$_{Theme}$ is transformed.

(17)   a.   CAUSE ([   ]$_i$, [GO ([   ]$_{Theme}$; [TO [$_{Thing}$ *peasant*]$_{Base}$])])
       b.   CAUSE ([   ]$_i$, [GO ([$_{Property}$*peasant*]$_{Base}$; [TO [   ]$_{Theme}$])])

Why does *peasantize* not mean 'supply with peasants' (ornative interpretation), or 'make someone go to a peasant' (locative)? First of all, the spatial-ornative meaning is not attested but is certainly possible. A village, for example, could be peasantized by making more peasants live there. This type of meaning is actually attested with two derivatives out of the large group of forms that relate to a country or group of people, e.g. *Anglicanize, Baskonize, Cubanize, Czechize, Mongolianize, Nigerianize, Scandinavianize, Turkicize, Vietnamize*. While most of these derivatives only show the causative meaning 'render X in character', the resultative meaning 'turn into an X' is also attested. The said ornative forms are *Romanianize* and *Filipinize* 'supply with Romanians/Filipinos' (cf. the quotations in the *OED*), which is exactly parallel to the putative ornative formation *peasantize (a village)*.

But why is the locative interpretation apparently ruled out? Generalizing from the previous examples it seems that the semantic-categorial interpretation of the arguments largely depends on the inherent semantics of these arguments. Thus certain nouns like *hospital* or *ghetto* are prone to spatial-locative interpretations, while nouns denoting persons never seem to adopt this meaning. The reason for this is not obvious, but it seems that with verbs like *hospitalize* non-locative interpretations are indeed possible. Thus, if *hospitalized* was not lexicalized with its spatial-locative meaning, it is conceivable that the conversion of an institution (say, a child-care center) into a hospital (i.e. a change-of-state) could be referred to with the verb *hospitalize*. The inherent semantics of *hospital*, in which the 'location' meaning is more prominent than the 'institution' meaning, strongly favors the locative interpretation.[8] A similar reasoning holds for the non-attested, but possible interpretation of locatives like *containerize* as causatives/resultatives 'make (into) a container'. Coming back to the problem of *peasantize*, the interpretation of *peasant* as a location could be ruled out along the same lines, since the semantic information concerning the Property is more prominent than the possibility of being a location. However, the latter interpretation would not be excluded on structural grounds, nor is it obvious that it should be. Consider the derivative *Vietnamize*, which was cited above as belonging to the same group as, for example, *Cubanize*. The interesting point with *Vietnamize* is that its attested meaning is not the causative but the locative 'make something go to Vietnam', in the sense of 'handing over to the state of Vietnam'. Compare the quotation from the *OED*:

(18)   **1969** *Daily Tel.* 25 Oct. 5/3: It was learned .. that America had handed over another base to South Vietnam. Two of the United States major port facilities, including the one in Saigon, were next on the list to be 'Vietnamised'.

To summarize, it is unclear whether any account of *-ize* derivatives should include principled mechanisms that would strictly prevent items like *peasantize* from being interpreted as a locative derivative, and how such a mechanism would still allow the correct interpretation of items like *Vietnamize*. We will leave this issue to further research.

Coming back to the difference between the resultative and causative categories we have seen that the only formal difference lies in the syntactic category of the base (N vs. A) and in the paraphrase ('make X' vs. 'make into X'). Both differences are naturally accounted for under the analysis proposed here. Reference to the syntactic category of the base is superfluous, and the difference in the paraphrase does not have a correlate in the semantics but merely shows that paraphrases of this kind are not an appropriate meta-language.

---

[8]   Furthermore, the putting of patients into a hospital is culturally more salient than the conversion of hospitals into other institutions. Given the importance of frequency for lexicalization in general, it is this salience that is responsible for the lexicalization of the locative meaning of *hospitalize*.

Consider another example, *fantasize*, of which one reviewer of this chapter says that it is not adequately described by the proposed model. According to the LCSs above, this derivative could be analyzed as a causative/resultative formation in the sense of 'making (into) a fantasy'. The reviewer quotes the *COBUILD* dictionary's definition of *fantasize* to show that the above LCSs cannot capture the "rich meaning" of *fantasize*: "If you *fantasize*, you think about a pleasant event or situation which you would like to happen but which is unlikely to happen." (*COBUILD*:515). However, one should not equate dictionary definitions with semantic structures. Thus, the dictionary gives three definitions of the base word *fantasy*, one of which is almost entirely identical with the definition of the derivative *fantasize*: "a pleasant situation or event that you think about and hope will happen, although it is unlikely to happen" (*COBUILD*:516). This meaning of *fantasy* seems to be derived from the more general meaning "a story or situation that someone creates from their imagination and that is not based on reality". From these definitions of the base word and the LCS above, the meaning of *fantasize* can be predicted rather precisely as a straightforward causative/resultative, 'making (into) a fantasy'. The rest follows from the "rich meaning" of the base word.

Having shown that resultatives can also be subsumed under the LCS (13), we may turn to the discussion of inchoatives. The label 'inchoative' is usually attached to derived verbs that are intransitively used and whose meaning can be paraphrased as 'become X'. In the corpus of neologisms this meaning is not very frequent, but it seems that most transitive derivatives expressing a change-of-state can potentially also be used intransitively. I propose the following LCS for inchoatives:

(19)   LCS of inchoative *-ize* verbs
    $[[\quad]_{Base}$ *-ize*$]_V$
    NP$_{Theme}$ _____
    $[GO ([_{Thing, Property} \quad]_{Theme}; [TO [_{Thing, Property} \quad]_{Base}])]$
    (e.g. *aerosolize, grammaticalize, primitivize*)

The difference between the LCSs in (14) and (19) is that the latter lacks the function CAUSE, and that - consequently - the Agent argument of CAUSE is also lacking. Finally, the Theme occurs in the surface subject position and not in the object position. The LCSs of the previously discussed derivatives and the inchoative ones are unified in (20):

(20)   LCS of locative/ornative/causative/resultative/inchoative -*ize* verbs
[[   ]$_{BASE}$ -*ize*]$_V$
NP$_i$ ___ NP$_{Theme}$
$\underline{CAUSE}$ ([.....]$_i$, [GO ([$_{Property, Thing}$]$_{Theme / Base}$;
                                                [TO [$_{Property, Thing}$]$_{Base / Theme}$])])

Following the arguments and conventions presented in Jackendoff (1990:73), the dashed underline signals that the CAUSE function is optional. If it is applied, we are dealing with the locative/ornative/causative/resultative meanings discussed above, if it is not, we are confronted with an inchoative meaning. Before we turn to the problem of the syntactic realization of the Theme as the subject in inchoative structures, let us first illustrate (20) with an example from the corpus for which both transitive and intransitive variants are attested. *Primitivize* is characterized by the *OED* as 'trans. and intr.* To render primitive; to impute primitiveness to; to simplify; to return to an earlier stage'. The possible LCSs look as follows, with the mnemonic categorization given at the end of each line:

(21)   LCS of *primitivize* (on the basis of (20))
   a.   'ornative'
        CAUSE ([   ]i, [GO ([*primitive*]$_{Base}$; [TO [   ]$_{Theme}$])])
   b.   'causative'
        CAUSE ([   ]i, [GO ([   ]$_{Theme}$; [TO [*primitive*]$_{Base}$])])
   c.   'inchoative/ornative'
        GO ([*primitive*]$_{Base}$; [TO [   ]$_{Theme}$])
   d.   'inchoative'
        GO ([   ]$_{Theme}$; [TO [*primitive*]$_{Base}$])

(21a) formalizes the meaning 'impute primitiveness to', (21b) spells out as 'render primitive', and (21d) 'become primitive' corresponds to the *OED*'s 'to return to an earlier stage'. The interpretation (21c) would be dispreferred with the base *primitive*, because the transfer of a Property to a Thing usually requires an Agent, i.e. the CAUSE function. A structure like (21c) should, however, not be ruled out *a priori* as a possible structure. In the case of *oxidize* the structural parallel to (21c) is entirely appropriate, because of the inherent semantics of the base:

(22)   LCS of *oxidize* (only inchoative meanings given)
    a. GO ($[oxide]$ Base; [TO [   ] Theme])
    b. GO ([   ] Theme; [TO $[oxide]$ Base])

The meanings as given by the *OED* for intransitive *oxidize* match exactly the ones described by (22). Thus, interpretation (22a) is a formalization of the *OED*'s 'become coated with oxide', and (22b) corresponds to 'become converted into an oxide'. The reason for the adequacy of (22a) is that the base can be interpreted as a Thing that is transferred to [ ] Theme without visible instigation. Such an interpretation is less likely with (21c). The examples show again how the correct interpretations can be construed on the basis of the general LCS of -*ize* verbs in interaction with the inherent semantics of the arguments involved.

    Let us turn to the problem of subjecthood. In the LCS (20) it is left unclear how, when and why the Theme should appear in subject position. Two solutions to this problem are possible, a local, i.e. lexical one and a more general one.

    The lexical solution would mean that the object/subject alternation is encoded in the LCS itself, i.e. some device in the LCS regulates that in the case of the non-presence of NP$_i$, NP$_{Theme}$ occurs in the subject position. A LCS of this kind could take the following form:

(23)   LCS of locative/ornative/causative/resultative/inchoative -*ize* verbs
    [[   ] BASE -*ize*] V
    {NP$_i$ ___ NP Theme, NP Theme ___ }
    CAUSE ([.....] $_j$, [GO ([Property, Thing   ] Theme / Base;
                                            [TO [Property, Thing   ] Base / Theme])])

According to (23), -*ize* verbs may occur either transitively, i.e. in the syntactic frame [NP$_i$ ___ NP Theme], or intransitively, i.e. in the frame [NP Theme ___]. In those cases where the underlined function is lacking, the second frame applies automatically.

    Although this lexical solution works properly for -*ize* verbs, there are strong arguments in favor of a more principled solution. Such arguments are based on the observation that the subject/object alternation of Theme arguments is not restricted to a particular class of derived verbs but a rather wide-spread phenomenon. A standard example is the verb *open*, whose Theme may appear as the subject of the intransitive form or as the object of the transitive form. A number of principled analyses of such mismatches between syntactic and conceptual relations have been proposed (see Jackendoff 1990:155ff for an overview), an evaluation of which is beyond the scope of this investigation. Since the problems of a principled analysis are still hotly debated, I will adopt the more conservative lexical solution here. Future research will show how the proposed lexical mechanisms can be eliminated in favor of more general principles (see Jackendoff 1990: chapter 11 for some suggestions). In any case, the decision on this problem does not substantially affect the proposed analysis of *-ize* verbs.

Another problem concerns the optionality of the CAUSE function in the LCS (20). The formulation of (20) suggests that any *-ize* verb may be used as an inchoative, which is certainly not the case. Locative and ornative derivatives necessarily take three arguments, and a putative intransitive form *hospitalize* can therefore only be interpreted as 'become a hospital'.

Since inchoatives lack an overt instigator one can expect intransitive forms typically with Events where Agency is either unclear or unnecessary to specify. This prediction is borne out by the data. Consider for example *aerosolize*, which in its intransitive form denotes a process that is governed by the laws of physics (cf. the quotation given by the *OED* "Six per cent. of the total amount of penicillin aerosolized").

So far, our treatment may have suggested that intransitive derivatives are automatically interpreted as inchoatives. This is, however, not true. In some cases we find intransitive forms that do not correspond to the analysis of inchoative derivatives as put forward above. This group of non-inchoative intransitive *-ize* derivatives is the one that was labeled 'performatives' in (6), and whose meaning can be paraphrased as 'perform X', e.g. *anthropologize*, or *apologize* (Lieber's example, not a 20th century neologism). Let us consider in some detail the intransitive form *anthropologize* '*intr.* to pursue anthropology' (*OED*) as in *John anthropologized in the field* (a slightly modified *OED* quotation). In such cases, the Theme argument remains unexpressed, while there is a clear Agent expressed by the subject NP (in this case [*John*]). This suggests that there is yet another syntactic frame for *-ize* verbs, namely [NP_i ___]. Incorporating this frame into (23) yields the following LCS:

(24)   LCS of *-ize* verbs (generalized)
   $[[\quad]_{\text{BASE}} \, \text{-}ize]_{\text{V}}$
   $\{ \text{NP}_i \, \underline{\quad} \, \text{NP}_{\text{Theme}}, \text{NP}_{\text{Theme}} \, \underline{\quad}, \text{NP}_i \underline{\quad} \}$
   $\underline{\text{CAUSE}} \, ([\,\ldots\ldots\,]_i, [\text{GO} \, ([\,]_{\text{Property, Thing}} \,]_{\text{Theme / Base}};$
   $\qquad\qquad\qquad\qquad [\text{TO} \, [\,]_{\text{Property, Thing}} \,]_{\text{Base / Theme}}])])$

The LCS of *John anthropologized (in the field)* looks then as in (25):

(25)   LCS of *John anthropologized (in the field)*
 a. 'ornative'
  CAUSE ([*John*]$_i$, [GO ([*anthropology*]$_{Base}$; [TO [   ]$_{Theme}$])])
 b. 'inchoative'
  GO ([*John*]$_{Theme}$; [TO [*anthropology*]$_{Base}$])])

Given the lack of an overt object, only two syntactic structures can be mapped onto the semantic representation, namely [NP$_{Theme}$ ___] and [NP$_i$ ___]. Thus [*John*] can be either interpreted as [NP$_i$], yielding the interpretation (25a), or as [NP $_{Theme}$ ___], with the interpretation (25b). (25a) can be paraphrased as 'John applied anthropology to an unmentioned object', while (25b) would paraphrase as 'John became anthropology', which is an interpretation that can be ruled out on pragmatic grounds. Thus the introduction of a third syntactic frame naturally solves the syntactic and semantic problems with the group of derivatives called 'performatives' above, which can, like the other groups, be subsumed under the LCS (24).

I have already critically mentioned Lieber's example *economize*, which, although not a 20th century innovation, would nicely fit into the performative group (instead of Lieber's 'manner' group (5d)). One of the meanings of the base word *economy*, and surely the pertinent one in this case, is given by the *OED* as 'Frugality, thrift, saving'. Accordingly, and correctly I think, the intransitive derivative *economize* is defined by the *OED* 'To practise economy', which parallels our analysis of verbs like *apologize* or *anthropologize*. Under Lieber's approach these similarities are not ackowledged and *apologize* and *economize* are taken as examples of different, even homophonous categories. As already pointed out in section 6.1.2., another disadvantage of Lieber's model is that the transitive use of performative -*ize* derivatives is left unexplained, whereas the present model predicts that transitive use is in principle possible.[9]

We may now turn to the last cluster of derivatives, called 'similatives', which are often paraphrased as 'act like X', 'imitate X', and which seem like an entirely separate class of derivatives, mostly with proper nouns as their bases. Lieber's analysis of these forms as in (5d) is therefore not at all far-fetched. However, both the traditional paraphrases and Lieber's LCS (5d)

---

[9] That is not to say that all of the performative verbs *must* have a transitive variant. Examples like *apologize* show that this is not the case. Note, however, that one can *apologize for something*, in which case the normally unexpressed Theme surfaces syntactically as an adjunct phrase.

cannot cope with the problem that most, if not all of the pertinent derivatives are transitive. I will show that these formations can be subsumed under the general LCS of -*ize* derivatives. The corpus contains the following
forms, among others: *Coslettize, Hooverize, Lukanize, Maoize, Mandelize,
Marxize, Powellize, Stalinize, Sherardize, Taylorize.* Let us examine how
they fit into the LCS of -*ize* verbs by looking briefly at the form *Marxize,*
as in *The socialists Marxize the West* (adopted under slight modification
from an *OED* quotation), and the form *Taylorize.* For reasons of space and
clarity only the transitive forms will be considered; the analysis of intran-
sitives can be done in a parallel fashion (see the discussion above):

(26)   LCS of *The socialists Marxize the West*
    a.   CAUSE ([*The socialists*]$_i$, [GO ([*Marx*]$_{Base}$;
                                        [TO [*the West*]$_{Theme}$])])
    b.   CAUSE ([*The socialists*]$_i$, [GO ([*the West*]$_{Theme}$;
                                        [TO [*Marx*]$_{Base}$])])

Two interpretations are structurally possible. The first is that [*Marx*] is
induced in [*the West*], the second is that [*the West*] is transferred to [*Marx*].
Both interpretations only make sense if the base *Marx* is not interpreted as
the name of a person but metonymically as a framework of ideas. Such
cases of metonymy are a rather frequent phenomenon, which can be illustrated by a sentence like

(27)   Marx is rather out-dated these days.

The referent of *Marx* in (27) is not Marx himself, but his ideas, usually
referred to by the form *Marxism.* Reference to metonymic meanings is also
attested in other areas of word-formation, e.g. with the suffix -*(i)an.* A
Chomskian may have nothing to do with Chomsky himself, but follows the
master's ideas. Coming back to the structures in (26), we can paraphrase
them as either 'the socialists induce Marxism in the West' or 'the socialists
make the West adopt Marxism'.
    Let us briefly discuss the second example, *Taylorize,* which is para-
phrased by the *OED* as 'To introduce the Taylor system into'. In other
words, we are confronted with an ornative meaning where the base *Taylor*
stands metonymically for the system invented by Taylor (similar arguments
apply with the other derivatives mentioned). In sum, the oft-cited meaning
'act like X, imitate X' (formally encapsulated in Lieber's LCS (5d)) is the

result of the inference that if one applies the ideas or manners of a certain person, one acts like that person.[10]

As was already pointed out above, previous approaches have difficulties in explaining the transitive use of similative derivatives. However, analyzing similatives as special kinds of ornatives, as suggested above, can nicely account for this fact. Furthermore, the proposed analysis explicates the relationship between the similative and the other interpretations of *-ize* verbs. If there were no such relationship, as suggested by the advocates of the homonymy position, the very existence of a similative interpretation would be totally unwarranted.

To summarize the discussion of each of the semantic categories mentioned in (6), we can say that all of them are derived from a single LCS, which I repeat here for convenience:

(28)   LCS of *-ize* verbs (generalized)
$[[\quad]_{\text{BASE}}\ \text{-ize}]_V$
$\{\ \text{NP}_i\ \underline{\quad}\ \text{NP}_{\text{Theme}},\ \text{NP}_{\text{Theme}}\ \underline{\quad}\ ,\ \text{NP}_i\ \underline{\quad}\ \}$
$\underline{\text{CAUSE}}\ ([\ \underline{\dots}\ ]_i,\ [\text{GO}\ ([_{\text{Property, Thing}}\quad]_{\text{Theme / Base}};$
$[\text{TO}\ [_{\text{Property, Thing}}\quad]_{\text{Base / Theme}}])])$

This LCS can account for the vast majority of 20th century neologisms in *-ize*. In the remainder of this section, I want to discuss the very few derivatives in the corpus that seem to be impossible to interpret on the basis of the proposed LCS. These derivatives are *prisonize* ' To cause (a person) to adapt himself to prison life', *weatherize* 'To make weatherproof', *winterize* 'To adapt or prepare (something) for operation or use in cold weather', *ecize* 'of plants: to become established in a new habitat', and *cannibalize* 'To take parts from one unit for incorporation in, and completion of, another (of a similar kind)' (all definitions *OED*).

In the case of *cannibalize*, the derivative has only a remote semantic relationship to the base word's meaning. Without the appropriate context, or knowledge of the lexicalized form, the correct meaning cannot be inferred. *Cannibalize* may well have been coined in analogy to derivatives with a similative meaning 'act like a cannibal', but, if so, it is unclear, why it does not mean 'eat someone of your own species'. In other words, *cannibalize* is

---

[10]   Sometimes such inferences contribute to a complete loss of productivity of a given rule. Van Marle (1988) is a detailed study of semantic diversity leading to the downfall of a morphological category.

semantically not transparent and has only a very remote relationship to productively formed *-ize* derivatives.

Not quite as remote seems to be the relationship between regular *-ize* words and the forms *prisonize, weatherize* and *winterize*. Although these forms cannot be interpreted in terms of (28), they do denote the inducing of a property in the Thing denoted by Theme. However, this property is not denoted by the base. Rather these forms could be paraphrased as 'adapt something to X', with X being the base word. These deviant forms seem to be based on the inference that adaptation always implies a change of Properties. As shown by van Marle (1988), such inferences are not uncommon and often lead to the development of a greater semantic diversity of a derivational category. Hence, the three forms can be regarded as being derived by a creative extension of the original semantics of regular *-ize* formations.

Turning to the derivative *ecize*, it is clear from the quotation given in the *OED* that this form has been intentionally coined by biologists on the basis of *ecesis* (cf. Greek οἰκίζειν 'to colonize'), apparently in analogy to other nouns in *-sis* (e.g. *hypothesis, metathesis*) which in their majority may undergo *-ize* suffixation (e.g. Raffelsiefen 1996). In general, the words of this type show the kind of polysemy discussed in connection with the LCS in (28). Thus, *ecize* (like e.g. *metamorphosize* and *metathesize*) belongs to the performative group, while others may be considered resultatives or locatives (*e.g. hypothesize*, not a 20th century neologism), or ornatives (e.g. *metastasize*) etc. Semantically, *ecize* is thus a regular formation.

In sum, even the putatively idiosyncratic formations can be shown to be at least remotely related to the general semantics of *-ize*. Given that idiosyncratic, lexicalized meanings are a rather common phenomenon with derivational categories, these isolated exceptions do not challenge our overall analysis. Quite to the contrary, the fact that they are so small in number supports the semantic coherence of *-ize* derivatives as expressed by the LCS in (28).

An additional argument for the suggested analysis comes from the relative stability of *-ize* affixation over the centuries and from its present productivity. Van Marle (1988) argues that semantically diverse morphological processes tend to lose their productivity, unless their diversity is still transparently related. The latter is crucially the case with all processes that display polysemy proper, like, for example, Dutch subject nouns (Booij 1986). The fact that *-ize* is definitely a productive verb-deriving process in English is another indication that we are dealing with a semantically transparent, polysemous process.

Lieber (1996) questions the semantic transparency of -*ize* derivatives and calls this suffix only 'partially determinate'. She claims that it is more determinate than, for example, N to V conversion, but less determinate than the formation of denominal verbs in *de-* (such as *debug, deflea, dethrone*). This view rests on two questionable assumptions. The first is that "the more transparent the meaning, the more productive the pattern of word formation" (1996:10). While a significant relationship between semantic transparency and productivity cannot be denied, it seems that this relationship is not of the kind assumed by Lieber. Thus, there are completely unproductive derivational processes in English that are nevertheless semantically highly transparent (e.g. nominal -*th*, verbal -*en*). However, there seems to be no process that is semantically non-transparent and nevertheless productive. These considerations boil down to the more moderate and more accurate generalization that productive processes are always transparent.

Based on her questionable assumption, Lieber then puts forward that the greater productivity of denominal *de-* is an indication of the fact that -*ize* is semantically less determinate than *de-*. First of all, it can seriously be doubted that *de-* is in fact more productive than -*ize*. Unfortunately, Lieber does not give any source for her "recent calculation of P for *de-* ... $P=0.0465$" (as against $P=0.0072$ for denominal -*ize* and 0.0138 for deadjectival -*ize*), but if CELEX was used, the figures cannot be trusted (see the discussion in chapters 2 and 5 above). My own calculation on the basis of the *OED* (again 20th century neologisms) yields a different result. Including denominal, deverbal, and parasynthetic formations with *de-*, I arrived at 115 types, which is less than half the number of -*ize* neologisms in this source.[11]

Secondly, it is unclear what, if anything, such purely quantitative assesssments of productivtiy can tell us about the semantics of a morphological process, since even unproductive processes can be transparent. Thus, even if *de-* had a higher P than -*ize*, this could be simply due to non-semantic (e.g. phonological or morphological) restrictions that constrain -*ize* formations but not *de-* formations. Attempts to base semantic conclusions on a simple comparison of purely quantitative measures are therefore totally unconvincing.

In sum, Lieber's arguments against the semantic coherence of -*ize* derivatives are not compelling.

---

[11]   A quantitative analysis of *de-* in the Cobuild corpus was not carried out.

6.1.4. Conclusion

In the foregoing discussion I have put forward a unified analysis of the meaning of the suffix *-ize* and its derivatives in English. The investigation of a large corpus of neologisms has provided strong evidence for the semantic coherence of *-ize* formations, a coherence hitherto not recognized in the linguistic literature. On the basis of the LCS suggested in (28), the polysemy of *-ize* verbs can be described, predicted and formalized in a straightforward manner. The semantic interpretation of a given derivative can be construed by mapping the different participants and the base onto the semantic representation as expressed in the LCS.

This analysis has certain advantages over previous approaches. First, the proposed model can not only account for the semantic diversity between different derivatives, but can also explain the attested or possible divergent meanings of individual formations, which is a problem largely neglected by previous authors. Second, it was shown explicitly how the different meanings of *-ize* formations are related, with the consequence that the apparent semantic diversity of productively formed *-ize* derivatives turned out to be a case of polysemy, not homonymy. Third, the specification of the syntactic category of the base word was shown to be superfluous, which leads to a welcome simplification of the morphological machinery. These findings have a number of implications for some theoretical issues in morphology such as the status of affixes and word formation rules in the lexicon.

The analysis of *-ize* derivatives put forward here provides strong arguments against purely syntactic models of derivational morphology (such as E. Williams 1981a, 1981b, Lieber 1992, Hale and Keyser 1993). These arguments are essentially the same as those provided and discussed in Lieber's (1996) analysis of *-ize*, the main point being that the intricacies of the semantics cannot be captured by purely syntactic formalisms. Since this point is laid out convincingly and in considerable detail in Lieber (1996), it need not be elaborated here, and I will focus my attention on another theoretical problem, the format of word formation rules.

In standard generative approaches word formation rules contain, among other things, information on the semantics of the suffix and the syntactic category of the base. Furthermore, word formation rules are considered as operations on a possible input with a predictable output. Both assumptions are called into question by my findings.

Consider again Gussmann's (1987) approach, which was already briefly mentioned in chapter 5. He claims that there is a so-called rule of derivation, i.e. a "uniform semanto-syntactic formula whereby adjectives become verbalised" (1987:82) with the meaning 'make (more) X'. This rule of derivation is spelled out by the rival affixes *-ize*, *-ate*, *-ify*, etc. While the postulated meaning 'make (more) X' is intuitively plausible, these rules can neither account for the other widely-attested meanings nor can they explain why many of the verbalizing affixes (including *-ize*) also take nouns and bound roots as their bases. In Gussmann's framework one would have to posit yet another - denominal - rule (plus a number of additional derivational rules that express the other possible meanings). Streamlining the denominal and deadjectival rules by making reference to a syntactic feature like [+ N][12]common to both adjectives and nouns would achieve greater descriptive adequacy, but would not eliminate the stipulation as such. Under the approach presented above nothing needs to be stipulated, but it follows from the LCS itself that the syntactic category may be a noun or an adjective, and not, say, a verb.

Thus, the case of *-ize* strongly challenges the traditional practice (generative and non-generative alike) of treating the information about the syntactic category of the base word as crucial for derivational processes. Generalizing from *-ize*, one could even come up with the strong hypothesis that with any given productive affix, the syntactic category of potential base words is only a by-product of the semantics of the process. Such a hypothesis would find some support in a recent study of the person noun forming suffix *-ee*, in which it is shown that some existing denominal derivatives can naturally be accounted for if the semantics of *-ee* is properly defined (Barker 1996[13]). Future research will show whether such a strong hypothesis is indeed tenable.

The problem of the syntactic specification of the base word is symptomatic of a more general problem, namely the architecture of word formation rules. Such rules are usually seen as operations on a more or less well-defined class of possible input structures which derive a class of possible output structures. The account of *-ize* I propose here shifts emphasis from the possible input to the possible output by rephrasing the traditional input-output relation between base, affix and derivative as a general condition on

---

[12]   Following Aronoff (1976:48), and Scalise (1984:139).

[13]   Note that Barker himself does not advocate this in his paper. Rather, he assumes that the denominal forms are based on an underlying zero-derived verb even if such a verb is not attested (e.g. *festschriftee* < **festschrift* $_V$ + *-ee*). This analysis seems rather ad hoc, especially in view of the fact that the pertinent data can be accounted for in the purely semantic terms developed by Barker.

the output, with desirable empirical and theoretical consequences. Such an analysis of derivational morphological processes has been advocated earlier for example by Plank (1981), and, in regard to inflection, by Bybee and Slobin (1982), Bybee and Moder (1983), and links up with similar recent trends in other areas of linguistics. Thus, in phonology and syntax frameworks like Optimality Theory or the Minimalist Program (e.g. Prince and Smolensky 1993b, Chomsky 1993, respectively) incorporate a major shift from derivational to representational mechanisms. That output-oriented approaches lead to new insights into the nature of morpho-phonological alternations has already been shown in a growing number of studies[14] and will be demonstrated also in the next section, when the phonology of *-ize* derivatives will be dealt with. The findings presented above call for an extension of representational mechanisms to the syntactic and semantic aspects of morphological processes.

6.2. The phonology of *-ize* derivatives

6.2.1. Introduction

Having outlined the semantic properties of *-ize* derivatives, we will now focus on the phonological restrictions operating on these forms. It has been observed that verbs derived by the suffixation of *-ize* feature some peculiar and apparently variable phonological properties. Thus base-final segments are often deleted (as in *emphasis - emphasize*), base-final consonants may change (as in *Celtic - Celticize*), vowels may alternate (as in *géntile - géntilìze*[15]), consonants appear to be inserted between the base and the suffix (as in *stigma - stigmatize*) and even stress may be shifted (as in *cátholic - cathólicìze*) or reduced (as in (*fértile - fértilìze*)). To complicate matters further, the application of these phonological manipulations of the base word seem to be rather unpredictable. Some words are affected, others are not for no obvious reason. Apart from these allomorphy problems, one has to account for the fact that the possibility to attach *-ize* to a given base

---

[14]   See e.g. McCarthy and Prince (1993b), Golston and Wiese (1996), Neef (1996), Raffelsiefen (1996), Booij (1998), and many of the papers listed in the Rutgers Optimality Archive.
[15]   Following established conventions, I use acute accent to mark primary stress, grave accent to mark secondary stress.

word seems to depend on certain phonological properties of the base. In particular, monosyllables and words with final primary stress almost never appear as stems in *-ize* formations.

Although these phenomena are well-known, it has remained unclear which mechanisms can best account for the phonological alternations and the phonological productivity restrictions of *-ize* words. Basically, two kinds of models have been proposed, one based on the application of phonological rules (e.g. Gussmann 1987, Kettemann 1988), the other on well-formedness conditions (Raffelsiefen 1996). Hence, on the theoretical level, the debate on the phonology of *-ize* derivatives reflects the more general controversy about derivational versus representational theories in linguistics. I will argue here that the phonological behavior of derived verbs can best be accounted for if we assume a number of violable output constraints as in Optimality Theory (henceforth OT) instead of input restrictions and/or morpho-phonological rules.

There are cursory remarks on the phonology of *-ize* in numerous linguistic sources but only very few in-depth studies of the phonological properties of *-ize* derivatives (Gussmann 1987, E. Schneider 1987, Kettemann 1988, and Raffelsiefen 1996).[16] These studies will serve as a reference point for the account to be presented below. It will be shown that the earlier attempts are flawed in many respects and that they should be replaced by an account according to which the phonological well-formedness of potential *-ize* formations crucially depends on the prosodic structure of the derivative. I will also argue for violable constraints of the type proposed in OT and show that non-violable well-formedness conditions as put forward, for example, by Neef (1996), are less adequate.

The next section (6.2.2.) presents a short introduction to the basic concepts and machinery of OT. Readers already familiar with this theory may wish to skip this section and immediately move on to section 6.2.3., which reviews previous studies of *-ize* verbs. In section 6.2.4. I discuss some hitherto neglected empirical facts about *-ize* derivatives, and in 6.2.5. we turn to the presentation of a new constraint-based model of the phonology of *-ize* derivatives. Section 6.2.6. summarizes the results and discusses the theoretical implications of the proposed account.

---

16 There is one notable account of the stress pattern of *-ize* derivatives, namely Danielsson (1948). This historically oriented study presents a wealth of data, but leaves the reader with the impression that hardly any generalizations can be drawn. Danielsson lists a whole range of attested stress patterns, but it remains unclear what, if anything, conditions the diverging patterns.

6.2.2.   Optimality Theory: An introduction

Optimality Theory is a theory about the organization and nature of grammar, most notably phonology. It is a theory that does not make use of clas-
sical derivational rules but of a set of ranked violable well-formedness
conditions against which possible output forms are evaluated in parallel. In
this section I will outline the basic architecture of this theory, with special
focus on those aspects that will be relevant for the discussion of derived
verbs in English. Due to this focus the following introduction to OT is
necessarily simplified and incomplete. For a more detailed discussion the
reader should consult the primary literature (e.g. Prince and Smolensky
1993, McCarthy and Prince 1993b) or the introductory treatments in
Archangeli and Langendoen (1997) or Sherrard (1997), for example.

   In OT, Universal Grammar (UG) provides a set of well-formedness
conditions, called constraints, from which grammars are constructed. The
grammar of a particular language consists of an ordered ranking of these
constraints, which is specific to this language. The grammars of other languages are characterized by different constraint rankings. How do these
constraints operate? Given an underlying representation as input, a component of UG (called *Gen*) generates a whole range of possible outputs (so-
called *candidates*) of which the one is chosen as optimal which best satisfies the constraints.

   What mainly differentiates OT from other non-derivational theories is the
assumption that the constraints are violable. The hierarchical ranking of the
constraints ensures that a constraint must always be satisfied unless doing
so would involve the violation of a more important constraint. For
illustration consider the surface realizations and syllabifications of the
input forms /tata/, /pap/ and /aka/ in a given language L. For the sake of the
argument, let us assume that only two constraints are responsible for syllabification, ONSET and NOCODA (e.g Prince and Smolensky 1993), and
that there are two constraints that work against the deletion or epenthesis
of segments, MAX and DEP (McCarthy and Prince 1995):

(29)   a.   Constraints on syllable structure:
            ONSET: Syllables must have onsets
            NOCODA: Syllables must not have codas
       b.   Constraints against deletion/epenthesis
            MAX: No deletion of underlying segments
            DEP: No epenthesis

Let us further assume that in language L ONSET, NOCODA and MAX are ranked higher than DEP. Such rankings are usually expressed as in (30a) or (30b):

(30)   a.   ONSET, NOCODA, MAX >> DEP
       b.   ONSET, NOCODA, MAX
                      |
                    DEP

Considering first only four likely output candidates for the input /tata/, we can construct a tableau as in (31) below, which shows the computation of the optimal candidate. A few notational conventions are necessary for the interpretation of an OT tableau. The output candidates are listed in the leftmost column, with the optimal candidate being marked by the pointing hand ('☞'). Violations are marked by an asterisk and exclamation marks indicate fatal constraint violations, i.e. those which eliminate a candidate. The optimal candidate is the one that rates better on the higher constraints than the competing candidates. If two candidates both violate the same high constraint, the decision is passed on to the next lower constraint. Solid lines between colomns indicate hierarchical ranking, broken lines are used between constraints that are not ranked with respect to each other.

(31) ONSET, NOCODA, MAX >> DEP

/tata/	ONSET	NOCODA	MAX	DEP
☞ ta.ta				
tat.a	*!	*!		
ta.tat		*!		*
tat		*!	*!	

In (31), [ta.ta] is the optimal candidate because it violates none of the constraints in the tableau. All other candidates violate at least one constraint and are therefore ruled out. The syllabification *tat.a*, for example, is illicit due to the filled coda of the first syllable (i.e. a NOCODA violation) and the onsetless second syllable (i.e. an ONSET violation). Note that in our example [ta.ta] emerges as the optimal candidate under any ranking of the constraints because it violates none of them. The next sample input /pap/

shows, however, that the ranking is crucial for the selection of the optimal output:

(32) ONSET, NOCODA, MAX >> DEP

/pap/	ONSET	NOCODA	MAX	DEP
☞ pa.pa				*
pap.a	*!			*
pap		*!		
pa			*!	

In (32) [pa.pa] is selected as the optimal candidate, because the high rank of NOCODA necessitates either vowel epenthesis or deletion of the final consonant. Since the constraint against deletion (i.e. MAX) is higher-ranked than the constraint against epenthesis (i.e. DEP), the DEP violation is more easily affordable than the MAX violation. Under a different ranking, another candidate is optimal. For example, if DEP were ranked higher than MAX, vowel epenthesis would be ruled out, and the candidate involving a MAX violation would emerge as optimal. If both MAX and DEP were ranked above NOCODA, [pap] would be optimal.

The last example shows how constraint violation becomes unavoidable because of conflicting constraints. Given a consonant-final input form, it is impossible to have CV syllables without either epenthesis or deletion, satisfying high-ranked NOCODA. Thus, of the three constraints NOCODA, MAX and DEP, two can be satisfied at the expense of the third, but never all three of them at the same time. Let us finally consider the input /aka/:

(33) ONSET, NOCODA, MAX >> DEP

/aka/	ONSET	NOCODA	MAX	DEP
☞ ʔa.ka				*
a.ka	*!			
ka			*!	

With the given input in (33), ONSET requires either deletion or epenthesis. The higher rank of MAX again leads to epenthesis as the preferred repair strategy.[17] Ranking both MAX and DEP higher than ONSET would make [aka] the optimal candidate.

Having outlined the basic machinery, we may now turn to the nature of constraints in more detail. Obviously, one of the central problems in OT is to constrain the use of constaints in some way or another. Which constraints should be allowed in the theory and which others should be ruled out? Ideally, each constraint can be motivated on cross-linguistic grounds. Thus the constraints against filled codas and for filled onsets mirror the crosslinguistic tendency towards CV as the unmarked syllable structure (e.g. Jakobson 1962, Vennemann 1988, Blevins 1995) and have been used to establish a factorial typology of syllabic structures (Prince and Smolensky 1993: chapter 6). Unfortunately, not all constraints that can be found in the literature have been justified in an equally satisfactory manner and a good deal of the present discussion in OT is devoted to this question. Currently the following types of constraints are widely acknowledged:

(34)   Types of constraints in OT
    a.   markedness constraints
    b.   alignment constraints
    c.   constituency constraints
    d.   faithfulness constraints

Markedness constraints reflect the preference for certain types of structures. For example, it has been suggested that, cross-linguistically, obstruents make better syllable margins than sonorant consonants or vowels. This fact can be formalized in OT as a hierarchy of constraints against certain types of syllable margins (M), according to their sonority, as in (35) (cf. Prince and Smolensky 1993):

(35)   *M/a >> *M/i >> *M/l >> *M/n >> *M/t

A more detailed discussion of markedness constraints is not necessary for the purposes of this study.

Let us therefore turn to alignment constraints, which regulate the adjacency or coincidence of linguistic objects. Alignment constraints are fre-

---

[17]   Essentially, this is the kind of situation we find in a language like German, where underlyingly vowel-initial syllables in certain prosodic positions (i.e. word- or foot-initial) are realized with a glottal stop in onset position (see, for example, Wiese 1996a:58-60 for discussion).

quently used to analyze the metrical behavior of words. The general format of alignment constraints is given in (36), with a perhaps more accessible formulation in (37) (see McCarthy and Prince 1993a):

(36)   Align (Cat1, Edge1, Cat2, Edge2)
       ∀ Cat1 ∃ Cat2 such that Edge1 of Cat1 and Edge2 of Cat2 coincide
       Where   Cat1, Cat2 ∈ PCat ∪ GCat
       Edge1, Edge2 ∈ {Right, Left}

(37)   Align (Cat1, Edge1, Cat2, Edge2)
       "for each element of Cat(egory)1 there is an element of Cat(egory)2 such that Edge1 of Cat(egory)1 and Edge2 of Cat(egory)2 coincide. Cat1 and Cat2 may be prosodic or grammatical (i.e. morphological or syntactic) categories. An Edge is either a left or a right edge of such a category."

To give only one illustrative example, consider the syllabification of the word *helpless*. Most native speakers would probably agree that the syllable boundary should be placed between *help* and *less* (*help.less*). However, in terms of the standard syllabification principles of English, we would expect *hel.pless* instead, because both *hel* and *pless* are well-formed syllables and because this syllabification would better satisfy the maximal onset principle (Selkirk 1982b). Compare, for instance *im.ply* and **imp.ly*, *com.plain* and **comp.lain*, which illustrate this point. What these examples show is that syllabification interacts with morphology in such a way that with words such as *helpless*, the morphological boundary must coincide with the a syllable boundary. In the theory of generalized alignment (McCarthy and Prince 1993a), this can be achieved by the high ranking of the pertinent alignment constraint ALIGN-Stem-σ as against the lower ranking of the constraints that ensure maximal onsets:

(38)   ALIGN-STEM-σ
       Align (stem, R, σ, R)
       "The right edge of the stem must coincide with the right edge of a syllable"

For the vowel-initial verbal suffixes such a constraint does not play a crucial role, since in these derivatives the stem-final consonant (if not truncated) fills the onset position of the last syllable, as exemplified by *wea.ken, fe.de.ra.lize, per.so.ni.fy, hy.phe.nate.* This means that ONSET is ranked higher than ALIGN-STEM-σ.

Constituency constraints refer to the prosodic hierarchy (e.g. Nespor and Vogel 1986) and govern the extent to which, for example, syllables are dominated, or 'parsed', by feet, feet by prosodic words, etc. Such constraints are especially relevant for an analysis of extrametricality. For example, a trisyllabic input can be footed in several ways. Under the assumption that footing proceeds from left to right and that feet must be either mono- or disyllabic, but not trisyllabic, there is one completely footed candidate $(\sigma\sigma)(\sigma)$[18] and one 'extrametrical' candidate $(\sigma\sigma)\sigma$. Footing from left to right is achieved by the alignment constraint ALLFEETLEFT (short for Align (Ft, L, PrWd, L)[19]), the parsing of syllables into feet by PARSE-σ ("All syllables are parsed into feet"). The choice of the optimal candidate now depends on the ranking of these two constraints (*ceteris paribus*):

(39)   ALLFEETLEFT >> PARSE-σ

	ALLFEETLEFT	PARSE-σ
☞ $(\sigma\sigma)\sigma$		*
$(\sigma\sigma)(\sigma)$	$\sigma\sigma$![20]	

(40)   PARSE-σ >> ALLFEETLEFT

	PARSE-σ	ALLFEETLEFT
$(\sigma\sigma)\sigma$	*!	
☞ $(\sigma\sigma)(\sigma)$		$\sigma\sigma$

The tableaux show that unparsed syllables are only allowed if PARSE-σ is ranked below ALLFEETLEFT. Under such a ranking PARSE-σ needs to be violated in order to satisfy the more important ALLFEETLEFT.

Let us turn to the family of constraints that can be considered the most important in the context of this study, faithfulness constraints. These con-

---

[18]   I adopt the standard convention that parentheses indicate feet.
[19]   Ft=foot, PrWd=prosodic word, L=left, R=right
[20]   Two sigmas indicate that the offending foot is two syllables from the left margin of the prosodic word.

straints regulate the degree of identity which ideally exists between input and output. Thus, traditional rule-based analyses (e.g. *SPE*) have often been criticized as implausible on the grounds that many of the proposed underlying representations were too far removed from their respective surface forms, a problem that has become known as the problem of abstractness. Much of the most recent OT literature is devoted to a principled solution of this problem in terms of a sub-theory called correspondence theory (McCarthy and Prince 1995).

The essence of faithfulness between input and output is that both members should be identical, which is achieved mainly by the constraints MAX and DEP, which we have used already above and which we can now define in a more appropriate fashion in terms of correspondence theory:

(41)   a.   MAX ('maximality')
            "Every input segment has a correspondent segment in the output" (="no deletion")
       b.   DEP ('dependency')
            "Every output segment has a correspondent segment in the input" (="no epenthesis")

Featural identity between input and output is achieved by parametrized constraints of the family IDENT (F), where F stands for a distinctive feature:

(42)   IDENT (F)
       "Output correspondents of an input segment have the same value for the feature F"

A number of additional input-output (I-O) faithfulness constraints have been proposed to account for other kinds of correspondence relations between input and output, for example constraints against metathesis, but we will not discuss those any further (see for example McCarthy and Prince 1995: Appendix A for an overview).

Let us turn instead to another type of faithfulness that only very recently has attracted the attention of researchers, namely output-output (O-O) faithfulness. O-O faithfulness has been employed in a growing number of studies (e.g. Alber 1998, Alderete 1995, Benua 1995, 1997, Kager 1997, Kenstowicz 1996, McCarthy 1995, Pater 1995) to account for some intriguing morpho-phonological phenomena. It will be shown that O-O faithfulness is also of crucial importance for the phonological effects that can be observed with derived verbs in English. To mention only one illustrative example that has nothing to do with derived verbs, consider truncated hypocoristics in English. Benua (1995) observed that the truncated form of *Larry* (and similar forms) is pronounced [læɹ] in many dialects of American English, although in these dialects the low front vowel [æ] ordinarily does not occur before a tautosyllabic [ɹ]. Consider, for example, [kɑɹ]/[kɑɹd]/*[kæɹ]/*[kæɹd] as against [kæ.ɹɪ]. In other words, truncated words are exempt from constraints on vowel quality in syllables with a rhotic coda. Why should this be the case? The answer to this question lies in the simple but fundamental insight that derived words have to be sufficiently similar to the words they are derived from. For our example this means that the constraint which ensures surface similarity (i.e. O-O vowel identity) between *Larry* and *Lar* must rank higher than the phonological constraints which prohibit the occurrence of [æɹ.].

Having briefly outlined the basic concepts of OT we may now turn the analysis of derived verbs in English. As we will proceed, a number of problems concerning the ranking and the nature of the constraints involved with these classes of words will be discussed in more detail.

6.2.3. Previous analyses

In the literature there are four studies that describe the phonology of *-ize* derivatives in some detail: Gussmann 1987, E. Schneider 1987, Kettemann 1988, and Raffelsiefen 1996.

In his article on deadjectival *-ize*,[21] Gussmann focuses on the segmental structure of the base words and proposes that the suffix attaches to "Latinate adjectives ending in a vowel followed by one or more sonorant consonants" (1987:95). On the same page, some counterexamples are presented (*stabilise, malleablise,*[22] *legitimatise, objectivise, collectivise*[23]), but Gussmann dismisses them as being "very infrequent" and thus "in the permanent lexicon" (1987:95). In addition to the most frequent sonorants [l, r, n] Marchand lists [s] as the next frequent segment, and [t], [d] and [m] as

---

[21] In the subsequent discussion, we will not distinguish between deadjectival and denominal *-ize* derivatives because this distinction is neither phonologically not semantically relevant.

[22] The forms *stabilise* and *malleablise* only count as counterexamples on the assumption that the base words end in syllabic /l/.

[23] The examples are cited in the orthographical form of the original.

the least frequent segments preceding -*ize*, which at least partially refutes Gussmann's claims, since three of the seven segments mentioned are obstruents, not sonorants. In the neologism corpus, more counterexamples to Gussmann's generalization are revealed. Among the derivatives with adjectival bases we find *absolutize, academicize* (and many more in -*ic-ize*),[24] *comprehensivize* (and many more in -*ive-ize*), *finitize, infinitize, instantize, permanentize, polyploidize, privatize, rigidize, ruggedize*. With denominal derivatives even vowels are attested as final segments with a number of bases (e.g. *ghettoize, virtuize*). The great number of attested forms and their regularity (-*ic-ize*, -*ive-ize*) is a strong indication that Gussmann's rule is too restrictive with respect to the base-final segment. As we will shortly see, it is also too weak in that it does not take into account restrictions of a prosodic nature, which, as shown by Raffelsiefen (1996), are much more pervasive for the distribution of -*ize* than segmental restrictions.

In his brief but insightful remarks on the phonology of -*ize* derivatives (1987:102ff), E. Schneider states that there are no restrictions concerning the base-final segments, but detects some interesting facts relating to the prosodic structure of the words from which -*ize* words are derived. On the basis of his corpus of 744 items he finds a strong tendency towards polysyllabic base words (only 5 monosyllabic stems, as in *dockize*), and an equally strong tendency towards antepenultimate stress, with only sporadic stress shift. Disyllabic bases are usually consonant-final, with two exceptions, *heroize* and *zeroize*. Unstressed base-final vowels of trisyllabic words are deleted (*summary - summarize*) and base-final secondary stress is often reduced (*fértile - fértilìze*). Finally, E. Schneider finds peculiar allomorphy effects with Greek bases (e.g. *system-systematize*) including stress shift (e.g. *plátitude-platitúdinize*). In sum, in spite of its brevity, E. Schneider's account is very detailed and empirically well-founded. However, no attempt is made to provide a unified explanation for the observed facts. Furthermore, the large data-base including a high number of long-established forms brings in so many idiosyncratic forms that we are faced with an abundance of counterexamples to the proposed generalizations. Hence, E. Schneider comes to the conlusion that the properties of -*ize* (and of the other suffixes he investigates) can only be described in terms of quantitative tendencies, but not as categorical (1987:109). As we will see

---

[24]   According to Gussmann, -*ic* is generally truncated. The *OED* data refute this statement. For a more detailed discussion of truncation see below.

below, it is possible to provide a more adequate account of the phonology of -*ize* derivatives by restricting one's data-base to recent formations.

Kettemann's book (1988) deals with the phonological alternations triggered by derivational affixes in English. He accounts for the alternations in -*ize* formations either by introducing phonological rules or by assigning the alternation to the word's individual lexical entry. For example, he states that stress shift in the base should be assigned to the individual lexical entry of the word (p. 207), but for the majority of the segmental alternations he proposes phonological rules, such as [∅ ↔ n] for the alternation in the pair *Plato - platonic* (p. 210). While he can describe most existing derivatives in this manner, his model is unable to predict whether a given base will undergo a certain alternation, and if so, which kind of phonological or phonetic change can be expected. Thus, from his list of possible segmental alternations it is not clear which morphophonological conditions trigger the observed alternation, or, in those cases in which the trigger is mentioned, it is not said whether the alternation is obligatory. Indeed, in many cases it is not. In sum, the phonological description of -*ize* derivatives in Kettemann (1988) is insufficient in its generalizations and predictive power.

We will now turn to the most detailed and sophisticated account of the phonology of -*ize* to date, Raffelsiefen (1996). She correctly notes that "Although the rule [of -*ize* suffixation] is generally productive, it almost never applies to monosyllabic or iambic words" (see also Goldsmith 1990:270 for a similar statement). Thus, words like *obscéne* or *secúre* cannot take -*ize* as a suffix, contrary to the predictions in Gussmann. Note that Kettemann's model does not make any predictions at all here. Using violable OT-type constraints, Raffelsiefen proposes a number of ranked phonological constraints that are held responsible for the shape of -*ize* derivatives and the gaps that arise from these constraints. In the following I will first summarize her findings and then show that her account is not sophisticated enough to explain all problematic data.

Raffelsiefen's constraints are given in (43):

(43)   IDENT: The stem of the derived word must be identical to the
               base.
        *CLASH: Two adjacent stressed syllables are prohibited.
        M-PARSE: Morphemes are parsed into morphological constituents.
        *LAPSE: Two adjacent stressless syllables are prohibited.
        IDENT(S): Each stressed syllable in the base must correspond to a
               stressed syllable in the derived word.

*O$_i$RO$_i$[25]: Adjacent syllables must not have identical onsets.
*VV: Adjacent vowels are prohibited.

The constraints are ranked as in (44):

(44)   IDENT(S) >> * O$_i$RO$_i$, *VV >> *CLASH >>
        M-PARSE >> IDENT >> *LAPSE

*LAPSE is the lowest constraint in the hierarchy because it can easily be violated by *-ize* formations (e.g. *féderalìze*). The IDENT constraints ensure that candidates that preserve the segmental and prosodic make-up of the base are preferred to those candidates that do not. M-PARSE ensures that with certain derivatives the morphologically unparsed candidate is optimal, to the effect that words of this kind cannot be derived. For instance, Prince and Smolensky (1993:49) argue that the impossibility of attaching the comparative suffix *-er* to words of more than one foot, such as *violet*, is due to the fact that the violation of the one-foot constraint is evaded by not attaching *-er* at all. In Raffelsiefen's model, M-PARSE ensures that unaffixed structures are preferred to ones involving, for example, a stress clash. *CLASH prohibits forms such as *corrúptìze*, thus naturally accounting for the fact that *-ize* almost never attaches to monosyllabic and iambic words. *VV is responsible that, for example, base-final [ɪ] is truncated in words like *mémorìze* or *súmmarìze*. The fact that *mémorìze* is a better candidate than *mémoryìze* is expressed by ranking *VV over IDENT in the hierarchy. *O$_i$RO$_i$ prohibits forms like *máximumìze or *fémininìze, which both have identical onsets in their last two syllables.[26] The strongest constraint is IDENT(S) which dictates that the stress pattern of the base word is not altered by the suffixation of *-ize*. The high rank of IDENT(S) as against the low rank of IDENT is responsible for the fact that stem allomorphy in the form of loss of base-final segments is rather frequent, but stress shift is virtually impossible. In other words, phonetic material of the base can be rather freely truncated, but the prosody of the base remains largely intact.

These constraints can account quite elegantly for a wide range of problematic or non-occurring *-ize* formations, thereby showing that many of the

---

[25]   In Raffelsiefen's notation, 'O' stands for onset and 'R' for rhyme.
[26]   The derivative *memorize* also violates *O$_i$RO$_i$, but since all likely candidates equally violate the constraint, *memorize* is the optimal candidate (in view of the other constraints).

lexical gaps are systematic in nature. Nevertheless, Raffelsiefen's analysis is not entirely convincing, for the following reasons:

- The constraints are both too weak and too strong, because they still allow structures that are systematically impossible, and they rule out structures that appear to be systematic.
- Sometimes contradictory constraint rankings are necessary to explain certain subsets of data.
- Some striking regularities are unconvincingly treated as idiosyncrasies.
- A number of additional constraints are mentioned by Raffelsiefen in footnotes, but it is unclear how they can be incorporated into the overall model.
- The constraints are not integrated into a more general model of English prosodic morphology.[27]

In the next section I will illustrate the main problems of Raffelsiefen's approach by discussing a much wider range of data than any of the previous authors (apart from E. Schneider, see above). It will become clear that some striking regularities have gone unnoticed by these authors, and that their approaches cannot account for them. Based on these regularities, I will propose a more fine-tuned model of prosodic constraints in section 6.2.4.

6.2.4.   *Towards well-formedness conditions on* -ize *derivatives*

6.2.4.1. Hiatus and stress

The first major problem we will discuss is the *VV constraint, postulated by Raffelsiefen to bar forms with adjacent vowels, such as **summaryize* or truncated forms like **emphasiize*. As we will shortly see, this constraint involves a number of empirical and conceptual problems.

Raffelsiefen herself mentions a few counterexamples (*dandyize, Toryize, ghettoize, zeroize, echoize, statuize, virtuize, Zuluize*). In view of these

---

[27]   I use the term 'prosodic morphology' in the wide sense of McCarthy and Prince (1998:283) as referring to "a theory of how morphological and phonological determinants of linguistic form interact with one another in grammatical systems".

formations, Raffelsiefen tries to save her constraint by proposing a "correlative pattern *Xize* -> *Xism*" (p.201, note 21), i.e. for each word in *-ism* there is a word in *-ize,* such as *Toryize - Toryism.* It is, however, unclear what the status of correlative pairs should be in Raffelsiefen's model. Can correlative pairs override any constraint? And why should they be allowed to? It seems that Raffelsiefen evokes correlative pairs as an escape hatch whenever the model encounters systematic constraint violations that would otherwise falsify the proposed constraints (see, for example, the discussion of *t*-epenthesis below). The existence of correlative pairs is of course interesting, but it is a fact that is in need of an explanation itself. Thus, one could venture the hypothesis that the phonological and semantic restrictions *-ize* and *-ism* impose on their bases or derivatives are very similar or identical, which then inevitably leads to the existence of correlative pairs. In other words, correlative pairs present evidence for the operation of (similar or identical) constraints and not for their violation.

These problems aside, there is more empirical evidence against *VV that can neither be explained away with the notion of correlative pairs, nor can it be accounted for by the kinds of constraints proposed by Raffelsiefen. The following 20th century neologisms can be added to the *VV violators mentioned above: *Maoize, radioize, jumboize, scenarioize, virtuize* (Raffelsiefen's *ghettoize* and *zeroize* are also in the *OED* list of neologisms). Omitting words labeled as rare or obsolete, there are in addition numerous non-20th-century forms listed in the OED which further illustrate the proliferance of adjacent vowels in *-ize* words: *altruize, centoize, cockneyize, flunkeyize, Harveyize, heroize, hinduize, libraryize, shintoize, toddyize, trollyize, vestryize.* Among the *-ize* derivatives that are only attested as participials, we find *dolbyize.* From such data one can only conclude that *VV is either not operative, or that it must be ranked lower than IDENT, in order to allow the existence of adjacent vowels. But the truncation of vowels in words like *summarize, memorize* had required the opposite constraint ranking, so that Raffelsiefen's account faces an empirical problem here. Alternatively, the counterexamples would have to be labeled as idiosyncratic, which, as we will shortly see, they are not.[28]

The counterexamples display a regularity which calls for an explanation. Thus, all of the attested *VV violators (except *libraryize,* a nonce-formation in the *OED*'s eyes, and *scenarioize,* both to be discussed below)

---

[28] Note also that, contra Raffelsiefen, most of the putative counterexamples do not have a correlating form in *-ism.*

share the striking characteristic that the base words are all disyllabic with initial stress, i.e. they have trochaic rhythm. This stands in remarkable contrast to the syllabic make-up of all the forms cited by Raffelsiefen to support *VV, which are all polysyllabic with antepenultimate primary stress, followed by two unstressed syllables (*mémory, jéopardy, epítomy, súmmary, fántasy,* etc.). In other words, it is only with the latter group of bases that the final vowel is truncated, but not with the former. Under Raffelsiefen's approach, these facts are coincidental, and the disyllabic non-truncating forms must be assigned the status of unsystematic exceptions.

It seems, though, that it is neither the constraint *VV nor the sheer number of base syllables that is responsible for the toleration of *VV violations, but rather the stress pattern. Thus, we can make the generalization that *-ize* attaches to vowels only if the base has penultimate main stress, which is trivially the case with trochaic bases. Although not attested in the *OED* data, it seems that trisyllabic vowel-final bases with penultimate stress may indeed take *-ize*, again contra the *VV predictions. This can be illustrated by the invented examples !*muláttoìze,* !*conféttiìze*,[29] which appear to be at least phonologically, if not also semantically, well-formed. But even if some speakers reject these words, they would probably still prefer them to truncated forms like *muláttìze* or *conféttìze*, which would exhibit a stress clash. Notably, under Raffelsiefen's analysis the null-parsed candidate would emerge as optimal because M-PARSE is ranked lower than both *CLASH and *VV. Hence Raffelsiefen would wrongly predict that there is a gap.

Thus, it is clear that the truncation of final vowels cannot be the effect of a putative *VV constraint alone but must be the result of some interaction with other constraints. For the moment, let us capture the facts by the following generalization:

(45)   Stress lapses are only allowed if a consonant precedes *-ize*.

For illustration of (45), consider a form such as *féderalìze*, which shows a stress lapse, and a form like **súmmaryìze*, which is ruled out by *VV in Raffelsiefen's model. The base *féderal* ends in a consonant, the stress lapse is therefore permissible. Items like **súmmaryìze* violate (45), because the last two syllables are unstressed. Derivatives with disyllabic trochaic bases

---

[29]   I use '!' to mark unattested, but possible forms. Asterisks indicate impossible words.

such as *dandyize* do not show a stress lapse and are therefore in accordance with the generalization in (45), and therefore possible words (if they are otherwise well-formed).

We may now turn to another problem that occurs with vowel-final bases. It can be observed that there is one vowel that never occurs immediately before *-ize*, namely schwa. This generalization is formulated in (46):

(46)   *-ize* may not be preceded by schwa

Violations of this constraints are avoided either by the occurrence of [t] between the putative base word and the suffix, as in *rhematize, stigmatize,* etc, or by truncation of schwa as in *patinize.* Raffelsiefen claims that "there is an undominated constraint ruling out any type of epenthesis in *-ize*-formations" (p.200, note 19) and argues against a phonological rule of t-epenthesis, "since it is unlikely that the nasal in *-ma* conditions *t*-epenthesis". Again she attributes the data to the existence of correlative pairs (*Xmatize -> Xma*), a notion whose questionable value we have already discussed above.

In my view, two other observations are important. First, intermediate [t] does not only occur with base words ending in *-ma*, as claimed by Raffel-siefen. Thus, the *OED* also lists *Asiatize.* Second, *t*-epenthesis is restricted to words of Greek origin, which have stem allomorphs ending in [t]. This kind of stem allomorph does not only occur with *-ize*, but also with other suffixes, such as *-ic* (cf. *asiatic, asthmatic, aromatic,* etc. with concurrent stress shift) or *-ous* (as in *eczematous, hematomatous*). In all such cases we are dealing with Greek bases that have a bound stem allomorph which is exclusively used in word-formation.[30]

The preliminary generalization in (46) will be further discussed below. With regard to the insertion of consonantal material, Kettemann proposes a rule of *n*-epenthesis for items such as *platonize* or *solemnize.* Although there are at least two more forms with this kind of alternation (the *OED* lists *Neronize, Plutonize* in addition to the two mentioned by Kettemann), both the scarcity and the age of the derivatives (first attestation in the 14th to 17th century) indicate a lexicalized alternation.[31] Kettemann's rule of

---

[30]   It can be assumed that occasionally non-Greek base words like *opera* can be-have like Greek words on the basis of analogy, if their phonological structure is similar. *Opera - operatize* is a case in point (the only one listed in the *OED*).

[31]   Note that the much younger form *autumnize* (first attested in 1829) does not show [n] insertion.

[ɪn] insertion in derivatives like *attitudinize* is also lexically governed and does not occur in the neologism corpus.

6.2.4.2. Haplology and stress

We now move on to the discussion of $*O_iRO_i$, which is argued by Raffel-siefen to account not only for the truncation of base forms suffixed by *-ize* (e.g. *feminize*), but also to be operative with other suffixes like *-ity* or *-ify*. If this were feasible, this constraint could be an important step towards the long-sought solution to the notorious problem of morphological haplology.[32] However, the constraint as it stands seems to be too powerful because it rules out a whole range of attested complex and simplex forms. Raffelsiefen herself concedes that this constraint "is often violated in English words" (1996: 199), but explains this away by restricting the constraint to *potential* words. *Actual* words may violate this constraint without any consequences. But even if $*O_iRO_i$ is restricted to possible words, too many counterexamples come to mind. Raffelsiefen only mentions the lexicalized words *entity, identity, quantity, sanctity*, but the following counterexamples of the putatively illegal $*nRn$, $*rRr$, $*sRs$, and $*tRt$ combinations with *-ize* can be added, namely *strychninize, mirrorize, terrorize,*[33] *classicize, potentize, dilletantize.*

Thus it seems that other constraints must be ranked higher than $*O_iRO_i$. However, ignoring the effect of M-PARSE, the constraint ranking given by Raffelsiefen (see (44) above) would predict that truncated forms like **classize* or **strychnize* would be optimal, since they would only violate lower-ranked constraints (in this case *CLASH and IDENT). But if M-PARSE is taken into account, violators of $*O_iRO_i$ will never surface at all, because M-PARSE is ranked lower. A similar argument applies to the other forms mentioned. In any case, we are again faced with wrong predictions concerning the absence or presence of certain forms.

It is obvious that the truncation of the base in some of the derivatives mentioned would lead to a derived form whose base is no longer recogniz-

---

32   See e.g. Stemberger (1981), Menn and McWhinney (1984) for discussion. More recent approaches to haplology are Yip (1996), and Plag (1998), both within the framework of OT.

33   Raffelsiefen considers *terrorize* a French borrowing. According to the *OED* this is incorrect. Semantically, this word is also completely regular (cf. section 6.1 above).

able, which may be an important general factor constraining the deletion of base-final segments in complex words. Raffelsiefen mentions this problem in a footnote and proposes an additional constraint to restrict possible truncations. She claims that minimally the first two syllables in the base must correspond to identical syllables in the derived form (p. 202). This putative constraint, like some others Raffelsiefen mentions in passing, is not incorporated into her tableaux, nor into the constraint ranking she advocates, which makes its status somewhat unclear. In any case, the constraint is designed to ensure the presence of enough phonological material so that the base can still be related to its non-affixed forms. Thus a form like *crisize* (instead of the $*O_iRO_i$ violator *crisisize*) would be ruled out because it is no longer recognizable as derived from *crisis*. However, Raffelsiefen's putative constraint on truncation is inadequate since it rules out all licit formations with consonant-final disyllabic bases like *randomize*. With such derivatives, the last segment of the stem is syllabified as the onset of the new final syllable (*ran.do.mize*). This means that in such cases there are no two identical syllables in the base and the derivative (cf. *ran.dom*). Thus *cri.si.size* would violate Raffelsiefen's base-recognition constraint just as *cri.size* would. Going strictly by the constraint ranking in (44), truncated forms like *potenize*, *potize*, or *classize* would be better candidates than the attested ones. It seems that a more adequate solution is needed to account for the truncation restrictions.

In sum, the empirical evidence for the operation of $*O_iRO_i$ with -*ize* is equivocal[34], and the analysis of some counterexamples makes contradictory constraint rankings necessary. Thus with her examples, $*O_iRO_i$ is ranked higher than IDENT, but with the counterexamples IDENT must be ranked higher than $*O_iRO_i$.

A reconsideration of the contradictory data reveals, however, a striking regularity, namely that all base words where one of the identical onsets is deleted are polysyllabic (*emphasis, metathesis, feminine, maximum*, etc.), whereas all base words with surviving identical onsets (except one, *dilletante*, to be discussed shortly) are disyllabic. At first sight the constraint appears to be sensitive to the number of syllables. However, the stress pattern is also different between the violators of $*O_iRO_i$ on the one hand, and

---

[34] Some of the examples Raffelsiefen mentions in favor of her identical onset constraint could be ruled out on independent grounds, like for example *Hittitize* (stress clash), and *horrorize* (blocked by *horrify*). The existence of *Leninize* is a problem for Raffelsiefen's model, so is the form *Leninite*, which equally violates $*O_iRO_i$.

the conformers on the other. Thus, all the conformers have base words with antepenultimate stress followed by two unstressed syllables i.e. they are dactyls, while none of the violators has a base word that exhibits a stress lapse. That this stress-based description is superior to the simple counting of syllables is corroborated by the behavior of *dilletántìze*, whose base word has a main stress on the final syllable (which all the other polysyllabic forms cited lack). In sum, the operation of *O$_i$RO$_i$ needs to be restricted to those cases in which two unstressed syllables precede *-ize*. This is similar to the situation concerning Raffelsiefen's *VV constraint discussed above, where stress lapses are in general only tolerable if the final segment of the base is a consonant. Therefore, the haplology facts should be related to the stress lapse generalization formulated in (45), as it is proposed in (47):

(47)   Stress lapses are only allowed if a consonant precedes *-ize*, and if the coda and the onset of the base-final syllable are not identical.

By way of illustration, a form like **femininìze* exhibits a stress lapse, which would only be tolerable if the onset and the coda of the were not identical (as in forms such as *féderalìze, sénsitivìze*). Since they are identical, **femininìze* is an illicit formation. Derivatives like *térrorìze* do not exhibit a stress lapse, hence they behave according to the generalization. With vowel-final dactyls, stress lapses are avoided by vowel truncation (*mémory - mémorìze*)

   In section 6.2.5. I will propose a more sophisticated constraint model to account for the variable toleration of identical onsets in *-ize* formations.

6.2.4.3. Truncation and stress

The next problematic point concerning the phonology of *-ize* is truncation. It is clear that possible bases of *-ize* may lose final segments, but we have seen that it is still unclear how this can be restricted. Raffelsiefen proposes two auxiliary constraints to account for truncation restrictions. The first one, already mentioned above, dictates that two syllables of the base must remain intact, the second one "requires all onsets in the base to correspond to identical onsets in the derived form" (Raffelsiefen 1996:200, note 19). Unfortunately, these constraints are not discussed in detail in her article, and it is left unclear how they should be incorporated into the constraint ranking given in (44). However, our above remarks have already shown that the first constraint is inadequate. The second one is more promising, however.

It can be observed that only entire word-final rhymes and not just word-final consonants may be truncated. In Raffelsiefen's model the deletion of a single consonantal coda is made impossible by other constraints, like *VV, which is evoked to rule out forms like *emphasiize*. However, it is still left unclear as to why the final segment in complex codas is never deleted (cf. the discussion of words like *potentize/*potenize* above). In a preliminary fashion these facts can be generalized as in (48):

(48)   Only the base-final rhyme may be deleted.

We may now turn to the stress clash constraint. Both Goldsmith (1990:270ff) and Raffelsiefen (1996) point out that stress clashes are generally avoided in possible words.[35] So far, we have frequently referred to this constraint, but, in view of the numerous counterexamples, its exact formulation and status remain problematic.

I assume that we have to distinguish three degrees of stress in English. Syllables may have primary stress, non-primary (i.e. secondary) stress,[36] or no stress (cf., e.g., Giegerich 1985). This trichotomy is corroborated by both phonological and phonetic facts (see Giegerich 1992). The stress behavior of *-ize* derivatives can now be largely predicted from the segmental structure of the suffix. Since the syllabic structure of *-ize* involves a branching rhyme with a diphthong, the suffix will attract secondary stress.[37] Given that stress clashes tend to be avoided in complex words, we can predict that *-ize* usually does not occur after stressed syllables. Coun-

---

[35]   For Goldsmith (1990:271), the prohibition of stress clashes is dependent on an intervening word boundary. Raffelsiefen argues against this dependency on the grounds that it also holds for cases where stem allomorphy is involved, i.e. where there is only a morpheme-boundary. Furthermore, she claims that stress clashes are historically often unstable, as shown by the replacement of quantity-sensitive stress by alternating stress in words like *mobile, abdomen, advertise* and the like. We will return to this issue below.

[36]   I do not use 'secondary' in the sense of *SPE* stress 2, but simply as a label for syllables that have non-primary stress. For a detailed criticism of the *SPE* stress numerology see e.g. Hogg and McCully (1987).

[37]   We ignore here the possibility that *-ize* may receive primary stress. See below for discussion.

terexamples like *banálìze* and *routínìze*,[38] are, however, occasionally coined, which shows that speakers may violate this constraint if no other possibility is available to avoid the clash (for example through truncation). Although the stress clash constraint seems to be important and necessary, Raffelsiefen cannot account for some derivatives like *rádiòize* which are impossible formations in her model, because they violate both *VV and *CLASH, whereas the corresponding truncated form *rádìize* would only violate *VV and the lower ranked IDENT constraint. Again, the constraints as proposed by Raffelsiefen do not make the correct predictions.

Another stress-related problem is that with some isolated forms involving secondary ultimate stress, *-ize* attachment may lead to the destressing of secondarily stressed syllables. Consider the following pairs:

(49) a. *ánòde - ánodìze*   [əʊ] → [ə]
      b. *láterìte - láteritìze*   [aɪ] → [ɪ/ə]
      c. *pódzòl - pódzolìze*   [ɒ]   → [ə]
      d. *sílàne - sílanìze*   [eɪ] → [ə]
      e. *strýchnìne - stríchninìze* [i/ɪ] → [ɪ][39]

Similar alternations are discussed by Kettemann who proposes individual rules of vowel reduction ([ɑ] ↔ [ə], [aɪ] ↔ [ə], [æ]↔ [ə]), but explains them as instances of the Auxiliary Vowel Reduction Rule (Halle and Keyser 1971:35) in connection with *SPE*'s Vowel Reduction Rule (1968:126). In essence, these alternations seem not to be specific to *-ize* derivatives but follow from general principles of stress assignment and foot construction in English (see also Giegerich 1992, Goldsmith 1990:259). In other words, the forms in (49) are more fully integrated into the general metrical system

---

[38] The stress patterns indicated follow the information given in the *OED*. Note, however, that, at least in American English, *routinize* is pronounced usually with primary stress on the first syllable, followed by an unstressed syllable. In other words, there is a stress shift. Note also that there are at least two dialect clusters which exhibit primary stress on *-ize*, Hiberno-English and Caribbean English. Dialectal variation in stress patterns of derived words in general is certainly in need of further investigation, but will not be dealt with systematically here.

[39] I adopt here the pronunciations given by the *OED*. Some speakers prefer the pronunciation [stɹɪknaɪn] for the base word, but this does not have any effect on the pronunciation of the derived verb, because even these speakers pronounce the verb [stɹɪknɪnaɪz]. For these speakers *strychninize* patterns like *lateritize* in (49b).

of English than forms that feature two adjacent stressed syllables. However, not all base-final secondarily stressed syllables are affected by destressing, but only those that end in a consonant. For example, *ghettoize* and *radioize* (and all other pertinent forms) preserve their secondary stress. In other words, we are faced with another incidence where the segmental structure interacts with the metrical structure in an interesting way. In section 6.2.5. we will see how this interaction can be explained.

Note that the syllable which carries primary stress is never reduced or destressed. This is what one would expect if stress shift were possible, but, apart from some rare exceptions, the main stress of the base word is never shifted by productive -*ize* attachment. There are only five forms in the corpus of 284 20th century neologisms in which the main stress of the base seems to be altered, namely *bácterìze, lyóphilìze, lysógenìze, multímerìze,* and *phagocýtìze*. These forms will be discussed in some detail towards the end of section 6.2.5.

6.2.4.4. Summary: Hiatus, truncation and stress

Let us summarize the most important points of the foregoing discussion. We have seen that Raffelsiefen proposes interesting explanations for the intricacies of the phonological restrictions on -*ize* derivatives. From the broad range of data in appendix 1 a number of significant generalizations emerged that present serious empirical and theoretical problems for Raffelsiefen's model. Any attempt to formalize and explain the observed generalizations must account for the peculiar interaction of metrical and segmental structures, in particular the dependance of truncation, stem allomorph selection, and stress assignment on both the segmental and metrical make-up of the base or the derivative. None of the existing treatments of -*ize* provides such an analysis.

6.2.5.   Phonological constraints on -ize *derivatives: A new account*

In this section I will propose an alternative model of the phonology of -*ize* derivatives in which the observed generalizations can be explained in a straightforward manner. The model will be formulated in the framework of OT, and an attempt will be made to integrate the phonological behavior of -*ize* derivatives into a more general model of English prosodic phonology and morphology.

I will adopt Pater's (1995) general OT-model of primary and secondary stress assignment in English nouns as a frame of reference for the description of the prosodic behavior of derived verbs (see also Benua 1997 for an approach similar to Pater's). Pater's model is especially attractive because it can account for a number of hitherto unresolved problems in English prosody, such as the nonuniformity of weight-to-stress and stress preservation effects (e.g. Liberman and Prince 1977, Hayes 1982, Halle 1973, Kager 1989). My central claim is that *-ize* verbs in principle follow the prosodic pattern of nouns as proposed by Pater (1995), with some affix-specific constraints that enrich the general constraint hierarchy and trigger the observed prosodic effects.

6.2.5.1. Stress assignment in English nouns: Pater's (1995) OT model

In this sub-section I will briefly outline the general constraint hierarchy responsible for the stress patterns in English nouns, omitting a number of constraints not directly relevant for the present purposes. The specific phonological properties of *-ize* verbs result from the operation of constraints that occupy a lexically specified position in the general hierarchy. This is in line with the idea frequently expressed in the literature (e.g. Alber 1998, Benua 1995, 1997, Urbanczyk 1995, 1996) that members of derivational categories are subject to the general prosodic constraints of a language, but that these categories involve further faithfulness relations which enrich the general constraint hierarchy of the language. As we will see, such constraints do not only influence stress assignment, but also segmental stem alternations as those that can be observed with *-ize* derivatives.

The following of Pater's constraints are most important for the analysis of *-ize* verbs. They are also the ones that are highest in Pater's hierarchy. The constraints and their definitions are given in (50a), their hierarchical ordering is given in (50b):

(50)   a.   FOOT BINARITY (=FT-BIN):
             "Feet are binary at some level of analysis (mora, syllable)"
             TROCHEE (=TROCH):
             "Feet are trochaic"
             NONFINALITY (=NONFIN):
             "The head foot of the prosodic word must not be final"

ALIGN (PrWd, R, Head(PrWd), R) (=R-ALIGN-HEAD):
"Align the right edge of the prosodic word with the right edge
of the head of the prosodic word"

b. FT-BIN, TROCH, NONFINALITY
|
R-ALIGN-HEAD

Basically, it is these four constraints that are responsible for the well-
known generalization that English nouns are stressed on the penultima if it
is heavy, and on the antepenultimate syllable if the penultima is light. (e.g
Giegerich 1992:187, Burzio 1994:43). Let us see how this works. The
constraints NONFINALITY and R-ALIGN-HEAD are in direct competition
with each other. If NONFINALITY is ranked above R-ALIGN-HEAD, this
forces main stress, and the main stressed foot, off the final syllable. R-
ALIGN-HEAD nevertheless forces the main stress to be as close as possible
to the right edge of the word, with each syllable intervening between the
head syllable and the edge counting as one violation. Thus the minimal
violation of R-ALIGN-HEAD which satisfies NONFINALITY is main stress on
the penult. Consider the stress assignment in *agenda* and *Canada* (from
Pater 1995:17-18):

(51) penultimate stress in nouns (heavy penult)

agenda	FT-BIN	TROCH	NONFIN	R-ALIGN-HEAD
☞ a(gén)da				σ
(ágen)da				$\sigma\sigma$!
(agén)da		*!		σ
(àgen)(dá)	*!		*!	

The optimal candidate involves only one R-ALIGN-HEAD violation,
whereas the competing candidates either violate higher ranked NON-
FINALITY or show an additional R-ALIGN-HEAD violation. Note that, obviously, PARSE-σ must be ranked lower than R-ALIGN-HEAD, because the
optimal candidate has two unparsed syllables. TROCH rules out the iambic
candidate *(agén)da*, whereas Ft-BIN has no effect with these candidates.
Turning now to words with non-heavy penult, we see that stress must be

placed on the penultima in order to satisfy either of the top-ranked constraints:

(52) antepenultimate stress in nouns (light penult)

Canada	FT-BIN	TROCH	NONFIN	R-ALIGN-HEAD
☞ (Cána)da				$\sigma\sigma$
Ca(náda)			*!	σ
Ca(ná)da	*!			σ
(Caná)da		*!		σ

Candidates that have a light penultima cannot have penultimate stress because in that case they would either have a final prosodic head, as in *Ca(náda)*, or non-binary foot, as in *Ca(ná)da*, or an iambic foot, as in *(Caná)da*. With either of these candidates, one of the top-ranked constraints is violated.

Let us now turn to -*ize* derivatives, which show the same kind of basic stress pattern as nouns, in that they never have ultimate primary stress.[40] They thus markedly differ from other verbs, which usually carry their stress on the last syllable, especially if it is superheavy (e.g. Burzio 1994: chapter 3). Consider the following data:

(53)   prevént   rándomìze
       decíde   áuthorìze
       constráin   colónialìze
       condúct   mémorìze
       permít   ghéttòize

The behavior of canonical verbs must be due to a different ranking of the constraints in (50a) above. Thus, it could be argued that with underived verbs NONFINALITY ranks below R-ALIGN-HEAD. The details of such an account still need to be worked out, but need not concern us here any further. The basic points are that nouns behave differently from verbs, that

---

[40]   As mentioned already in note 13, Hiberno-English and many varieties of Caribbean English place ultimate primary stress on -*ize* derivatives. The analysis to be proposed here does not extend to these varieties.

derived verbs behave differently from underived verbs and that -*ize* verbs behave in general like nouns, but with some requirements that are specific to this class of words.

Note that it is not only derived verbs that do not behave like their underived counterparts, but that also certain derived nouns and adjectives show an aberrant behavior. Thus, nominal derivatives in -*ee* and -*eer*, or adjectives in -*esque* pattern with canonical verbs in that they have ultimate primary stress. The reasons for this anti-canonical prosodic behavior of certain classes of derived words certainly merit further investigation, but in general we can say that suffixes may bring in their own requirements which may disturb the general pattern.

Let us now turn to one of the most striking properties of -*ize* verbs, the preservation of main stress.

6.2.5.2. Preservation of main stress

As frequently mentioned above, -*ize* derivatives never exhibit a stress shift. This suggests the operation of a high-ranking constraint against stress shift (IDENT-HEAD). Given that stress is not an underlying property in English, the constraint ensuring stress identity must necessarily be an output-output constraint, and can be defined as in (54):

(54)   IDENT-HEAD:
       "The prosodic head of the base must be identical to the prosodic head of the derived word"

The following tableau shows that IDENT-HEAD must be ranked higher than R-ALIGN-HEAD.

(55)   FT-BIN, TROCH, NONFINALITY, IDENT-HEAD >> R-ALIGN HEAD

random-ize	FT-BIN	TROCH	NONFIN	IDENT-HEAD	R-ALIGN-HEAD
a. ☞ (rándo)(mìze)					$\sigma\sigma$
b. (ràndo)(míze)			*!		
c. ran(dó)(mìze)				*!	σ
d. (randó)(mìze)	*!			*!	σ

The optimal candidate satisfies the highest general constraints FT-BIN, TROCH, NONFINALITY and the constraint demanding preservation of main stress. The elimination of candidate (55c) shows that two violations of R-ALIGN-HEAD are less costly than a violation of IDENT-HEAD, which is a clear indication for the higher rank of IDENT-HEAD over R-ALIGN-HEAD. Disregarding haplology effects for the moment, the proposed ranking makes the right predictions also for consonant-final dactylic bases such as *hóspital*:

(56)   IDENT-HEAD >> R-ALIGN-HEAD

hospital-ize	IDENT-HEAD	R-ALIGN-HEAD
a. ☞ (hóspi)ta(lìze)		σσσ
b. ho(spíta)(lìze)	*!	σσ

Unlike underived nouns, words like *hóspitalìze* have primary stress on the pre-antepenult. In other words, R-ALIGN-HEAD is violated three times. This could in principle be remedied by shifting the main stress further to the right, but the high ranking of IDENT-HEAD does not permit this, as candidate (56b) shows.

6.2.5.3. Vowel deletion: dactylic bases

Although the ranking in (55) and (56) rules out all kinds of candidates which do not preserve the prosodic head of the base, possible candidates involving the truncation of segments under preservation of main stress would emerge as optimal because of their better satisfaction of R-ALIGN-HEAD. The puzzling fact now is that consonant-final dactyls are always left intact (on the cost of R-ALIGN-RIGHT), whereas vowel-final dactyls always lose their final vowel (on the cost of some MAX constraint). The pair *hóspital - hóspitalìze* as against *mémory - mémorìze* are canonical examples of this generalization. In terms of OT, this means that a constraint against the deletion of consonants (MAX-C) must be ranked above R-ALIGN-HEAD and that a constraint against the deletion of vowels (MAX-V) must be ranked below R-ALIGN-HEAD:

(57)   MAX-C:
       "Every consonant in the input has a correspondent in the output"
       MAX-V:
       "Every vocalic element in the input has a correspondent in the output"

This splitting up of MAX into one vocalic and one consonantal constraint has been proposed before by Kager (1997) to account of rhythmic vowel deletion in Macushi Carib and South-eastern Tepehuan. What English -ize derivatives and these two languages have in common is that the deletion of vowels is conditioned by constraints on rhythmic structure (such as R-ALIGN-HEAD).

Let us compare the selection of optimal candidates with consonant-final and vowel-final dactylic bases, using *hóspitalìze* and *mémorìze* as canonical examples:

(58)   MAX-C >> R-ALIGN-HEAD >> MAX-V

a. C-final dactylic base

hospital-ize	MAX-C	R-ALIGN-HEAD	MAX-V
☞ (hóspi)ta(lìze)		σσσ	
(hóspi)(tìze)	*!	σσ	*

b. V-final dactylic base

memory-ize	MAX-C	R-ALIGN-HEAD	MAX-V
(mémo)ry(ìze)		σσσ!	
☞ (mémo)(rìze)		σσ	*

So far this accounts only for the non-uniformity of truncation with V-final and C-final dactylic bases. Disyllabic vowel-final bases will be dealt with below.

There are a number of derivatives in the corpus that go against the predictions made by our model as it stands. As we will shortly see, the only unsystematic counterexample is *libráryìze*. With regard to this form, the constraint model would predict the truncation of the base-final vowel instead of stress shift, contrary to the fact as given in the *OED*.[41] Since *líbráryìze* is the only counterexample of this kind, it should be treated as exceptional.

Apart from *líbráryìze*, putative counterexamples involve Greek bases ending in schwa. It was already argued above that the epenthesis of [t] is conditioned by the selection of the pertinent bound stem allomorph. The alternative to stem allomorph selection would be the assumption that the insertion of [t] is forced by prosodic constraints. This assumption faces two major problems. First, it is empirically inadequate, since, according to the proposed ranking of the constraints, truncated forms like **cinemize* should be more optimal than the attested *cinematize* because vowel truncation is more easily tolerated than stress lapses (i.e. three violations of R-ALIGN-HEAD). Of course one could argue that possibly additional constraints are needed and/or different constraint rankings. However, this is unlikely in view of the firm generalizations that fall out from the constraint ranking as proposed above, and, more importantly, in view of the fact that intermediate [t] almost exclusively occurs in a very special, well-defined set of words, those of Greek origin. Thus it seems that we are dealing here with borrowed morphology.

This becomes more evident if we consider the second major problem, which is that [t] as an epenthetic consonant cannot be independently justified. The default epenthetic consonant in English (as in many other languages) is the glottal stop, and not [t]. This can be observed, for instance, in colloquial speech, when speakers do not use the expected allomorph of the article before a following vowel ([ði] or [ən]), but instead separate schwa and the following vowel by a glottal stop. Hence the selection of [t] is phonologically highly unnatural. As already mentioned, putative epenthetic [t] surfaces only in words of Greek origin or occasionally also in words that are coined in analogy to the Greek examples. In essence, we are faced with two different stem allomorphs (both borrowed from Greek), one occurring in free forms and compounds, the other in suffixed forms. The important difference between the stem allomorphy of the Greek bases and the stem allomorphies of the other bases discussed in this study is that the latter are truly phonologically conditioned, whereas the Greek allomorphs are lexically conditioned, i.e. derivatives in *-ize* on schwa-final Greek bases

---

41   Note, however, that the penultimate stress of *líbráryìze* relates the verb to *li-bbrárian*. Thus it could even be argued that there is no stress-shift. The semantics and the fact that the verb is not *!librarianize*, however, do not suggest that *librarian* is the base word.

must obligatorily be based on the bound stem allomorph, the one ending in [t]. Perhaps one reason why this kind of exceptional behavior survives in English is that the derivatives coined in that way fit into the overall prosodic structure of *-ize* derivatives: those with penultimate stress (e.g. *rhématìze, arómatìze*) are totally unproblematic and those involving a stress lapse have a base-final consonant (cf. *cínematìze*). In both cases the generalizations in (46) and (47) are unviolated. It has to be noted, however, that in the case of schwa-final Greek bases morphology (i.e. lexically conditioned allomorphy) overrules the phonological constraints (cf. **cinemize* vs. *cinematìze*).

This account leaves us, however, with the problem of schwa-final bases that are not of Greek etymology. Unfortunately, there is only one form of this type among the neologisms, *pátinìze*. Another pertinent derivative mentioned in the *OED* is *íotìze* (rare, based on *iota*), which is however not a 20th century innovation (first attested in 1880). It seems that no additional machinery is necessary to select *pátinìze* as optimal, since it is evaluated in the same fashion as derivatives like *mémorìze* in (58) above. the final schwa is truncated in order to satisfy more highly ranked constraints:

(59)   R-ALIGN-HEAD >> MAX-V

patina-ize	R-ALIGN-HEAD	MAX-V
☞ (páti)(nìze)	$\sigma\sigma$	*
(páti)na(ìze)	$\sigma\sigma\sigma$!	

6.2.5.4. No vowel deletion: trochaic vowel-final bases

Unlike vowel-final dactyls, vowel-final trochees never lose their final vowel under *-ize* attachment (cf. *dándyìze*). According to the constraints introduced so far, this contrast is unexpected since the deletion of the final vowel (as in **dándìze*) would equally lead to a better satisfaction of the higher ranked R-ALIGN-HEAD. In view of these facts there must be yet another constraint that supersedes R-ALIGN-HEAD, thereby mitigating against truncation. I propose that truncated candidates like **dándìze* are ruled out because they violate a constraint against the adjacency of a stressed syllable and the prosodic head of the word, **CLASH-HEAD.

(60) *CLASH-HEAD
"No stressed syllable may be adjacent to the head of the prosodic word"

This constraint is identical with Pater's STRESS-WELL (see also Halle and Vergnaud 1987:238), but I have chosen what I consider a more mnemonic label for it. In essence, *CLASH-HEAD is a stronger version of the well-known prohibition of adjacent stresses (see Prince 1983, Hammond 1984, or Raffelsiefen's *CLASH constraint). *CLASH-HEAD must be ranked above R-ALIGN-HEAD, to the effect that the better satisfaction of R-ALIGN-HEAD does not save the candidate violating *CLASH-HEAD:

(61)   *CLASH-HEAD >> R-ALIGN-HEAD >> MAX-V

dandy-ize[42]	*CLASH-HEAD	R-ALIGN-HEAD	MAX-V
☞ dándyìze		$\sigma\sigma$	
dándìze	*!	σ	*

There is reason to believe, however, that an additional constraint is at work which only becomes visible with disyllabic schwa-final bases (and with bases ending in a stressed vowel, as we will see below). This constraint has the effect that it prohibits the adjacency of schwa and a following vowel. Although no examples of schwa-final disyllables can be found among the neologisms, evidence for the operation of such constraints can be gleaned from older attested forms and from nonce words. The *OED* lists the following formations on the basis of schwa-final bases (none of them 20th century innovations): *hebraize, judaize, Mithraize, Utopia-ize*. The interesting thing now is that the first three forms are given with a pronunciation in which the schwa-syllable of the base is pronounced [eɪ] in the derived word. The *OED* does not give a pronunciation of *Utopia-ize*, but its spelling with a hyphen strongly suggests a phonological oddity, namely the

---

[42]   *Dandyize* is chosen as the canonical example of a vowel-final trochaic base although it is not a 20th century neologism. The reason is that, in spite of their being fully systematic coinages, the corpus did not contain the relevant forms. As pointed out above, the corpus of attested participials features the parallel form *dolbyize*, and similar nonce forms are equally possible.

insertion of a glottal stop. If forced to pronounce nonce words such as *!moraize*, native speakers insert a glottal stop between base and suffix. Thus, it seems that concerning new formations, consonant epenthesis (i.e. insertion of a glottal stop) is optimal with schwa-final trochees of non-Greek origin. In contrast to that, schwa deletion is optimal with dactylic bases.

The constraint prohibiting the adjacency of schwa and *-ize* is a special kind of hiatus restriction, which is most likely the effect of a number of different constraints on featural and syllabic constraints (see, for example, Casali's 1997 OT account of hiatus resolution in a number of different languages). Since the details of the English schwa-vowel hiatus restriction are beyond the scope of this chapter I will use *SCHWA-V as an abbreviation of what is probably the combined effect of a number of interacting constraints:

(62)   *SCHWA-V:
       "Schwa may not immediately precede another vowel within a pro-
       sodic word"

*SCHWA-V as a constraint has not been proposed before in the OT litera-ture, but can be independently justified by the allmorphy of articles in English. As is well-known, both definite and indefinite articles have two allomorphs, whose use is governed by the following segment. A vowel triggers [ði] or [ən], respectively, whereas a following consonant demands the allomorphs [ðə] and [ə], respectively. What unites the different allo-morphies of definite and indefinite articles is the fact that schwa may never precede a vowel. I argue that this generalization can be captured by the proposed constraint *SCHWA-V, which is not only operative with articles but also with (certain) suffixes. Note that the constraint becomes active only below the level of the prosodic word and the clitic group (Nespor and Vogel 1986), as is shown by the unproblematic occurrence of schwa-vowel between phonological words, as in *Indian[ə ɪ]s wonderful.*[43] Suffixes like *-ize* only expand prosodic words, but are not prosodic words themselves.

---

[43]   If such sequences occur across phonological words, so-called 'intrusive *r*' can
       be inserted in non-formal speech (e.g. *idea*[r]*of*). Note, however, that the class
       of possible vowels allowing intrusive *r* is not restricted to schwa but includes
       all non-high vowels (e.g. Giegerich 1992:283).

With regard to the ranking of *SCHWA-V, the surface form of the potential word !*móraìze* shows that *SCHWA-V must be ranked above R-ALIGN-HEAD:

(63)   *SCHWA-V, *CLASH-HEAD >> R-ALIGN-HEAD

mora-ize	*SCHWA-V	*CLASH-HEAD	R-ALIGN-HEAD
☞ (móra)([ʔ]ìze)			σσ
(mór[ə])(ìze)	*!		σσ
(mór)(ìze)		*!	σ

*SCHWA-V cannot be replaced by a more general constraint that prohibits hiatus (such as Raffelsiefen's *VV), because, as we have seen, vowel-final trochees that end in a different vowel behave differently. The optimal candidate in (63) obviously violates the constraint against epenthesis, DEP, which must be ranked below *SCHWA-V and *CLASH-HEAD. DEP does not interact with R-ALIGN-HEAD:

(64)   *SCHWA-V, *CLASH-HEAD >> R-ALIGN-HEAD, DEP

mora-ize	*SCHWA-V	*CLASH-HEAD	R-ALIGN-HEAD	DEP
☞ (móra)([ʔ]ìze)			σσ	*
(mór[ə])(ìze)	*!		σσ	
(mór)(ìze)		*!	σ	

That glottal stop insertion is triggered by *SCHWA-V and *CLASH-HEAD, and not by a high-ranking ONSET is evidenced by verbs such as *dándyìze*, which do not necessitate glide insertion.[44]

The proposed constraint rankings solve the problem of the non-unifomity of vowel-deletion with V-final trochaic bases and V-final dactylic bases. In

---

[44]   There is a pronunciation possible which involves glide insertion, as in *dandy*[j]*ize*. In this case ONSET would rank above DEP but still below *CLASH. For full discussion of DEP and ONSET see chapter 7.

essence, disyllabic bases are never truncated because this would lead to a clash of secondary and primary stress in the derivative.

6.2.5.5. Non-uniform preservation of secondary stress

There is yet another class of V-final, non-dactylic derivatives that need to be discussed, namely those with bases ending in a secondarily stressed vowel such as *ghéttòize* or *rádiòize*. The base-final vowels in such derivatives survive intact, i.e. they are neither deleted nor destressed. However, consonant-final bases which end in a secondarily stressed syllable (e.g. *ánòde*) exhibit destressing of their final syllable under *-ize* attachment (cf. *án[ə]dìze*). How can this non-uniformity effect be accounted for?

With disyllabic bases such as *ghéttòize*, *CLASH-HEAD already rules out truncation of the final vowel (cf. *ghéttìze*), but this does not explain why base words such as *rádiò* are not truncated. In their case, truncation would not lead to a *CLASH-HEAD violation, but to a better satisfaction of R-ALIGN-HEAD. These facts suggest that a constraint against the deletion of stressed vowels must be ranked higher than R-ALIGN-HEAD. Assuming that faithfulness constraints may be specified for privileged prosodic positions such as onsets, root-initial positions or stressed syllables (Beckman 1998), I propose the constraint in (65), which prohibits the deletion of stressed vowels:

(65)   MAX-$\acute{\sigma}$-V
       "Every stressed vowel in the base form must have some correspondent in the derived form"

This constraint must be ranked above R-ALIGN-HEAD, as shown in the following tableau.

(65)   MAX-$\acute{\sigma}$-V >> R-ALIGN-HEAD

radio-ize	MAX-$\acute{\sigma}$-V	R-ALIGN-HEAD
☞ (rádi)(ò)(ìze)		σσσ
(rádi)(ìze)	*!	σσ

The truncated candidate *(rádi)(ìze)* better satisfies R-ALIGN-HEAD but violates the higher ranked MAX-ó-V.

With disyllabic bases such as *géttòize* the question arises why the final vowel is not destressed as it can be observed with consonant-final base words that have a secondarily stressed ultima (cf. *ánòde* - *án[ə]dìze*). Informally speaking, the affixation of *-ize* to such base words gives the opportunity to avoid the stress clash present in the underived output form *(ánòde)*. In other words, a *CLASH-HEAD violation is avoided on the cost of some other constraint which demands that stressed syllables in the base form be stressed in the derived form (this is again an output-output constraint):

(66)   STRESS-IDENT
        "stressed elements in the base form must be stressed in the derived
        form"[45]

This yields the tableau in (67):

(67)   *CLASH-HEAD >> STRESS-IDENT

anode-ize	*CLASH-HEAD	STRESS-IDENT
☞ án[ə]dìze		*
án[əù]dìze	*!	

Note that MAX-ó-V is not violated by the optimal candidate because there is still some correspondent in the output.

Returning to base forms such as *radio, ghetto* or *virtue*, destressing would involve a *SCHWA-V violation, which is obviously not desired, as the final vowel regularly remains stressed in the derivatives. Thus, a stress clash is preferred to schwa-vowel adjacency. These facts suggest the ranking as exemplified in (68):

---

[45]   See Pater (1995) for a slightly different formulation of this constraint.

(68)   *SCHWA-V >> *CLASH-HEAD

a. *virtuize*

virtue-ize	*SCHWA-V	*CLASH-HEAD
☞ vírtùìze		*
vírt[(j)ə]ìze	*!	

b. *ghettoize*

ghetto-ize	*SCHWA-V	*CLASH-HEAD
☞ ghéttòìze		*
ghétt[ə]ìze	*!	

The tableaux in (67) and (68) capture the generalization that secondarily stressed vowels are reduced, if this does not lead to a *SCHWA-V violation

However, a violation of *SCHWA-V could also be avoided by the insertion of a glottal stop, as in *ghétt[əʔ]ìze*. As we saw above, DEP is ranked lower on the hierarchy, which is corroborated by the fact that glide insertion is otherwise tolerated (cf. *rádiò[w]ìze, vírtù[w]ìze*). One possibility is to rank DEP above *CLASH-HEAD, but given the considerations in the previous sub-section (see (64)), this is not a viable solution. The crucial observation concerning the pertinent data is that STRESS-IDENT may be violated only if it is not accompanied by a DEP violation. This is the kind of situation for which Smolensky (1993, 1995, 1997) has introduced the idea of local conjunction of constraints. According to this proposal, two constraints may form a composite constraint which is violated, if and only if each of the conjoined constraints is violated in some given domain. The conjoined constraint only has tangible effects if some other constraint(s) is/are ranked between the conjoined constraint and the individual constraints that together make up the conjoined constraint (see also Ito and Mester (1998) for discussion).

In our case the conjoined constraint STRESS-IDENT & DEP is ranked above *CLASH-HEAD, with each of the individual constraints STRESS-IDENT and DEP being ranked below *CLASH-HEAD. Now the correct optimal candidate emerges:

(69)   *SCHWA-V, STRESS-IDENT & DEP >>
        *CLASH-HEAD >> STRESS-IDENT, DEP

a. *virtuize*

virtue-ize	*SCHWA -V	STRESS- IDENT & DEP	*CLASH- HEAD	STRESS- IDENT	DEP
☞ vírtùìze			*		
vírt[(j)ə]ìze	*!			*	
vírt[(j)əʔ]ìze		*!		*	*

b. *ghettoize*

ghetto-ize	*SCHWA -V	STRESS- IDENT & DEP	*CLASH- HEAD	STRESS- IDENT	DEP
☞ ghéttòìze			*		
ghétt[ə]ìze	*!			*	
ghétt[əʔ]ìze		*!		*	*

c. *anodize*

anode-ize	*SCHWA -V	STRESS- IDENT & DEP	*CLASH- HEAD	STRESS- IDENT	DEP
ánòdìze			*!		
☞ án[ə]dìze				*	

d. *radioize*

radio-ize	*SCHWA -V	STRESS- IDENT & DEP	*CLASH- HEAD	STRESS- IDENT	DEP
☞ rádiòìze					
rádi[əʔ]ìze		*!		*	*
rádi[ə]ìze	*!			*	

There are three derivatives in the neologism corpus that do not behave as demanded by the proposed constraints, *Locarnize* (< *Locárnò*), *fínìtize* (< *finite*) and *sátellìze* (< *sátellìte*). The two latter forms should exhibit de-stressing of the base-final syllable (i.e. !*fín*[ɪ]*tìze*, !*sátell*[ɪ]*tìze*) instead of stress preservation and truncation, respectively. They must be regarded as idiosyncratic formations. With *Locárnìze*, the base-final vowel of *Locárnò* is deleted inspite of the fact that this leads to a violation of both MAX-ó-V and *CLASH-HEAD. In other words, this is again an idiosyncratic form which the proposed model cannot account for, and which illustrates the fact that even newly created forms may occasionally violate well-formedness conditions on complex words.

6.2.5.6. Trochees preferred

Let us now deal with the fact that *-ize* attaches overwhelmingly to prosodi-cally left-headed words. There is a whole class of forms that in Raffel-siefen's account are treated as exceptional, namely those derivatives formed on the basis of words with ultimate primary stress, and monosylla-bles. What the iambic derivatives show is that IDENT-HEAD must be ranked higher than *CLASH-HEAD, because they never shift the main stress to a preceding syllable. Consider for example *banálìze*:

(70)   IDENT-HEAD >> *CLASH-HEAD

banal-ize	IDENT-HEAD	*CLASH-HEAD
☞ banálìze		*
bánalìze	*!	
bánìze	*!	*

With monosyllabic bases, a violation of *CLASH-HEAD seems inevitable, because such derivatives cannot be improved by stem allomorphy (cf. *Márxìze*). The violation of these highly ranked constraints makes the at-tested derivatives highly marked and therefore dispreferred *-ize* words. In our corpus of 284 20th century neologisms only the following forms are attested: *banálìze, cyclize* (trisyllabic pronunciation is preferred), *Czechize, ecize, Maoize* (again, trisyllabic pronunciation is preferred), *Marxize, quantize, routínìze*.

In Raffelsiefen's model, derivatives involving primary stressed immediately before -ize are completely ruled out by the M-PARSE constraint, because this constraint is ranked lower than *CLASH. Hence, the optimal candidate is one in which the affix is not attached at all, which, according to Raffelsiefen, leads to a lexical gap. In the next chapter, I propose a different reason for the near-absence of iambic or monosyllabic base words with -ize, namely the competition with -ify. The present model therefore dismisses M-PARSE as a necessary constraint for -ize derivatives.

There are only four derivatives in the neologism corpus that could possibly be classified as stress-shifted, i.e. as violators of IDENT-HEAD: *bácterize* (*bactéria*), *lyóphilìze* (*lýophìle/lýophil*), *multímerìze* (*múltimer*) and *phagocýtìze* (*phágocỳte*). However, *bácterize* could well be argued to be coined on the basis of the bound stem *bacter-*, which would naturally account for the existence and the prosodic structure of the attested cadidate. If *bactéria* (instead of *bacter-*) were the base, we would expect !*bactériìze* as optimal.[46] Forms such as *bácteroid* show that there is a bound stem allomorph *bacter-* available and forms such as *bactèriólogy* indicate the general possibility of schwa deletion (with the main stress of the base form surviving as a secondary stress). The form *multímerìze* is only considered as a minor variant in the *OED*, whereas the non-stress-shifted *múltimerìze* is presented as the standard pronunciation (also with the participles listed). This bears witness to the exceptionality of the stress-shifted form.

The remaining two forms (*phagocýtìze* and *lyóphilìze*) should be treated as exceptions. However, it is remarkable that both forms share their unusual stress patterns with other derived forms of their word families. Thus, in *lyóphilìze* the secondary stress of *lyòphilizátion* surfaces as main stress. This suggests that it might be a back-formation from the *nomen actionis*. The aberrant stress pattern of the -ize derivative makes the verb more similar to the nominalization than to the underived base word, and this may be exactly what the coiners and users aim at. Hence the *nomen actionis* is the output form with which stress correpondence is established. Evidence for this claim can be gleaned from the dates of the first citations of the forms as given in the *OED*. Thus *lyóphilìze* is first attested in the same text as the corresponding *nomen actionis*, respectively.

With the base word *phágocỳte*, we would predict the candidate *phágoc*[ɪ]*tìze* to be optimal. Notably, this candidate is also cited in the

---

46   Perhaps for orthographic reasons (unusual clash of two <i>s) !*bacteriize* is avoided in written language.

OED in its participial form (*phágocytìzed*), with a primary stress on the first syllable. Thus there are in fact two competing forms attested, one of which is in accordance with the predictions of our model. Furthermore, a converted form *to phágocỳte* is attested with the same meaning, which might also be interpreted as indicative of the oddity of *phagocýtìze*. But again, the stress shift is reminiscent of other derived forms such as *phagocýtal* and *phagocýtòse*.

We may now turn to another intriguing property of -*ize* derivatives, the non-uniformity of haplology effects.

6.2.5.7. Haplology effects

Plag (1998) proposes a theory of morphological haplology according to which morphological haplology results from a family of constraints named OCP, which prohibit adjacent identical elements in the output.[47] The Obligatory Contour Principle (OCP) was originally suggested to ban adjacent identical tones from the lexical representation of a morpheme in tone languages (e.g. Leben 1973), but it seems that the concept can be fruitfully extended to non-tonal phenomena. In the case of -*ize* derivatives at least one OCP constraint plays a significant role, the one against identical onsets in adjacent syllables (OCP-ONSET):

(71)   OCP-ONSET:
        "No identical onsets in adjacent syllablcs"

Note that OCP-ONSET is only terminologically different from Raffel-siefen's $*O_iRO_i$. The reason for renaming this constraint is that my terminology expresses the fact that seemingly different phenomena can be subsumed under one family of related constraints on the repetition of identical phonological structures (see Plag 1998 for elaboration and discussion).

As already mentioned above, disyllabic base words are never affected by haplological truncation, whereas dactylic bases always are. This patterning can be explained if we introduce OCP-ONSET into the hierarchy we have

---

[47]   See also Yip (1996:7) who assumes the following OCP constraints: OCP (feature), OCP (segment), OCP (affix), OCP (stem). The latter two, however, are not phonological in nature. In Plag (1998) the extension of OCP constraints to morphological elements is rejected. See that paper for a more detailed discussion.

established so far. The data show that OCP-ONSET must be ranked between *CLASH-HEAD and R-ALIGN-HEAD. As we will shortly see, OCP-ONSET must be crucially non-ranked with respect to MAX-C. Crucial non-ranking is expressed by a dotted line in the tableaux below and by '=' in the constraint hierarchies. Pertinent derivatives are evaluated in the tableaus in (72) and (73):

(72) OCP-ONSET = MAX-C >> R-ALIGN-HEAD

feminine-ize	OCP-ONSET	MAX-C	R-ALIGN-HEAD
☞ (fémin)(ìze)		*	$\sigma\sigma$
(fémi)ni(nìze)	*		$\sigma\sigma\sigma$!
(fémi)ni(ìze)		*	$\sigma\sigma\sigma$!

Although it may seem at first sight that MAX-C is violated in order to satisfy OCP-ONSET, we see that it is really the alignment constraint which triggers deletion with *féminìze*. Recall that C-final dactylic bases not leading to identical onsets (*hóspitalìze*) cannot be truncated due to MAX-C. If either MAX-C or OCP-ONSET *must* be violated, the candidate with the least violations of R-ALIGN-HEAD is optimal.

   *CLASH-HEAD becomes operative only with trochaic bases, as we can see in (73):

(73)   *CLASH-HEAD >> OCP-ONSET = MAX-C >> R-ALIGN-HEAD

strychnine-ize	*CLASH-HEAD	OCP-ONSET	MAX-C	R-ALIGN-HEAD
a. (strých)(nìze)	*!		*	σ
b. ☞ (strýchni)(nìze)		*		$\sigma\sigma$
c. ?☞ (strýchni)(ìze)			*	$\sigma\sigma$

The minimally truncated form (73c), *strýchniìze*, emerges falsely as optimal in this tableau, but this is only because the effects of DEP and ONSET are not presented. Thus candidate (73c) either violates DEP (if a glide is inserted in onset position) or ONSET (if no glide is inserted). The attested candidate (3b) violates neither of these constraints and is therefore selected as optimal.

6.2.5.8. Summary

We are now in a position to summarize our findings. The rankings established in the foregoing discussion are repeated below, with a brief description of their effect on *-ize* derivatives:

(55)   FT-BIN, TROCH, NONFINALITY, IDENT-HEAD >> R-ALIGN HEAD
       Effect: noun-like stress, no stress-shift (*rándomìze, hóspitalìze*)

(58)   MAX-C >> R-ALIGN-HEAD >> MAX-V
       Effect: deletion of stem-final vowels, but not of stem-final consonants (*mémorìze* vs. *hóspitalìze*)

(61)   *CLASH-HEAD >> R-ALIGN-HEAD >> MAX-V
       Effect: no deletion of stem-final vowels with disyllabic trochaic bases (*dándyìze*)

(64)   *SCHWA-V, *CLASH-HEAD >> R-ALIGN-HEAD, DEP
       Effect: glottal stop insertion with disyllabic bases ending in schwa (*móra[ʔ]ìze*)

(65)   MAX-ó-V >> R-ALIGN-HEAD
       Effect: no deletion of stressed vowels (*rádiòize*)

(67)   *CLASH-HEAD >> STRESS-IDENT
       Effect: destressing of base-final syllables (*án[ə]dìze*)

(69)   *SCHWA-V, STRESS-IDENT & DEP >> *CLASH-HEAD >> STRESS-
       IDENT, DEP
       Effect: non-uniformity of destressing (*án[ə]dìze* vs. *ghéttòize*)

(70)   IDENT-HEAD >> *CLASH-HEAD
       Effect: no stress-shift with iambic bases (*banálìze*)

(73)   *CLASH-HEAD >> OCP-ONSET = MAX-C >> R-ALIGN-HEAD
       Effect: OCP-effects and their non-uniformity (*féminìze* vs. *strýchninìze*)

Aggregating these rankings in one hierarchical tree structure yields the figure in (74) below, in which the constraints FT-BIN, TROCH, NON-FINALITY together are abbreviated as NOUN STRESS for expository purposes. The constraints in the top line are all unviolated:

(74)   Constraint hierarchy for *-ize* derivatives

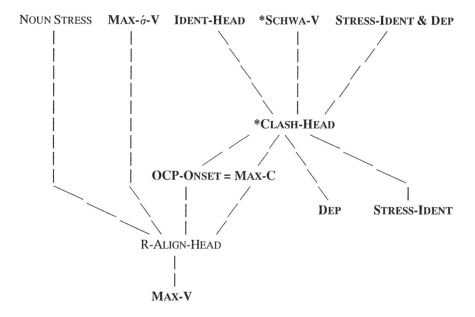

6.2.6. Theoretical implications

In the foregoing sections I have presented a model of phonological well-formedness conditions on English *-ize* verbs in the framework of OT. It has been shown that earlier approaches by E. Schneider, Gussmann, Kettemann, and Raffelsiefen are not satisfactory. A number of violable output constraints were proposed that can both account for the apparent phonological variability of recently formed *-ize* derivatives and predict the phonological make-up of possible derivatives.

The proposed analysis raises some important and controversial theoretical issues. The first of these concerns the controversy between rule-based and constraint-based theories in linguistics, the second the status of the proposed constraints within the prosodic system of English, and the third relates to the nature of the morphophonological mechanisms at work.

Let us start with the problem of rules vs. constraints. The analysis presented above does not only show the versatility of OT for the description of morphophonological phenomena in English but also makes a strong point against rule-based approaches to allomorphy, or word-formation in general. It was pointed out that rule-based approaches cannot cope ade-

general. It was pointed out that rule-based approaches cannot cope adequately with the obvious variability in the application of a putative rule. The non-uniformity of certain effects might be captured by imposing complex special restrictions on the rules, e.g. of the type "apply the rule except when...", similar to the generalization in (47) above, but such mechanisms are ad hoc and require an explanation themselves. As we have seen, violable constraints provide an empirically superior approach to morphophonological alternations.

Most recently, Neef (1996) has argued for non-violable well-formedness conditions in morphology instead of violable constraints of the OT type. At this stage it is unclear how his theory could handle the infrequent, but nevertheless attested, violations of some almost exceptionless well-formedness conditions of -ize, for example the near-non-occcurrence of stress shift or the rarity of iambic bases. In the present model, violation of constraints can be expected but it was argued that the high rank of certain constraints makes their violators highly marked - and therefore rare - structures. Although the exact relationship between type frequency and markedness remains to be studied (but see Golston and Wiese 1998 on German roots), the present model is preferable to Neef's, because in his approach such forms would have to be treated as truly idiosyncratic. Furthermore, generalizations (or 'word design conditions' in Neef's terminology) such as the ones put forward in section 6.2.4. are not fine-tuned enough to predict the different kinds of phonological alternations that occur, which means that the implementation of violable constraints yields the empirically more adequate results. But even if better word design conditions could be found, the same problems arise as with rule-based frameworks: why do we find these kinds of design conditions and not others? How can these conditions be independently motivated? In the model I have proposed, the violable constraints play a significant role in other areas of English phonology as well as in the phonological systems of other languages. Thus a growing number of studies in OT have demonstrated that constraints such as MAX, NONFINALITY, IDENT-HEAD etc. are universally relevant. Neef's design conditions, to the contrary, appear accidental and are necessarily language-specific.

The second theoretical problem raised by my analysis is that it entails a number of assumptions that are still under debate in OT. Thus I have argued that output-output constraints are needed to regulate stress preservation effects, that conjoined constraints are needed to account for some destressing effects, that crucial non-ranking of constraints is required to account for the observed OCP-effects and that morpheme-specific constraints can be integrated into the general hierarchy of constraints which is responsible for the prosodic structure of nouns in English. None of these points are original to this study but have been proposed by other scholars before in order to account for different phenomena in various languages (see the references above). An in-depth discussion of the theoretical problems involved would go beyond the scope of this investigation, but future research will show whether the proposed model is indeed tenable. More detailed evidence from a wider range of affixes is needed to find out more about possible and impossible constraints and their rankings and about the interaction of purely phonological constraints with those that only apply to morphologically complex words (e.g. output-output constraints).

The third problem concerns the - so far implicit - assumption that the stem allomorphy of *-ize* derivatives can be accounted for without making reference to the morphological structure of the base word. Thus, the shape of the optimal derivatives was solely determined on the basis of purely phonological constraints. It could, however, be argued that the constraints do not trigger phonological alternations in the putative base word, but that they either trigger the truncation of base-final morphemes, or that they only ensure the selection of the optimal stem allomorph. I will argue in the following that it is neither necessary nor possible to explain the stem allomorphy of *-ize* derivatives by making reference to morphological structure.

The strongest argument against phonologically governed allomorph selection or morphological truncation is of an empirical nature. Morphological truncation rules have been proposed, for example, in Aronoff (1976) or Booij (1977). The classic example of such a rule is the truncation of the verbal ending *-ate* when *-able* is attached (e.g. *demonstrate - demonstrable*). According to Aronoff (1976), this rule must make reference to the morphemic status of *-ate* since non-morphological *-ate* (as in *debate*) does not truncate (**debable*). As pointed out by Anderson (1992:280), these facts can equally well be expressed as a purely phonological generalization: only secondarily stressed *-ate* can be deleted, irrespective of the morphological status of the string [eɪt].

In general, it can be observed that truncation does often not involve morphological constituents. Corbin (1987:345), for example, provides a whole range of French data which demonstrate that the deleted sequence at the end of the base cannot be a morpheme, and the same is true for *-ize* derivatives. For example, the deletion of base-final [ɪ] in many of the neologisms under discussion can hardly be analyzed as the truncation of a putative morpheme *-y*, since [ɪ] does not seem to have morphemic status in words like *anthropólogy, (Madame) Bóvary, fántasy, mediócrity, Nórmandy* or *vaséctomy*. In particular, I am unaware of any claims that *-logy* or *-ity* are bi-morphemic suffixes, consisting of *-log* and *-y*, or *-it* and *-y*, respectively. What the six words really have in common is not the morphology of putative *-y*, but their prosody: they are dactyls that end in a vowel. As we have seen above, such a phonological structure leads to the truncation of the final vowel across the board, ignoring morphological structure: *anthropologize, bovarize, fantasize, mediocritize, Normandize, vasectomize*. This point is corroborated by the form *patinize*, where the final schwa of the base word *patina* does not represent a suffix either, but is nevertheles truncated because the base conforms to the kind of prosodic structure that necessitates the deletion of the final vowel when *-ize* is attached.

Similar arguments hold for the haplology cases, where *-ite* in *appetite* or *-is* in *metathesis* can hardly be regarded as English morphemes (if morphemes are units of sound and meaning). However, Kiparsky (personal communication, August 1997) pointed out to me that a form like *parallelize* may serve as evidence that perhaps only morphemes can be deleted, since, according to the proposed OCP constraints this derivative would be less optimal than the truncated **parallize*. Under an account that only allows the deletion of [əl] if it represents a morpheme, the existence of *parallelize* could be predicted.

This argument is not entirely convincing, however. First, *parallelize* is a very old form, first attested 1610, which means that it does not necessarily reflect the constraints of present-day English morphology. This is corroborated by the fact that native speakers generally prefer the synonymous converted verb *parallel* to *parallelize* (see also the respective entries in the *OED*). Second, it seems that suffixal *-al* is equally never truncated (cf. *federalize* and many more examples), so that the argument in favor of morphological truncation collapses. Third, even if we allow *parallelize* to be a possible derivative (and not only an actual one), it is still conceivable that OCP-ONSET needs to be further specified for phonological features. For example, [l] might be allowed to appear in identical onsets whereas other consonants might not. Unfortunately, there are no data that could show this, because all stems which can take adjectival *-al* and which end in [l] take *-ar* instead of *-al* as an adjectival suffix (cf. **polal* vs. *polar*).[48] In

---

[48]   This is an interesting fact by itself, because it shows the operation of another OCP constraint proposed in Plag (1998) which does not allow identical onset and coda in a single syllable. This constraint is obviously ranked lower with agentive *-er* since this suffix can be attached to stems ending in /r/, as in *murderer*. Note that the alternation between *-al* and *-ar* cannot be explained in

principle, however, the featural specification of OCP constraints is not unusual[49] and could perhaps also solve the problem at hand. In view of the arguments just presented it is however preferable to assign idiosyncratic status to the word *parallelize*.

In summary, the idea of morphological truncation has two main flaws. It necessitates the postulation of otherwise unmotivated morphological structure, and it cannot explain the robust phonological generalizations that hold across morphologically diverse derivatives.

The only remaining alternative to a purely phonological model is therefore to assume that *-ize* selects certain stem allomorphs in order to satisfy the constraints. Under this approach, the deleted material need not be a morphological constituent, but only the base would have to be a morphological unit, namely a bound stem. This idea is preferable to the one just dismissed because it makes it unnecessary to assign questionable morphological status to certain sound sequences at the end of words. The problem is, however, to provide in each case independent evidence for the existence of the respective bound stem. While this may still justifiable with a stem like *anthropolog-*, which also surfaces in words like *anthropolog-ical* and *anthropolog-ist*, there are words where the putative bound stem only occurs in combination with *-ize*. Consider *Normandize*, whose stem *Normand-* is not attested outside the base word *Normandy*, whereas all other complex words feature *Norman(n)-* as their base (*Norman-esque, Normann-ic, Norman-ish, Norman-ism*, etc.). Similar empirical problems emerge with words like *metathesize*, where there is no independent evidence for a bound stem *metathes-* (unless one assumes that *-is* is a nominal suffix of English, which would be a truly innovational but nevertheless unconvincing claim). To complicate the situation, the only bound stem allomorph that does exist ends in *-t-* (as in *metathetical*), and it is mysterious why *-ize* would not select this stem allomorph if it prefers bound stems with these kinds of base lexemes.

Apart from these problems, the allomorph selection approach faces similar difficulties as the morphological truncation approach in accounting for the observed phonological generalizations across the many different derivatives. These generalizations would be accidental by-products of stem

---

terms of phonological alternation but should be regarded as an instance of allomorph selection, with the allomorphs being inherited from Latin.

[49] For example, the occurrence of epenthetic schwa in English verbs and nouns involving the inflectional suffix *-s* has been explained by a constraint which prohibits adjacent sibilants (see, for example, Yip 1996, Russel 1997).

allomorphy because the stem allomorphs to be selected must be available *a priori*. But where and how do they originate? Under the present account, stem allomorphy is not (necessarily) a peculiar, given fact of the language, but can at least partially be explained as the result of independently motivated prosodic constraints that define the phonological make-up of a derivational category. In functional terms, stem allomorphy ensures the phonological coherence of the morphological category of *-ize* derivatives at the potential cost of reduced recognizability of the bases of individual derivatives. Sometimes these allomorphs are lexicalized or may become so, sometimes not. The important point is that under the selection model they *must* be lexicalized whereas under the present model they need not. The latter is clearly the more desirable solution.

On theoretical grounds, it seems that one should prefer an account that is most conservative in its assumptions. In the model proposed here, only one type of very general mechanism is needed to account for the data. Additional machinery like allomorphy selection should only be allowed if there is good independent evidence for it. The only derivatives where this is undoubtedly the case are those on the Greek bases discussed above. Note again that the selection of the Greek bound stem is not triggered by the phonological constraints, but by a purely lexical mechanism. The only other case where allomorphy selection might be involved are *-ize* derivatives on the basis of adjectives in *-ous*. It seems that these adjectives generally undergo truncation inspite of the fact that the non-truncated forms would be chosen as phonologically optimal in the above system. Thus, the only form which features the sequence *-ous-ize* listed in the whole *OED* is *graciousize* (obsolete/rare), with only one citation in 1701. Among the neologisms there is also only one form with a putative base in *-ous, indígenìze*. According to the model, this derivative is less optimal than the unattested !*indígenousìze*. However, this analysis presupposes that *indígenìze* is indeed based on the adjective and not on the bound stem *indigen-*. Under the assumption that there is indeed a bound stem *indigen-* which can serve as the basis for derivation, the attested form is also optimal. Due to the extremely low number of attested derivatives involving bases in *-ous* (truncated or not), I do not attempt to draw any firm conclusions with respect to bases ending in *-ous*. What the example of *indigenize* shows again, however, is that it is sometimes problematic to determine the base from which a complex word is actually derived. Thus it may well be the case that speakers coin words on the basis of bound stems, if available. Notably, this is not precluded by the model advocated above. What I have argued for is that the reliance on stem allomorphy selection as the general or the only mechanism can neither explain the kinds of stem allomorphy we observe nor the phonological generalizations that hold across morphologically diverse derivatives.

Although the foregoing discussion of the theoretical problems only concerned *-ize* derivatives, parallel arguments hold for the other complex derived by the affixation of *-ate, -ify, eN-* and *-en* and by conversion, to which we turn in the next chapter.

7. Rival morphological processes 3:
The structural properties of other verb-deriving processes

7.1. The structural properties of -*ify* derivatives

The number of attested neologisms in -*ify* is rather small in comparison to the number of -*ize* derivatives. It would seem at first sight that the small number does not allow for robust generalizations, but the following analysis will show that this is not the case. There is strong empirical evidence that -*ify* and -*ize* are phonologically conditioned allomorphs.

7.1.1.   The meaning of -ify derivatives

Since there are only 23 derivatives in the neologism corpus, I have listed them in their entirety in (1) (stress patterns are indicated as usual by grave and acute accents):

(1)   ammónifỳ   arídifỳ   ártifỳ   bourgeóisifỳ   géntrifỳ
       jázzifỳ   kárstifỳ   mássifỳ   múcifỳ   mýthifỳ
       Názifỳ   négrifỳ   opácifỳ   passívifỳ   probabílifỳ
       plástifỳ   sínifỳ   syllábifỳ   téchnifỳ   trústifỳ
       túbifỳ   yóuthifỳ   yúppifỳ

The meanings which verbs in -*ify* can express appear to be identical to the ones denoted by -*ize*. I therefore propose the same LCS for -*ify* derivatives in (2), with appropriate examples given in (3):

(2)   LCS of -*ify* verbs
       [[   ]Base -*ify*]v
       {NP$_i$ _____ NP$_{Theme}$, NP$_{Theme}$ _____ , NP$_i$ _____ }
       CAUSE ([.....]$_i$, [GO ([$_{Property, Thing}$]$_{Theme / Base}$;
                                                    [TO [$_{Property, Thing}$]$_{Base / Theme}$])])

(3)	locative	'put (in)to X'	*tubify*
	ornative	'provide with X'	*youthify*
	causative/factitive	'make (more) X'	*aridify*
	resultative	'make into X'	*trustify*
	inchoative	'become X'	*mucify*
	performative	'perform X'	-
	similative	'act like X'	-

Inchoatives are rarely attested, but seem to be possible cf. e.g. *mucify*, or *petrify* (the latter is not a neologism). The list in (2) reveals that there are no examples of the performative and similative interpretations. The comparatively small number of derivatives makes it impossible to definitely say whether the performative and similative meanings are systematic gaps, but this question is of limited interest anyway since, as was argued in the pertinent section on *-ize*, these two interpretations are special cases of the ornative meaning.

Given the rather flexible LCS in (2), the small number of neologisms in *-ify* is perhaps unexpected. However, in the next section we will see that this is largely the result of phonological factors.

7.1.2. *The phonology of* -ify *derivatives*

Mahn (1971) observed what I consider to be the most important prosodic property of *-ify* derivatives, namely that the syllable preceding *-ify* always carries main stress. Gussmann (1987) arrives at two generalizations, namely that *-ify* attaches to bases ending in the vowel /i/, which is deleted by a phonological rule, and to bases ending in an obstruent, followed by an optional sonorant. As he himself admits, these rules are insufficient because they overgenerate and do not cover all attested derivatives. In his analysis of 164 derivatives taken from the entire *OED,* E. Schneider (1987) again emphasizes the fact that *-ify* needs to be immediately adjacent to a main-stressed syllable, with the consequence that *-ify* tends to attach to monosyllables (as in *falsify*) and words with final stress (e.g. *divérsify*). With bases ending in an unstressed vowel, the final vowel coalesces with the suffix (*béautifŷ*) with consonant-final trochees as base words stress is shifted to the base-final syllable. As we will see, these generalizations (apart from stress shift) hold also for 20th century neologisms. Kettemann (1988) discusses a number of lexicalized stem alternations, but does not arrive at significant phonological constraints on *-ify* derivatives.

Of the 23 derivatives in the neologism corpus, 15 formations are based on monosyllabic stems or on iambic stems (*artify, bourgeoisify, jazzify, karstify, massify, mucify, mythify, negrify, opacify, plastify, sinify, technify, trustify, tubify, youthify*). Three forms have bases ending in an unstressed vowel, which is systematically truncated (*ammonia - ammonify, gentry - gentrify, Nazi - Nazify, yuppy - yuppify*). Stress lapses are absolutely prohibited, all derivatives have primary stress on the syllable immediately preceding the suffix. Stress shift is apparently a rare phenomenon (*passívify, probabílify, syllábify,* and *arídify*). Deletion of base-final consonants is not attested at all.

How can this behavior be accounted for? I propose that *-ify* is subject to the same constraint hierarchy as *-ize* derivatives, with the prosodic differences between the two types of derivatives resulting from the prosodic differences of the suffixes (one monosyllabic, the other disyllabic with a light penult).

A comparison of the prosodic properties of derivatives in *-ify* with those in *-ize* reveals that the phonological constraints lead to a (nearly) complementary distribution of the two suffixes: *-ize* is generally preceded by trochaic or dactylic bases, i.e. it needs an unstressed or secondarily stressed syllable to its left, whereas *-ify* always needs a main-stressed syllable to its left (stress shift is generally avoided).[1] Taking into account that, as argued in the preceding section, the two suffixes are synonymous, we can hypothesize that we are dealing with two phonologically conditioned allomorphs, more specifically with one of the rare cases of phonologically conditioned suppletion in derivational morphology. (cf. Carstairs-McCarthy 1988, Carstairs 1990).

In a rule based framework, this state of affairs would be expressed by two (or more) different rules which exhaust all possible environments. In an OT approach, both allomorphs are found among the candidates, which are evaluated in parallel by *only one* constraint hierarchy. As usual, the derivative which best satisfies the constraints is chosen as optimal (see e.g. Booij 1998 for illustration). Thus, if the two competing suffixes under discussion are indeed phonologically-conditioned allomorphs, two predictions can be made. First, the phonological shape of *-ify* derivatives and of *-ize* derivatives result from the same constraint hierarchy, i.e. the one al-

---

[1]   This would amount to perfect complementary distribution, if it were not for disyllabic bases ending in unstressed [ɪ], which trigger truncation of these rhymes. See below for discussion.

ready proposed for *-ize* derivatives. Secondly, the choice between *-ize* and *-ify* is determined by the very same hierarchy. As we will see, both predictions are correct.

Let us begin with the first prediction. As already mentioned, *-ify* derivatives have strictly ante-penultimate main stress. This pattern is exactly that of English nouns: polysyllables with a light penultima have antepenultimate main stress. Hence, stress placement results from the ranking in (4), which we already know from the preceding chapter:

(4)   FT-BIN, TROCH, NONFINALITY >> R-ALIGN HEAD

karst-ify	FT-BIN	TROCH	NONFIN	R-ALIGN-HEAD
a. ☞ (kársti)(fỳ)				$\sigma\sigma$
b. (kàr)(stí)(fỳ)	*!			σ
c. (kàrsti)(fý)			*!	
d. (karstí)(fỳ)		*!		

Due to the fact that *-ify* attachment automatically leads to a light penult in the derived form, two violations of R-ALIGN-HEAD are inevitable. Attempts to shift main stress further to the right in order to better satisfy R-ALIGN-HEAD are unsuccessful, because this entails violation of higher-ranked constraints (see candidates (4b), (4c) and (4d)). Notably, derivatives with iambic or monosyllabic bases fulfill these constraints optimally without any necessary stem allomorphy effects such as deletion of segments, destressing, or stress shift.

But why is it that *-ify* systematically does not attach to trochees or dactyls? If we include both *-ize* and *-ify* derivatives in the candidate sets the correct distribution emerges. With trochaic or dactylic bases, *-ize* derivatives necessarily involve one violation less than candidates with *-ify*, because *-ize* is monosyllabic:[2]

---

[2]   In those cases where the following tableaux also include *-ize* derivatives, only the optimal *-ize* derivative is given as a candidate. The exclusion of other *-ize* candidates was already shown in chapter 6.

(5)   allomorph selection: trochaic bases

random-ize/ify	FT-BIN	TROCH	NONFIN	R-ALIGN-HEAD
a. ☞ (rándo)(mìze)				σσ
b. (rándo)mi(fỳ)				σσσ!

Only a stress shift or the truncation of the base-final rhyme could improve the *-ify* derivative, but IDENT-HEAD and MAX-C are higher-ranked than R-ALIGN-HEAD, which rules out this option.[3] With dactylic bases parallel arguments can be adduced, to the effect that *-ize* attachment always emerges as more optimal than *-ify* attachment.

With monosyllabic bases, or bases ending in a main-stressed syllable, *-ify* is selected as the optimal allomorph:

(6)   allomorph selection: monosyllabic bases

karst-ify/ize	*CLASH-HEAD	R-ALIGN-HEAD
☞ kárstifỳ		σσ
kárstìze	*!	σ

(7)   allomorph selection: iambic bases

bourgeois-ify/ize	*CLASH-HEAD	R-ALIGN-HEAD
☞ bourgeóisifỳ		σσ
bourgeóisìze	*!	σ

As already mentioned in chapter 6, there are only very few exceptional cases where *-ize* is attached in spite of the resulting stress clash (*banálìze, Czéchìze, écìze, Márxìze, quántìze, routínìze*). These are exceptional formations because they are less optimal than the expected forms *!banálify, !Czechify* (cf. *Anglify, Russify*), *!ecify*, and *!Marxify*.

---

[3]   I assume that there are high-ranked faithfulness constraints that prohibit suffix allomorphy with both *-ize* and *-ify*. Hence no deletion of suffix material is possible, which rules out candidates such as **randomfy* or **randomif*, for example.

With regard to the selection of the optimal suffix, there is one problematic set of candidates, those on the basis of trochaic stems with an unstressed final [ɪ]. As pointed out by previous authors and as evidenced by the forms *gentrify, Nazify* and *yuppify*, such base words readily take *-ify* (under deletion of the base-final vowel), but as we have seen in the preceding chapter, such base words also may take *-ize* as a suffix (cf. *dolbyize*, see appendix 1, 6.1.). Hence our constraints should allow two optimal candidates. Interestingly, there are indeed at least two forms with doublets attested (both with their first citation before the 20th century): *Torify, Toryize* and *dandify, dandyize*. The form in *-ize* seems to be more optimal than the *-ify* derivative because it does not involve the deletion of the base-final vowel. However, the *-ify* derivative satisfies both ONSET and DEP. In other words, a violation of MAX-V (as in *Torify*) is sometimes preferred to a violation of either ONSET or DEP. Thus we are faced with a variable ranking of ONSET, DEP, and MAX-V:

The following tableaux illustrate this:

(8)

a.   MAX-V, ONSET >> DEP

dandy-ize/ify	MAX-V	ONSET	DEP
a. ☞ [dæn.dɪ.jaɪz]			*
b. [dæn.dɪ.aɪz]		*!	
c. [dæn.dɪ.faɪ]	*!		

b.   MAX-V, DEP >> ONSET

dandy-ize/ify	MAX-V	DEP	ONSET
a. [dæn.dɪ.jaɪz]		*!	
b. ☞ [dæn.dɪ.aɪz]			*
c. [dæn.dɪ.faɪ]	*!		

c.   ONSET, DEP >> MAX-V

dandy-ize/ify	ONSET	DEP	MAX-V
a. [dæn.dɪ.jaɪz]		*!	
b. [dæn.dɪ.aɪz]	*!		
c. ☞ [dæn.dɪ.faɪ]			*

If DEP or ONSET has the lowest rank, the *-ize* derivatives emerges as optimal. If MAX-V is lowest, *-ify* is attached. The emergence of different optimal pronunciations of *dandyize* is desirable, since, as already pointed out in chapter 6, both glide insertion and onsetless pronunciation are possible. The nature of this variation in constraint rankings and its theoretical implication certainly merit further investigation. For the purposes of this study we simply state that the observed variability can best be accounted for by a variable constraint ranking within a small subset of constraints in the overall hierarchy.

The ranking in (8c) can also account for the only remaining derivative based on a vowel-final stem, *ammonify*, which features otherwise unattested truncation (cf. *ammonia*). The pertinent constraints are RIGHT-ALIGN-HEAD, MAX-V, ONSET and DEP:

(9)   RIGHT-ALIGN-HEAD >> ONSET, DEP >> MAX-V

ammonia-ize/ify	R-ALIGN-HEAD	ONSET	DEP	MAX-V
a. ☞ [əmóʊnɪfàɪ]	σσ			**
b. [əmóʊnɪjàɪz]	σσ		*!	*
c. [əmóʊnɪàɪz]	σσ	*!		*

Candidate (9a) is optimal because it only violates low-ranked MAX-V. The singleton truncation effect is therefore straightforwardly explained by the proposed hierarchy.

The variable ranking of MAX-V, ONSET and DEP has consequences if we look again at *-ize* derivatives. In particular, we need to reconsider the behavior of schwa-final trochaic bases. In chapter 6 it was argued that such bases feature glottal stop insertion, if suffixed by *-ize* (cf. *!mora*[ʔ]*ize*). Even if competing candidates in *-ify* are taken into account, the proposed ranking in (8a) predicts that *!mora*[ʔ]*ize* as optimal. However, *!morify* is the optimal candidate under ranking (8c), because it only violates low-ranking MAX-V. Native speakers seem not to have strong intuitions about such words, and generally prefer syntactic constructions instead or alternative coinages where parallel forms are more frequent, such as !*moraicize*. One of the reasons for the insecurity of speakers may be that by looking exclusively at -*ize* derivatives no evidence for the ranking of MAX-V on the one hand and DEP and ONSET on the other can be found, because MAX-V does not interact with DEP and ONSET. In any case, the foregoing remarks about the behavior of schwa-final trochaic bases remain somewhat tentative. Given the rarity of potential base words of this phonological shape in English in general this is, however, a marginal problem.

The proposed rankings of MAX-V, DEP and ONSET lead to a slight modification of the lower part of the proposed hierarchy. The complete hierarchy is presented in (11), with variable rankings indicated by '%':

(10)   Constraint hierarchy for -*ize* and -*ify* derivatives

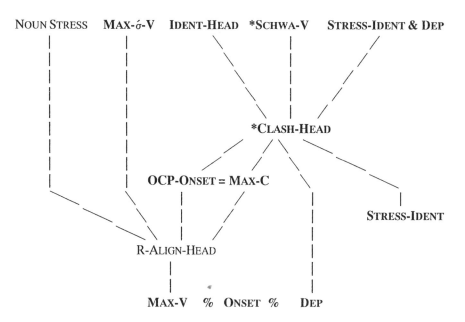

To summarize, the proposed constraint hierarchy for -*ize* and -*ify* derivatives does not only account for the stress pattern and allomorphy effects of -*ize* derivatives, but also for the phonological shape and restrictions on -*ify* derivatives and the distribution of the two competing suffixes. Thus, we can explain why monosyllabic bases avoid *-ize* but take *-ify* and why *-ify* only attaches to main stressed syllables. In informal terms, *-ize* is selected to make the main stress fall as far to the right as possible, whereas *-ify* is chosen to avoid a stress clash.

Only four of the *-ify* neologisms seem to go against the prediction of the proposed model, since they apparently exhibit a shift of the main stress (*passívify*, *probabílify*, *syllábify*, and *arídify*). I will discuss each of them in turn.

Passívify is an early 20th century rival of *passivate* and did not become established later, which can be interpreted as an indication of its slight oddness. Note also that *passívify* was subsequently never attested as a rival of *passivize*, which indicates the well-formedness of *pássivìze* as compared to *passívify*. *Probabílify* is attested with a meaning slightly different from that of *probábilìze*, and this meaning crucially is based on the noun *probabílity* rather than on the adjective *próbable* (cf. the quotations and definitions in the *OED*). Hence, there is evidence that *probabílify* is not derived from the base *probable*, but from *probabílity,* with the consequence that there is no IDENT-HEAD violation because the prosodic head of *probabílity* is the same as the prosodic head of *probabílify*.[4] *Syllábify* is a back-formation from *syllabification,* which in turn seems to be coined directly on the basis of Latin *syllabificare.* The only remaining odd form is *arídify*, whose analogy to the semantically related (and equally exceptional) form *humídify* is striking, the latter word being first attested some 40 years earlier (1884). In sum, the forms apparently violating IDENT-HEAD can either be explained on a paradigmatic basis by local analogy, or they did not survive for a longer period of time.

Contrary to this analysis, Kettemann (1988:92ff) argues that stress shift is a productive phenomenon with *-ify* derivatives. He bases his claim on a little experiment, where subjects had to suffix *-ify* to the nonce base *sarid,* which resulted in 70% answers involving a stress shift. In my view, this result, though impressive, does not demonstrate what Kettemann thinks it does, because the test item rhymes with adjectives such as *arid, humid, solid,* so that the choice of stress shift may well be triggered by this phonological similarity of the nonce forms with the attested and established forms *arídify*, *humídify*, *solídify.* Thus Kettemann's experiment should not be interpreted as a sign of productivity of stress shift. If stress shift were

---

[4]   In a similar fashion, the segmental alternation in *opacify* can be explained, cf. *opacity.*

indeed productive, I do not see any explanation for the almost complementary distribution of *-ify* and *-ize* based on the stress pattern of the base.
Why did none of the over two hundred trochaic and dactylic bases that
took *-ize* as a suffix chose *-ify* as a suffix with simultaneous stress shift? If
stress shift were productive, *-ify* should occur much more often with trochaic and dactylic bases.

To summarize the analysis, we can state that *-ify* and *-ize* are synonymous suffixes whose distribution is governed by the constraint hierarchy in
(10). Hence the two suffixes consitute a case of phonologically conditioned
suppletion, which is rarely found in derivational morphology, according to
Carstairs-McCarthy (1988) and Carstairs (1990).

7.2. The structural properties of *-ate* derivatives

Apart from *-ize* derivatives, verbs in *-ate* are the most frequent overtly
affixed verbs in our corpus of neologisms (72 types, see appendix 1).
While with *-ize* derivatives, the decision whether or not to count a form as
a proper *-ize* formation was rather straightforward, the discerning of proper
-ate formations turned out to be less clear-cut. As will be discussed in detail below, many forms display various phonological, morphological and
semantic peculiarities, which calls into question their status as forms resulting from the suffixation of *-ate*. As already mentioned in chapter 6, all
potentially doubtful cases were included in the corpus. First, in view of the
regularity of *-ize* verbs the observed heterogeneity of *-ate* verbs is an interesting fact in itself and requires some explanation, which can only be given
by also investigating the apparently problematic forms. Second, the heterogeneity of *-ate* verbs may have a bearing on the nature and representation
of the suffix itself, or its derivatives. Hence, I did not exclude forms on the
basis of a preconceived notion of what constitutes a properly suffixed *-ate*
verb.

7.2.1. *The meaning of* -ate *derivatives*

Having clarified this methodological point, let us first turn to the semantics
of the derivatives. Sources like Jespersen (1942) and Marchand (1969)
contain a lot of information about the history but very little about the
meaning of *-ate*. This may not be coincidental, since the semantics of *-ate*
derivatives appears to be extremely heterogenous, not to say messy. This

heterogeneity is not only reflected in the hundreds of forms that have entered the language in the past centuries but is also manifested in 20th century neologisms. Consider for example the following derivatives, which can be taken as instantiations of a number of different semantic categories. We find causatives (e.g. *passivate*), resultatives (e.g. *methanate*), inchoatives (e.g. *gelate*), instrumentals (*tambourinate*), statives (*dissonate* 'be dissonant') and a number of rather opaque forms (like, for example, *vagulate*).

7.2.1.1. Ornative/resultative -ate

In spite of the apparently wide range of meanings of *-ate* verbs I will argue that the meaning of the suffix *-ate* is in fact more restricted than the meaning of *-ize*. In particular, productive *-ate* expresses (only) an ornative-resultative meaning. This analysis of *-ate* can only account for one third of the derivatives in appendix 1, but we will shortly see that the majority of other forms are not derived through the suffixation of *-ate* but through other morphological processes, namely back-formation, conversion, local analogy, clipping, etc. We will first discuss ornative-resultative *-ate* before we turn to the other processes.

I suggest the following LCS for verbs with the derivational suffix *-ate*:

(11) LCS of *-ate* verbs
      $[[\text{'chemical substance'}]_{\text{Base}} \text{ -ate}]_V$
      { NP$_i$ ___ NP$_{\text{Theme}}$, NP$_{\text{Theme}}$ ___ , NP$_i$ ___ }
      CAUSE ($[_{\text{Thing}} \ldots]_i$, [GO ($[_{\text{Thing/Property}}$ $]_{\text{Base}}$; [TO $[_{\text{Thing}}$ $]_{\text{Theme}}$])])

In contrast to *-ize*, the LCS of *-ate* given in (11) is much more constrained. According to (11), *-ate* is productively suffixed only to bases that denote chemical substances. The derivatives denote either the physical transfer of such a substance to the entity denoted by NP$_{\text{Theme}}$, or, in its resultative interpretation, the inducing of the property denoted by the base in NP$_{\text{Theme}}$. Of the 25 verbs in our corpus that exemplify the given LCS, 16 are ornatives (see (12a)), eight instantiate the resultative meaning (see (12b), and one is attested with both meanings (see (12c)):

(12) a. alluviate   mercurate
          citrate   metalate
          fluorinate   nitrogenate

	fluoridate	nitrosate
	formylate	phosphorylate
	hydroborate	protonate
	hydroxylate	tarviate
	iodinate	tosylate
b.	gelate	silylate
	methanate	olate
	pupariate	solate
	sulphonylate	xanthate
c.	phosphate	

Even in this most homogeneous class of *-ate* verbs there are a number of peculiar forms, whose derivational history and phonology is deviant. The regular prosodic pattern of *-ate* verbs is characterized by alternating stress and a minimum of three syllables, with secondary stress on *-ate*. Five forms are different in this respect (*citrate, phosphate, gelate, olate* and *solate*), of which *citrate, phosphate* and *xanthate* exhibit a stress clash, whereas *gelate, olate* and *solate* even carry primary stress on *-ate*. For a detailed discussion of the phonological properties of *-ate* derivatives see section 7.2.2. below.

Although based on a new set of data, our ornative-resultative analysis of *-ate* is similar to Marchand's observation that *-ate* can be "freely used to derive verbs from Latin nominal stems, with the meaning 'combine, impregnate, treat with --' " (1969:258). The differences in formalization aside, our approach has two advantages. Firstly, we can also account for the attested resultative meanings, and secondly the denominal character of *-ate* need not be stipulated, but follows from the LCS itself.

We may now turn to the discussion of the other forms in our corpus, which I argue to be the result of a number of different morphological processes that do not involve the suffix *-ate* in the way described so far. As we will see, most of these processes are based on local analogies with other already existing complex words.

7.2.1.2. The role of back-formation

The most common of these processes is back-formation, which I take to be "the formation of a new lexeme by the deletion of a suffix, or supposed suffix, from an apparently complex form by analogy with other instances where the suffixed and non-suffixed forms are both lexemes" (Bauer

1983:64). The decision whether a form is a back-formation or not is some-times both theoretically and empirically controversial, but I will adduce three kinds of evidence to substantiate my analysis, namely the dates of the earliest attestations as given in the OED, the close semantic relationship between model form and back-formed verb, and the aberrant phonological properties of some of the back-formed verbs.

Of the 72 verbs in the corpus, 38 are first attested at least one year later than the complex noun from which they are presumably back-formed, and 18 are first attested in the same year, of which 12 are first attested in the same text as the related noun. These facts clearly indicate that a huge por-tion of *-ate* verbs, if not the majority, do not arise through the suffixation of *-ate* to a given base, but through back-formation from *nomina actionis* in *-ation*.[5] The reason for the high number of back-formations is rather obvious: the existence of the suffix *-ation* on the one hand, and the fact that all *-ate* verbs can be nominalized by the attachment of *-ion* on the other (see e.g. Raffelsiefen 1992, and section 4.3. above). Thus every noun in *-ation* is a possible candidate for the back-formation of a verb in *-ate*.

Although *-ation* has often been analyzed as a combination of *-ate* and *-ion*, both older and newer pairs like *declare-declaration* (noun first at-tested 1340) *derive-derivation* (noun: 1530), *starve-starvation* (noun: 1778) show that *-ation* also exists as a non-compositional suffix, since there are no corresponding forms ?*declarate*, ?*derivate*, ?*starvate*.[6] The neologisms and their related forms as given in the *OED* suggest that this non-compositional suffix is especially productive in the realm of chemical-technical terminology and primarily attaches to nouns (e.g. *epoxide - ep-oxidation*). This analysis of *-ation* runs counter to standard sources, which treat *-ation* as an exclusively deverbal suffix. The data indicate, however, that this cannot be the whole story and even Marchand states that "[s]ubstantives in *-ation* which go with verbs in *-ate* are, as a rule, older than the verbs." (1969:260). In view of these facts the most natural conclu-sion - not drawn by Marchand, however - would be to analyze most of these *-ate* verbs as back-formations.

There is, however, also the possibility that most of the putative *-ation* nouns are in fact nominalizations not of actual but of possible *-ate* verbs. The above-cited *epoxidation* (first attested 1945) would be a case in point,

---

5   There are only two back-formed verbs on the basis of other nouns. *Mono-chromate* is modelled on *monochromator*, *escalate*₁ on *escalator*.

6   See Haspelmath (1995) for a detailed discussion of affix reanalysis.

since !*epoxidate*, though not attested, is certainly a possible form. This escape hatch has in fact been used by Marchand to account for the existence of *sedimentation*, for which no verbal *-ate* base is attested. He submits that, for example, in the case of *sedimentation*, "*-ation* derives a noun from a verb that exists only virtually" (1969:261). Under this assumption the lack of an attested base verb for a given *-ation* noun is pragmatically conditioned, it is simply not needed. This type of approach would have wider implications also for the semantic analysis of *-ate*. Assuming that *-ation* nouns are all derived from possible *-ate* verbs, the meaning of a semantically transparent *-ation* noun would depend on the meaning of its base, i.e. the possible *-ate* verb. Given the heterogeneous meaning of *-ation* derivatives, we would have to assume that *-ate* is just as indeterminate in meaning as the action nominals putatively derived from it. Consequently, the LCS proposed above would be wrong, and the meaning of *-ate* would be as indeterminate as that of *-ation*, i.e. simply denoting an Event having to do with what is denoted by the base. Such an analysis will be proposed for denominal zero-derived verbs below, but, as we will see, it is not feasible for all *-ate* formations.

The decision for a very general verbal meaning (as against the LCS above) would hinge, among other things, on the acceptance of the claim that the *-ation* nouns are derived from possible but unattested *-ate* verbs. This claim is, however, most problematic. First, the existence of forms like *derivation, declaration, perseveration, starvation,* etc. clearly shows that *-ation* has an independent status as a non-compositional suffix. Second, as pointed out by Rainer (1993:99), the postulation of one compound suffix instead of two stacked ones is all the more plausible, the more often the compound suffix is attested without a corresponding single affix form. As conceded by Marchand, it is the rule rather than the exception, that the *-ation* form is attested earlier than the *-ate* form, and the same holds for the neologisms in our corpus. These facts are strong evidence against the successive suffixation of *-ate* and *-ion* in the cases under discussion.

Another major argument for the back-formation analysis is the close semantic relationship between model noun and back-formed verb. In general, the meaning dependency between a putatively back-formed word and its model is crucial evidence for a back-formation (see e.g. the discussion in Becker 1993a, 1993b). We would therefore predict that the indeterminacy of the meaning of *-ation* derivatives is reflected in the meaning of back-derived verbs. Under this approach, the heterogeneity of the *-ate* verbs turns out to be the direct consequence of their derivational history.

A full-fledged analysis of the semantic properties of *-ation* derivatives is beyond the scope of the present investigation, but as already mentioned above, the data suggest that action nominals in *-ation* merely denote an Event having to do with the entity denoted by the base. The postulation of a more specific meaning seems not to be justified in view of the semantic variation among the forms. On the basis of the meaning of *-ation* just proposed it can be (correctly) predicted that, for example, *cavitation* denotes an Event in which a cavity or cavities are involved in some manner. The lexicalized meaning 'The formation of bubbles or cavities in a fluid, esp. by the rapid motion of a propeller' (*OED*) is certainly more specific, but conforms to the general semantics of *-ation*. The semantics of the back-formed verbs directly reflect the semantics of the action nominal from which they are derived. This close relationship between verb and action nominal is especially striking in those cases where more idiosyncratic meanings are involved, but a parallel analysis applies to the less idiosyncratic cases.

Let us consider, for example, *escalate, formate* and *perseverate*. The verb *escalate* can have two meanings, each of which is derived from their respective model word. The first meaning, that of *escalate*$_1$, can be paraphrased as 'To climb or reach by means of an escalator ... To travel on an escalator' (*OED*), and is thus closely related to *escalator*. The second meaning, associated with *esacalate*$_2$, is roughly synonymous with 'increase in intensity', which is derived from *escalation*.[7] The second example, *formate*, is obviously coined in analogy to *formation*, as it is clearly indicated by the *OED*'s paraphrase 'Of an aircraft or its pilot: to take up formation *with*, to fly in formation'. Finally, the meaning of *perseverate*, a technical term used in psychology, is given by the *OED* as 'To repeat a response after the cessation of the original stimulus, in various senses of perseveration 2'. *Perseveration*$_2$ is paraphrased in the *OED* as 'The tendency for an activity to be persevered with or repeated after the cessation of the stimulus to which it originally responded'. In all of these examples the *-ate* verb is semantically dependent on the action noun, and the noun is also attested a number of years earlier than the verb.

The final argument for the back-formation analysis comes from phonological facts. As already mentioned above, there are a number of verbs that have prosodic patterns that do not conform to the regular one of *-ate*

---

[7] Note that the *OED* analyzes *escalation* as being derived by *escalate* + *-tion*. The dates of the first attestations, however, indicate a back-formation relationship (*escalation* 1938, *escalate* (in this sense) 1959).

verbs. Of these, the following are attested in the same year or later than the corresponding action nominals in *-ation*:[8]

(13)   formáte, geláte, lènáte, notáte, oláte, predáte, soláte, solváte

The derivatives in (13) all have primary stress on the last syllable. The aberrant phonological behavior of these forms is however naturally accounted for if we assume that they simply have preserved the stress pattern of their model form, i.e. the *nomen actionis*, which has primary stress on *-átion*. In sum, the phonologically aberrant behavior of these forms, together with their semantics, stresses the role of back-formation in the creation of *-ate* verbs.

The reader should note that eleven of the 25 ornative-resultative *-ate* verbs given in (12) discussed above are also attested later than their related action noun, which can be interpreted in such a way that these forms are not derived by suffixation, but are back-formations. This does, however, not challenge our analysis of ornative-resultative *-ate* verbs, but merely shows that the relationship of ornative-resultative *-ate* verbs with the corresponding *-ation* nouns is probably one of cross-formation (see Becker 1993a). The LCS in (11) should not be confused with a traditional word formation rule on the basis of which all ornative-resultative *-ate* verbs must be formed. What I have proposed instead is a semantic well-formedness condition for possible *-ate* verbs which does not entail claims about the morphological operation (affixation, back-formation, or conversion) by which they come into existence.

7.2.1.3. Other non-affixational operations

Let us look in more detail at other non-affixational operations leading to *-ate* verbs. Four forms seems to be the product of conversion (*citrate, hydroborate, phosphate, xanthate*)[9], one is a back-derived or clipped form (*patriate < repatriate*), and four derivatives are coined in analogy to other forms. Thus, *inactivate, radioactivate* and *stereoregulate* have models in the pairs *active-activate, regular-regulate*, while *plasticate* seems to follow

---

[8]   The derivatives in (13) include those that do not conform to the LCS of productive *-ate*.

[9]   I have treated derivatives as resulting from conversion if their segmental and prosodic form is unalterted.

masticate, both technical terms in rubber production (cf. the first quotation for *plastication* in the *OED*). There are five or six derivatives that are rather idiosyncratic: *dissonate* is unique because it is the only verbal derivative encountered so far that expresses a stative meaning, 'be dissonant'. Apart from this derivative, the stative meaning is never attested in neologisms involving overt affixes, but only with some zero-derived verbs. *Fidate* is a semantically opaque technical term in chess, which is most probably an intentional invention. *Pathosticate, vagulate,* and *tambourinate* are creations that only surface in the literary works of their inventors, i.e. the writers Shaw, Woolf, and Mackenzie, respectively. These forms are based on local analogies at best. *Coventrate* is apparently a loan-translation from German and an example of the kind of derivatives where *-ate* only serves to indicate the verbal category.[10]

7.2.1.4. Summary

Having discussed all types of *-ate* formations in the neologism corpus, the following picture emerges. There is a productive suffix *-ate* that has a rather restricted LCS on the one hand, and there are numerous *-ate* derivatives that do not conform to the LCS proposed for *-ate* on the other hand, and which arise from a number of different non-affixational morphological operations. With the latter group of forms it can be argued that *-ate* is merely a marker of the word's verbal status (with the pertinent syntactic and semantic implications). Quite strikingly, the two kinds of *-ate* formations reflect two different dimensions of word-formation, the syntagmatic and the paradigmatic. The postulated ornative-resultative suffix *-ate* works on a primarily syntagmatic basis in that the suffix interacts with the form it attaches to in a predictable manner. The other processes, be they back-formation, local analogy, or conversion, are paradigmatic in the sense that they crucially involve elements in absentia. Consequently, the semantic and phonological properties of the derivatives of these processes do not so much depend on the properties of the concatenated elements, i.e. bases and affixes, but on their relationship with other, non-present, elements.

---

[10]   Alternatively, *coventrate* could be analyzed as a resultative form with concomitant metonymy of *Coventry.* Under this analysis, *coventrate* is closely linked to the LCS proposed for *-ate* formartions above.

How does this analysis relate to previous accounts of *-ate*? This question takes us back to the problem that the proposed analysis could be either too general or too restrictive. In particular, one might argue for a different LCS, or for a dismissal of any specific LCS and simply take *-ate* as a category-indicating suffix. Both analyses have been proposed in the literature. Gussmann (1987), for example, assumes that *-ate* is a semi-productive causative suffix turning adjectives into verbs. Although many established *-ate* verbs exhibit this type of pattern, our data show that if it ever was a productive pattern, it no longer is. The very few adjective-based derivatives are best explained as local analogies, and not as the product of a productive or semi-productive rule. Under the analysis I propose, the lack of adjectival forms is a natural consequence of the derivational history of the forms in that the vast majority of forms either conform to (11), which excludes adjectival bases, or are back-formed on the basis of action nominals that are themselves derived from nominal bases.

Plank (1981), speaking of established *-ate* verbs, states that "with the vast majority of English *-ate* verbs, [...] there is no relationship to a lexemic base" (1981:214, my translation). He therefore suggests that *-ate* in such forms should not be regarded as "the encoding of a derivational category but as an indicator of the verbal character of the lexeme" (1981:214, my translation). A similar point is made by Marchand who finds that with a number of forms the suffix has "merely a functional value" (1969:258). As argued extensively above, the rather high number of idiosyncratic forms among both the *OED* and the Cobuild data corroborates this view of *-ate* formations.

Both Plank and Marchand, however, also acknowledge the existence of a derivational pattern with *-ate* on the basis of nouns (the former without giving a semantic analysis). This denominal pattern is formalized in the LCS given above. Discarding the proposed LCS altogether would have the strong disadvantage that it would remain unclear as to why a significant portion of derivatives should conform to this semantic structure, given the abundance of possible verbal meanings that could in principle be expressed. Furthermore, the almost complete lack of adjectival bases would be unaccounted for.

In sum, there is a remarkable difference between the neologisms involving *-ate* and those involving *-ize*. In contrast to *-ize* formations, the neologisms featuring *-ate* are extremely diverse in terms of their derivation and their meanings. Nevertheless, it was shown that there is a subgroup of *-ate* formations that behaves as coherently as do the vast majority of *-ize* forms, whereas the rest of the derivatives are the result of a variety of different morphological processes.

Finishing our remarks on the semantics of *-ate*, we may speculate over the reason why, alongside with the regular forms, so many semantically (and phonologically) diverse innovative *-ate* formations are created. One possible answer is that it is the diversity and frequency of already existing *-ate* forms that prompts the diversity and comparative proliferance of the newcomers. The analysis of the Cobuild corpus has demonstrated that, in comparison to the other overt verb-deriving affixes, *-ate* occurs in an extremely high number of both tokens and types, with even the low frequency types being highly idiosyncratic. This state of affairs makes it hard for the speaker (and the linguist) to discern a productive pattern. In terms of an analogical model (e.g. along the lines of Becker 1990), it seems that there are simply too many different possible analogical models around, with only one (namely the ornative-resultative) being more prominent.

7.2.2. The phonology of *-ate* derivatives

In the above discussion we already briefly hinted at some phonological properties of *-ate* verbs. In this section I will investigate these properties in detail, restricting my remarks to the forms listed in (12), which conform to the LCS of productive *-ate* formations. However, the majority of the other *-ate* derivatives listed in the appendix also conform to the analysis to be proposed. In (14) the pertinent forms are repeated with their stress patterns:

(14) allúviàte   cítràte   flúoridàte
      flúorinàte   fórmylàte   geláte
      hỳdròbóràte   hỳdróxylàte   íodinàte
      mércuràte   métalàte   méthanàte
      nìtrógenàte   nítrosàte   phósphàte
      phosphórylàte   prótonàte   pùpáriàte
      sílylàte   soláte   sulphónylàte
      Tárviàte   xánthàte

Although there are a number of phonologically peculiar forms, the similarity to *-ize* derivatives is striking, and we will see that the constraint hierarchies of the two affixes differ only minimally.

To begin with, we can state that *-ate* derivatives basically follow the stress pattern of nouns as described in the previous chapter. Disyllabic trochaic base words survive intact, which is the result of a constraint ranking in which FT-BIN, TROCH, NONFINALITY and IDENT-HEAD dominate R-ALIGN-HEAD (cf. (55) in chapter 6). With base words stressed on the penultima, this ranking leads to main stress on the antepenult (of the derivative), with no stress shift. This is exemplified by the majority of derivatives, as given in (15):

(15)   flúorinàte
        flúoridàte
        fórmylàte
        hỳdróxylàte
        métalàte
        méthanàte
        prótonàte
        sílylàte
        tósylàte

The base words *fluorine, fluoride* and *silyl* can also be pronounced with a diphthong, i.e. secondary stress, on the ultima.[11] The constraint model as proposed in chapter 6 predicts for these forms that the secondarily stressed syllable of the base ends up destressed in the derivative, since *CLASH-HEAD is ranked above STRESS-IDENT (see (67) in chapter 6). This has the effect that *flúorinàte, flúoridàte,* and *sílylàte* are optimal for both kinds of base word pronunciations.

The crucial systematic difference between *-ize* derivatives and *-ate* derivatives concerns the position of R-ALIGN-HEAD. With *-ize* derivatives we saw that (only) vowel-final bases are truncated due to the ranking of R-ALIGN-HEAD between MAX-C and MAX-V (see section 6.2.4.3. in the preceding chapter for illustration and discussion). Derivatives in *-ate* show a different kind of behavior in that they allow truncation with both vowel- and consonant-final dactylic base words.

Thus *allúviàte, nítrosàte, pupáriàte* (with consonant-final bases *allúvium, nítrosyl, pupárium*) and *tárviàte, mércuràte* (with vowel-final bases *Tárvia* and *mércury*) truncate their final rhymes under *-ate* suffixation, which necessitates a ranking in which both MAX-C and MAX-V are ranked below R-ALIGN-HEAD:

---

[11]   I assume that *fluoride* and *fluorine* are disyllabic, no matter whether there is a secondary stress on the ultima or not.

(16) R-ALIGN-HEAD >> MAX-C, MAX-V

a. C-final dactylic base

allúvium-ate	R-ALIGN-HEAD	MAX-C	MAX-V
al(lúvi)u(màte)	σσσ!		
☞ al(lúvi)(àte)	σσ	*	*

b. V-final dactylic base

mercury-ate	R-ALIGN-HEAD	MAX-C	MAX-V
(mércu)ry(àte)	σσσ!		
☞ (mércu)(ràte)	σσ		*

In other words, base words are shortened under suffixation of *-ate* in order
to allow main stress as far as possible to the right. The fact that these forms
do not shift the stress to the right to better satisfy R-ALIGN-HEAD indicates
that IDENT-HEAD must rank above R-ALIGN-HEAD. If this were not the
case, at least some of the forms in (15) would end up with penultimate
stress. For example, **pròtónàte* would emerge as optimal, if R-ALIGN-
HEAD dominated IDENT-HEAD. This is independent evidence for the rankings established so far, given in (17):

(17) a. FT-BIN, TROCH, NONFINALITY, IDENT-HEAD >> R-ALIGN HEAD
      b. R-ALIGN-HEAD >> MAX-C, MAX-V
      c. *CLASH-HEAD >> STRESS-IDENT

However, a small set of derivatives exhibit stress shift, which means that in
those cases IDENT-HEAD must be ranked differently. The three forms
nìtrógenàte, phosphórylàte and *sulphónylàte* are based on words which
have primary stress on their first syllable. They are stress-shifted, which
means that IDENT-HEAD is violated in order to better satisfy R-ALIGN-
HEAD. Consider for example *nìtrógenàte*:

(18) exceptions: R-ALIGN-HEAD >> IDENT-HEAD

nitrogen-ate	R-ALIGN-HEAD	IDENT-HEAD
(nítro)ge(nàte)	σσσ!	
☞ (nì)(tróge)(nàte)	σσ	*

If the dactyls *nítrogen* and *phósphoryl* were suffixed in a systematic fashion, the constraints in (16) and (17) would trigger truncation, as exemplified with the parallel base form *alluvium* in (16a).

With *sulphónylàte* (base word: [sʌ́lfənàɪl]), truncation is impossible because of high-ranking MAX-ó-V ('don't delete stressed vowels'), but again IDENT-HEAD is exceptionally dominated by R-ALIGN-HEAD:

(19)   MAX-ó-V >> R-ALIGN-HEAD >> IDENT-HEAD

sulphonyl-ate	MAX-ó-V	R-ALIGN-HEAD	IDENT-HEAD
(súlpho)(nàte)	*!	σσσ	
☞ sul(phóny)(làte)		σσ	*

Although these forms do not obey the systematic ranking of IDENT-HEAD over R-ALIGN-HEAD, they still confirm the higher rank of *CLASH-HEAD over R-ALIGN-HEAD that was already established in the previous chapter. In spite of the fact that stress can be shifted (in these cases!), stress is not shifted to the penultima, i.e. a better satisfaction of R-ALIGN-HEAD is not possible, because this would lead to a *CLASH-HEAD violation:

(20)   *CLASH-HEAD >> R-ALIGN-HEAD

nitrogen-ate	*CLASH-HEAD	R-ALIGN-HEAD
(nìtro)(gén)(àte)	*!	σ
☞ (nì)(tróge)(nàte)		σσ

Since only three forms show the peculiar violation of IDENT-HEAD, they can be regarded as idiosyncratic in this respect. Another truly exceptional form is *í.o.di.nàte*, whose base word is trisyllabic ([aí.jəd.ɪn]/[aí.jə.daɪn]/[aí.jə.din]). If systematic, the optimal derivatives would either involve truncation (i.e. *í.o.dàte* on the basis of [a.jəd.ɪn]) or no truncation and no stress shift (i.e. *í.o.dì.nàte* on the bases of [aɪ.jə.daɪn] or [aɪ.jə.dɪn]). This is however not the case, hence *í.o.di.nàte* is the only exception to the strictly alternating stress we find with *-ate* derivatives.

Another unexpected set of derivatives appear to be disyllables with primary stress on *-ate* (*geláte, oláte, soláte*). However, as already mentioned above, these forms are back-formations on the basis of input nouns *-átion*, which suggests that they have preserved the main stress of their corresponding output form on the cost of a violation of NONFINALITY. This means that IDENT-HEAD ranks above NONFINALITY. Note that it was not possible to establish this ranking for *-ize* derivatives because there are no possible correspondents with primary stress on *-ize*. It is therefore possible to analyze *geláte, oláte, soláte* as completely systematic formations, only that they are coined on the bases of nouns in *-ation*, i.e. they have another complex form as their correspondent.

Finally, there is a class of base words with secondary stress on their ultima which does not behave as predicted, namely nouns ending in the suffix *-ate*, which denote "salts formed by the action of an acid on a base, as *nitrate, acetate, sulphate, carbonate, alcoholate, ethylate*" (*OED*). In general, these base words become *-ate* verbs by conversion, as evidenced by *cítràte, hỳdròbóràte, phósphàte* and *xánthàte*. This could be interpreted as a haplology effect, i.e. the avoidance of identical nuclei in adjacent syllables (OCP-NUCLEUS, see Plag 1998). It remains however unclear, why an OCP violation could not be avoided by destressing, cf. !*cítr*[ə]*tàte*. We will leave this issue to future investigations.

To summarize our phonological analysis of *-ate* derivatives, we can state that in spite of their apparent diversity, verbs in *-ate* exhibit a rather predictable phonological gestalt, which can be captured by almost the same constraint hierarchy as the one pertaining to *-ize* derivatives. The difference lies primarily in the ranking of MAX-C below R-ALIGN-HEAD, leading to strictly alternating stress. The data could not provide evidence for the ranking of some of the constraints operating over -ize derivatives, such as *SCHWA-V, STRESS-IDENT & DEP, and OCP-ONSET, but could indicate the higher rank of IDENT-HEAD with regard to NONFINALITY. The constraint hierarchy for *-ate* derivatives is summarized in (21):

(21) Constraint hierarchy for *-ate* derivatives

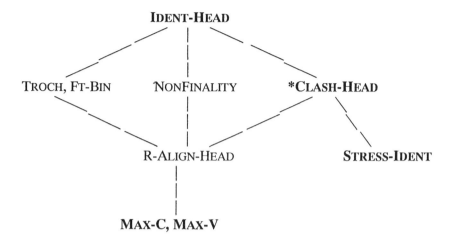

The slightly different ranking of these constraints has consequences not only for the kinds of stem allomorphy *-ize* and *-ate* may trigger, but also for the distribution of the two suffixes, as we will see in chapter 8.

7.3. Unproductive affixes: *eN-* and *-en*

I will finish the review of the structural properties of overtly marked verb-deriving processes in English by briefly looking at the attested neologisms involving the affixes *eN-* and *-en*. As indicated in table 5.1 in chapter 5, derivatives with these affixes are extremely rare, which warrants the conclusion that they are analogical formations and are not derived on the basis of a productive rule. Nevertheless, these forms share some interesting properties.

Derivatives with the prefix *eN-* seem to have a locative interpretation (*encode, endistance, envision, emplane, embus*), although an ornative meaning is also once attested (*enhat*), as well as a causative one (*embrittle*). Thus *eN-*, if used at all to create a new word, appears to be more or less reserved for the spatial meanings, which is in line with the analysis of *en-* as a spatial (prefixed) preposition, as proposed by Walinska de Hackbeil (1985).[12]

The suffix *-en* is attested with only two causative derivatives (*crispen, outen*), which notably also have earlier zero-derived equivalents. As previously mentioned, there is a phonological restriction on *-en* derivatives that the suffix may only be preceded by monosyllabic bases ending in one obstruent (optionally preceded by a sonorant). The two isolated neologisms in the *OED* at least partially conform to this restriction in that both bases end in an obstruent and are monosyllabic (*crispen, outen*).

7.4. Conversion

We may finally turn to the last of the productive processes discussed in this chapter, conversion. This process, more specifically denominal conversion, has been the most popular of all verb-deriving processes as a subject of linguistic inquiry. Accounts of the meaning of the zero-affix are extremely numerous and diverse, but all researchers agree that this is an extremely productive process. With regard to structural restrictions on this process, Bauer even states that "if there are constraints on conversion they have yet to be demonstrated" (1983:226).

Let us first take a look at the semantics of converted verbs.[13] I will not attempt to summarize the existing literature on this topic, but simply list a number of meaning categories (with examples) that have been proposed in the relevant studies (e.g. Kulak 1964, Marchand 1964, 1969, Rose 1973, Karius 1985):

---

[12]   Note that Walinska de Hackbeil's analysis also involves a zero-suffix as the head of the word, an analysis whose value seems questionable to me (see the discussion in the next section).

[13]   I use the term 'converted verb' for verbs derived by conversion.

(22) locative   'put (in)to X'   *jail*
      ornative   'provide with X'   *staff*
      causative   'make (more) X'   *yellow*
      resultative   'make into X'   *bundle*
      inchoative   'become X'   *cool*
      performative   'perform X'   *counterattack*
      similative   'act like X'   *chauffeur, pelican*
      instrumental   'use X'   *hammer*
      privative   'remove X'   *bark*
      stative   'be X'   *hostess*

Sometimes semantic categories have been suggested that cut across the ones proposed above, such as 'movement in time and space' (*jet, winter*), 'typical action of base' (*hammer*), 'typical function of base' (*cripple*), see Karius (1985). The relevance of these labels and their empirical and theoretical justification need not concern us here. What is important, however, is the growing consensus in the linguistic literature that the variety of meanings that can be expressed by zero-affixation is so large that there should be no specific meaning attached to the process of zero-derivation at all.

This position has been argued for in detail in Clark and Clark (1979) and Aronoff (1980) who claim that zero-derivation is a semantically impoverished morphological process.[14] Being a verb, the derived form must denote an Event, State, or Process. Being derived from another word, the verb must denote something that has to do with the base word. The diversity of meanings then "follows directly from the fact that the meaning of the verb is limited only to an activity which has some connection with the noun" (Aronoff 1980:747). The correct interpretation of the derived verb crucially involves non-linguistic knowledge (in a way we need not discuss here, see for example Clark and Clark 1979 for some discussion).

Let us turn to the data in the *OED*. As mentioned earlier, there are about one thousand verbs listed in the *OED* that are 20th century innovations which are not derived by suffixation. Among these are many back-derived verbs, verbs created by prefixation, parasynthesis, compounding and clipping. Excluding all these verbs plus the ones borrowed from other languages, 488 types remain of the class of verbs I was interested in, i.e. those

---

[14]   See Lieber and Baayen (1993) for a similar account of zero-derived verbs in Dutch.

words that have adopted the syntactic category of verb without any phonological marking on the surface.

These converted verbs can be classified into a number of groups with
interesting characteristics. For example, a significant proportion of derivatives have an onomatopoetic motivation (cf. e.g. *burp, chuff, clink-clank,
oink, ooh, pring,* etc.), while others have phrases as their bases (*blind-side,
cold-call, cold-cream,* etc.). A large group of forms are based on nouns,
and the smallest group is based on adjectives. Restricting ourselves to
nominal and adjectival bases, the neologisms nicely illustrate the semantic
indeterminacy of zero-derived verbs. Consider, for example, *eel,* which can
mean 'fish for eel' or 'to move ... like an eel', or *premature,* which is re-
corded as having the meaning 'Of a shell or other projectile: to explode
prematurely'. *Crew* can mean 'act as a (member of a) crew' or 'assign to a
crew', *young* is defined as 'to present the apparently younger side'
(paraphrases are cited from the *OED*). All of the meanings gleaned from
the linguistic literature and listed in (22) above are attested in the derivatives in appendix 1: locative *archive,* ornative *marmalade,*[15] causative *rustproof,* resultative *package,* inchoative *gel,* performative *tango,* similative
chauffeur, instrumental *lorry,* privative *brash,* stative *hostess.* Instrumental
derivatives seem to be the most frequent, which is in line with observations
by earlier authors, e.g. Kulak (1964), Karius (1985). In sum, converted
verbs can express all those meanings that overtly suffixed verbs can, and
many more.

Phonological restrictions seem not to be operative at all, but there are
indications of semantic and/or morphological restrictions. For instance, it
can be observed that the number of adjectival bases is rather small in comparison the number of nominal bases and onomatopoetic words. Of the 488
verbs, only 17 are derived from adjectives (*born, camp, cruel, dual, filthy,
hip, lethal, main, multiple, phoney, polychrome, premature, pretty, romantic, rustproof, skinny, young*). This is perhaps surprising in view of Gussmann's claim (1987:97) that this process is the most productive one deriving verbs from adjectives. The discrepancy between his claim and my

---

[15] There are a number of ornative verbs that are back-derived from adjectives
that are in turn derived by the suffixation of ornative *-ed* to nouns. Where
this could be discerned with some certainty (as for example with $monocle_V$ <
$monocled$ < $monocle_N$) the item was not included in the list of converted
verbs.

findings probably results from the fact that I have used only neologisms as a database whereas he has included all attested items.[16]

Gussmann (1987:82) also notes that derived adjectives do not undergo conversion. Although this generalization holds for the majority of our neologisms, it seems that it needs further qualification. Of the converted verbs, at least *filthy, partial, polychrome, premature, romantic, rustproof*, and *skinny* are based on homophonous morphologically complex adjectives. A more adequate constraint would perhaps be one which prohibits conversion from relational adjectives. Although no immediate explanation is available why this should be the case, a similar restriction is operative in nominalization, where "abstract suffixes forming quality nouns are only attachable to qualitative (or predicative) adjectives, but not to relational ones" (Rainer 1988:161). These phenomena certainly merit further investigation.

With respect to denominal conversion Marchand (1969:372) reached the conclusion that suffixed and prefixed nouns are impossible bases. Similar facts are reported for Dutch conversion into verbs by Don (1993). Marchand (1969: 372) and Bauer (1983:226) offer blocking as a possible explanation. As we have seen earlier, even if some kind of blocking effect (i.e. token-blocking) can be generally accepted as being responsible for the non-occurrence of certain kinds of formations, blocking does not totally exclude the occasional formation of doublets. Taking this into account, blocking is an uncompelling solution to the problem at hand, because there is an almost complete absence of doublets, which by itself suggests a stronger mechanism. It is unclear at the present stage what this mechanism could be.

Before we finish the discussion of zero-derived verbs let us briefly turn to the theoretical problems involved with zero-derivation. The first of these problems concerns the postulation of zero morphs, the second the input- or output-oriented nature of the rule.

There is a well-known controversy about the question of how to account for the category change of words without formal marking. Essentially two positions are conceiveable, one advocating a zero-affix of some sort, the other proposing a category change without any affixation. Most recently, Don (1993) has proposed a third, intermediate alternative, namely the af-

---

[16]   It might also be the case that the productivity of de-adjectival conversion is on the decline in contemporary English, but this question will be left to future research.

fixation of a morphosemantic AFFIX without any phonological affixation, not even Ø.

The former analysis is usually referred to as zero-derivation or zero-suffixation, the latter two as conversion. In all of the preceding discussion we have used the two terms interchangably without caring about the theoretical implications. It seems however, that the foregoing investigation has a bearing on the question of whether we are dealing with the affixation of a zero-morph or with conversion when we talk about formally unmarked derived verbs in English. I will not review all of the arguments for or against these two approaches, but simply discuss the arguments that emerge from the above examination of verbal derivation. These arguments concern the overt analogue criterion and the question of pre- vs. suffixation of zero, and seem to further undermine the zero-affix hypothesis.

The overt analogue criterion is investigated in detail in Sanders (1988), who formulates it as follows:

THE OVERT ANALOGUE CRITERION (RESTRICTED)
One word can be derived from another word of the same form in a language (only) if there is a precise analogue in the language where the same derivational function is marked in the derived word by an overt (nonzero) form.

(Sanders 1988:160-161)

Marchand implicitly uses this criterion to justify the existence of a zero-morph in English verbal derivation, as is illustrated by the following quotation:

If we compare such derivatives as *legalize, nationalize, sterilize* with vbs [verbs] like *clean, dirty, tidy*, we note that the syntactic-semantic pattern in both is the same: ... 'make, render clean, dirty, tidy' and 'make, render legal, national, sterile', respectively. ... As a sign is a two facet linguistic entity we say that the derivational morpheme is (phonologically) zero-marked in the case of *clean* 'make clean'.

(Marchand 1969:359)

Citing some interesting cases of some non-synonymous and some synonymous doublets, Sanders shows that zero and the putatively analogous overt affixes are not in complementary distribution and that zero is only sometimes, but not always in contrast with each of the overt suffixes.[17] In other words, zero and the overt suffixes fail to satisfy the overt analogue criterion. How does this relate to the present results?

The systematic investigation of the meaning of derived verbs in this chapter lends crucial support to Sanders' critical account. While Sanders' examples, though striking, could still be dismissed as isolated cases, the detailed semantic analysis of the individual processes presented above has clearly demonstrated that, while in certain areas their meaning may overlap, there are important and systematic differences between the processes. In the light of these findings, the facts presented by Sanders turn out to be systematic in nature, whereas in other approaches they must be explained away as idiosyncrasies.

The only way to satisfy the overt analogue criterion would be to assume a morphological model in which the semantics is completely separated from the phonological spell-out, such as Beard's lexeme-morpheme base morphology (e.g. 1995). I will postpone a discussion of separation theories until we have looked in more detail at the interaction of the rival processes, which will be done in the next chapter, where it is argued that separation is not a viable solution.

The second argument against a zero morph arises from the question whether the putative zero element is prefixed or suffixed. In general, the advocates of the zero morph favor zero-suffixation, a decision that is again based on the overt analogue criterion, since the rival morphs are suffixes. The zero-suffix assumption runs, however, into problems with the prefix *eN-*, as in *enlarge*, which may fulfill the same function and would therefore justify another zero-allomorph, a zero-prefix.[18] Taking into account the fact that *eN-* is no longer productive, the whole problem could of course be dismissed on the grounds that the prefixed verbs can be regarded as lexicalizations. Whereas this argument can perhaps solve the problem of *eN-*

---

17   Consider, for example, Sanders's examples *He patroned many fine artists* ≠ *He patronized many fine artists, I sectioned the article* = *I sectionized the article*. For a systematic discussion of such facts the reader is referred to the next chapter.

18   Walinska de Hackbeil (1985) has tried to solve the problem of *eN-* prefixation by positing a practically meaningless verbal zero-suffix in addition to the locative prefix *eN-*. Besides the unwarranted postulation of another zero-element (this time not only a zero-morph, but even a zero-morpheme), this anaylsis has the obvious disadvantage that it cannot account for non-locative formations like *enlarge*.

prefixation, it cannot be used to explain the problem of negative prefixation. In the domain of verb-forming affixation, negative, privative, ablative, and reversative meanings are exclusively expressed by prefixes, such as *un-*, *de-* and *dis-*, while all other possible meanings are expressed by suffixes (and the prefixes *eN-* and *be-*).[19] The problem now is that the putative zero-suffix can also express negative meanings, thus strongly suggesting the existence of a negative zero-prefix, if we follow the overt analogue criterion. Hence, advocates of the zero-affix would have to posit not only one, but two verb-deriving zero-affixes, one of them a suffix (with a rather general verbal meaning), the other a prefix (with negative, privative, ablative or reversative meaning). It seems that there is even less empirical and theoretical justification for two different verbalizing zero-affixes than there was for one.

The last theoretical problem to be mentioned is the nature of the rules involved. It was already pointed out that many linguists assume the existence of a nominal, and of an adjectival conversion or zero-suffixation rule. The data in appendix 1 indicate however, that, subject to the restrictions discussed above, any kind of sign may undergo conversion into verbs: nouns, adjectives, prepositions, echo words, and phrases.[20] Since semantically there is no reason to postulate different rules on the bases of syntactically different input categories, these findings call for an output-oriented rule of conversion.[21]

---

[19]   See, for example, Marchand (1973), Colen (1980/81). I am not aware of any convincing explanation for this firm generalization. Note that the morphological expression of negativity in Romance languages is also restricted to prefixes (e.g. Blank 1997). See Lieber and Baayen (1993) for an analysis of similar Dutch verbs.

[20]   This state of affairs is similar to compounding, where, as convincingly argued by Wiese (1996c), not only phrases may enter compounds (cf. *the Charles-and-Di-syndrome*), but even non-linguistic signs.

[21]   The fact that verbs do not seem to undergo conversion is straighforwardly explained. Conversion of verbs into verbs is both phonologically and semantically vacuous. An output-oriented rule of conversion has recently been advocated on the basis of phonological evidence by Kouwenberg (1997) for Papiamento, a Spanish-based Caribbean Creole language.

7.5. Summary

In this and the preceding chapter I have proposed a new structural analysis of the individual verb-deriving processes in English on the basis of a large number of 20th century neologisms. It was demonstrated that the semantically most versatile process is conversion, followed by *-ize/-ify*, and *-ate*, in this order. Interestingly, this ranking in terms of semantic versatility is very similar to the productivity ranking of these processes, which is unsurprising, because, other things being equal, the semantically most general process can be expected to give rise to the highest number of new formations. Another important finding is that, apart from *-ify/-ize* and contrary to statements found in the literature, the processes in question are semantically not identical, a fact whose consequences will be further discussed in the next chapter.

Furthermore, it was argued that restrictions concerning the syntactic category of the base can be disposed of because they fall out from the semantic properties of the process in question. In addition, it became clear that there are important and complex restrictions at work concerning the phonology of possible derivatives. These restrictions are accounted for in a straightforward manner by output-oriented constraints, which do not only influence the productivity of a process but also determine stem allomorphy, i.e. the phonological shape of the derivatives, and the choice between *-ize* and *-ify*. Thus, for example, the strikingly diverse morphophonological alternations accompanying the formation of *-ize* derivatives can be elegantly explained by a uniform set of prosodic and segmental output constraints.

Having outlined in some detail the individual structural properties of the rival morphological processes we are now well-equipped for an expedition into the strange land of suffixal rivalry, which will be explored in the next chapter.

8. Rival morphological processes 4: Where have all the rivals gone?

The central question I would like to answer in this chapter is which mechanisms regulate the selection of the appropriate affix with a given base. The solution of this problem has important consequences for certain theoretical issues such as the role of paradigmatic mechanisms in morphology or the modeling of morphological processes. It will turn out that the distribution of affixes is largely governed by the individual properties of the processes in question, complemented only by token-blocking and local analogy. This analysis supports a sign-based view of morphology and challenges separationist theories like Beard's (e.g. 1995).

In order to investigate their rivalry, the processes will be compared with each other, starting with *-ize* and *-ify*. Before we turn to this task, I will briefly define what is meant by the term 'rival'. In general, morphological processes are regarded as rival if they are phonologically distinct but semantically identical. This phenomenon is also often discussed under the label of affix synonymy, and in separationist approaches to morphology synonymy is one of the central arguments for these theories. On closer inspection, however, it turns out that many of the putatively rival processes are not really rivals in this sense.

For example, Baayen and Lieber (1991) claim that the English adjectival suffixes *-ous* and *-ish* are rivals, one attaching to Latinate bases, the other to Germanic bases. Malkiel (1977) demonstrates however that the two are not synonymous, *-ish* deriving a qualitative adjective indicating similarity, *-ous* being purely relational. The notorious couple *-ity* and *-ness* is a parallel case, since, as convincingly argued by Riddle (1985), these two suffixes exhibit subtle semantic differences. A similar point is made by Doyle (1992) with respect to Irish nominalizations. From these studies one can draw the conclusion that the domains in which two processes are actual rivals are often much smaller than standardly assumed. In some cases no overlap exists at all, making the assumption of rivalry an artefact of an insufficient analysis. The remaining overlap between domains may be further curtailed by additional restrictions, e.g. phonological ones, with the consequence that the number of cases where there is indeed a choice between affixes is further reduced.

What does this mean for the verb-deriving processes in English? As already mentioned in the previous chapter, the different affixes are not completely synonymous but merely overlap in meaning to varying degrees. This finding leads to a considerable reduction in the number of potentially rival forms. As we will shortly see, the phonological restrictions on the suffixes further diminish the potentially overlapping domains. The remaining truly rival domains are often very small, so that the number of actually competing derivatives is drastically diminished. It will become clear that in the remaining phonologically and semantically overlapping domains no additional restrictions can be discerned. In other words, the overall distribution of the affixes is only restricted by the particular combinatorial characteristics of each individual affix, i.e. its semantic and phonological properties.

8.1. *-ize* vs. *-ify*

As was shown in the preceding chapter, the derivatives in *-ize* and *-ify* are phonologically conditioned allomorphs whose distribution is regulated by the constraint hierarchy developed in the previous chapters. It was shown that the two allomorphs are almost complementarily distributed, with the domains of *-ify* and *-ize* overlapping only with vowel-final trochaic bases. Without making additional assumptions, one would predict the occurrence of doublets (at least with some less frequent words that fail to be token-blocked). *Dandify* and *dandyize* was mentioned as an example of such doublets. There are also a few doublets where *-ify* is attached to a monosyllabic bound root, whereas -ize attaches to the disyllabic stem:

(1)   sinicize/sinify, plasticize/plastify, technicize/technify

In sum, apart from the proposed constraint hierarchy no other mechanisms are needed to regulate the competition of *-ify* and *-ize*.

8.2. *-ize* vs. *-ate*

Productively formed derivatives in *-ate* can realize only a small subset of the meanings attested for *-ize* and *-ify* derivatives, with an additional semantic restriction on the potential base words. In van Marle's terms (1985, 1986), *-ate* could be regarded as the systematic special case in contrast to the more general cases of -*ize* and -*ify*. Assuming type-blocking to be operative, one would predict that -*ate* wins over -*ize* in its more specific semantic domain, if no other restrictions intervene. As we will shortly see, this prediction is wrong.

Phonologically, the domains of -*ize* and -*ate* overlap considerably, making -*ate* derivatives and -*ize* derivatives much more similar to each other than to verbs in -*ify*. Formations involving the former two suffixes have in common that both suffixes take secondary stress, both need an unstressed syllable preceding it, and both may involve the deletion of base-final segments. They differ in that formations in -*ate* have strictly alternating stress, while -*ize* may tolerate two preceding adjacent unstressed syllables under the specific conditions discussed in chapter 6. The stress pattern of the two kinds of derivatives may therefore contrast in such a way that -*ate* formations are always primarily stressed on the antepenult, while -*ize* verbs may also be stressed on the pre-antepenult. With trochaic bases the suffixes behave similarly.

With these semantic and phonological similarities in mind, let us look at potentially rival formations, i.e. those potential and attested forms that express the ornative-resultative meaning and conform to the semantic restriction on the base words ('chemical substance'). Consider first the derivatives in (2).

(2)   chémicalìze   !chémicàte
        dígitalìze   !dígitàte
        rádiumìze   !rádiàte
        sáccharinìze   !sáccharàte
        vítaminìze   !vítamàte

In the left column of (2) all attested neologisms in -*ize* are listed that conform to the semantics of -*ate* verbs and that also feature a stress lapse. Since -*ate* does not tolerate stress lapses at all (R-ALIGN-HEAD >> MAX-C), potential forms in -*ate* would have to involve the truncation of the base-final rhyme (as in the right column). Although none of the forms in the right column are attested in the *OED*, they are possible -*ate* verbs.[1]

_____

[1]   One reason for the non-attestation of the verbs in the right column might be the tendency towards phonological transparency in productive morphology. Thus, speakers may tend to avoid truncation if a semantically equivalent alternative is available that is phonologically more transparent (cf. Cutler 1981).

In (3) below I have listed *-ate* formations where the corresponding *-ize* word is not attested but seems entirely possible and well-formed, both in semantic and in phonological terms:

(3)   cannulate   !cannulize
       fluorinate   !fluorinize
       formylate   !formylize
       hydroxylate   !hydroxylize
       mercurate   !mercurize
       protonate   !protonize

Crucially, there are also neologims in *-ize* which are unparalleled by the equally possible *-ate* formations. Consider the data in (4):

(4)   !strychninate   strychninize
       !spheroidate   spheroidize
       !trypsinate   trypsinize
       !silanate   silanize

Finally, there are also two doublets, given in (5):

(5)   fluoridate   fluoridize[2]
       nitrógenize (1846-66)   nitrógenàte (1927)[3]

The data in (2) to (5) reveal that type-blocking does not play any role in the distribution of *-ize* and *-ate*. Rather, where both suffixes are semantically and phonologically licensed, both can in principle be attached. Sometimes, only one of the two is attested, sometimes the other, sometimes both. Again, the distribution can be accounted for without positing restrictions that go beyond the ones stated already for the individual affixes.

---

[2]   *Fluoridize* occurs as an adjectivally used present participle in the *OED* (see section 6.1., appendix 1). It is first attested in 1911.

[3]   Another doublet expressing an ornative meaning is *structurate - structurize*, which, however, does not conform to the semantic restriction that bases must denote chemical substances.

8.3. -ate vs. -ify

In general, a similar picture emerges here as with *-ize* and *-ify,* in that the domains of *-ify* and *-ate* do hardly overlap. Since *-ate* is monosyllabic and subject to almost the same constraint hierarchy as *-ize* derivatives, the distributional effects are very similar. Recall that *-ify* prefers iambic bases, *-ate* trochaic ones, with both types of derivatives needing strictly alternating stress. The only systematic overlap is (again) with disyllabic bases ending in an unstressed vowel, which, however, do not surface in the data, since the words denoting chemical substances do either end in other segments, or have more than two syllables. This makes, for example, *mercurate* (or !*mercurize*, for that matter) the only possible forms.

In sum, both suffixes may in principle form ornative/resultative verbs on the basis of nouns denoting chemical substances, but the actual domain where *-ate* and *-ize* are in competition is extremely small, due to the pertinent phonological restrictions.

8.4. Conversion vs. *-ize, -ify* and *-ate*

We may now turn to the discussion of conversion in relation to the overt suffixes. Semantically, conversion is the most general case in that the meanings of the derivatives with overt suffixes are a subset of the possible meanings of converted verbs. This means that all of the bases attested with the overt suffixes could, in principle, have undergone conversion instead of overt affixation. What made the speakers choose the overt affixes instead? It seems that one reason for this choice lies in the more specific meaning these suffixes express in comparison to the completely indeterminate meaning of conversion.[4] As was pointed out above, the interpretation of converted items relies on the linguistic and extra-linguistic context to an even greater extent than the interpretation of, say, *-ize* derivatives. Thus, from the view of perception, overtly affixed forms are better than converted items. Furthermore, conversion does not apply to certain kinds of derived adjectives nor to derived nouns, which makes these classes of base words exclusively susceptible to overt suffixation. A look at the neolo-

---

4   This effect may also be responsible for the slight preponderance of derivatives with the more specific *-ate* in (3) versus (4) above.

gisms in appendix 1 corroborates this, since, at least with *-ize*, a high proportion of base words are morphologically complex.[5]

In fact, of the 488 converted verbs only 79 (17 deadjectival and 62 denominal ones) actually express meanings that are also associated with the overt suffixes. If we compare this figure with the number of *-ize* derivatives, we see that it is only about one fourth of the number of *-ize* neologisms in the *OED*. This difference can be interpreted in such a way that conversion is certainly not the most productive process in important semantic domains. The semantically rival forms are listed in section 5 in appendix 1.

Incidentally, not all of the base forms of these 79 converted verbs could have been overtly suffixed, since there are other restrictions at work. One restriction holding for all overt suffixes which I have not yet discussed, is that compounds cannot be suffixed by *-ize, -ify* and *-ate*. However, as mentioned in the previous chapter, compounds may readily be turned into verbs by conversion. Of the compound-based converted verbs listed in appendix 1, the following express meanings that are also found with overtly suffixed verbs: *cobweb, cold-cream, highlight, mothball, pothole, rustproof, scapegoat, streamline, waymark*. A parallel restriction seems to hold for base forms involving the prefixed elements *multi- (multiplex), cross- (cross-reference)* and *super- (supercoil)*, which do not undergo overt suffixation either. The reason for this impossibility is probably not morphological but phonological. English compounds, as well as the forms with the said prefixes, seem to exhibit a stress pattern that is incompatible with the prosodic restrictions imposed on the derivatives involving overt suffixes.[6] Taking these restrictions into consideration the overlapping domain is further curtailed.

---

5   The high frequency of complex bases with *-ize* is not only due to its semantics but also due to the toleration of stress lapses. Many suffixed adjectives, for example, are dactyls or end in a dactyl (e.g. *federal*).

6   Thus, there seem to be no mechanisms available to accomodate compound stress to the stress patterns overtly affixed verbs must conform to. The details of this phenomenon still need to be worked out.

     Note that derivatives on the basis of words featuring *photo-* as their first element (*photoisomerize, photosensitize, photosynthesize*) are not compounds. This is evidenced by their stress pattern, which runs counter to the compound stress rule: the base words are pronounced with primary stress on the second element. In other words, *photo-* behaves like a combining form (Bauer 1983:213), and not like a noun. This analysis is in accordance with

With regard to the remaining group of truly competing formations a number of overtly suffixed forms are indeed attested (some of them 20th century forms). Consider the forms in (6), where the converted verbs are listed in the left column, their suffixed rivals in the right column:

(6)

carbon	carbonize
dolomite	dolomitize
dual	dualize
filthy	filthify
gas	gasify
gel	gelate
indemn	indemnify
lethal	lethalize
phagocyte	phagocytize
polychrome	polychromatize
propadanda	propagandize
pressure	pressurize
pretty	prettify
quinine	quinize
romantic	romanticize
satire	satirize
zero	zeroize

The majority of the derivatives on the left are synonymous to those on the right, which shows again that token-blocking is not to be expected with low frequency items.

The patterning of the data involving overtly suffixed forms as against converted verbs lead to the same conclusions as the findings presented in the previous sections. The semantic and phonological properties of the individual processes curtail the possible overlap of rival domains to a large extent. The number of actually competing forms is therefore much smaller than previously conceived, and in the truly rival domain all affixes are applicable.

---

the meaning conveyed by *photo-* in the above derivatives: 'having to do with light', not 'having to do with photographs'.

8.5. Summary

The foregoing discussion has clearly shown that it is the semantic properties of bases and individual affixes as well as affix-specific phonological
constraints that   govern the distribution of verb-deriving morphological
processes in English. In the remaining area, where no constraints are violated and semantic interpretations overlap, the choice of a particular process or affix is essentially arbitrary, i.e. it cannot be predicted on structural
grounds. This area is however, much smaller than standardly assumed. The
notion of type-blocking was shown to be inadequate and should be dismissed. The only paradigmatic forces at work are token-blocking and different kinds of local analogies, both of which are mechanisms independently needed in any adequate morphological theory.

8.6. Theoretical implications: Against the separation of form and meaning in morphology

The findings presented in this and the preceding chapter have important
implications for a central issue in morphological theory, the relation of
form and meaning in complex words. I will argue in this section that the
properties of verb-deriving processes provide strong arguments for a sign-
based model of morphology, and against theories that try to separate form
and meaning in morphology (e.g. Beard 1995, Don 1993, Gussmann 1987,
Szymanek 1985). It is important to note that the label 'sign-based' should
not be confused with 'morpheme-based'.[7] My use of the former term refers
to the output-oriented nature of morphological processes which I have
frequently pointed out in the preceding chapters, and which has recently
been argued for in detail by Orgun (1996).

My central arguments against separation as they emerge from the foregoing investigation concern two points, the polysemy of individual processes and the putative synonymy of competing processes. A similar approach is taken in Booij (1986). His objections against separationism are,
however, almost exclusively based on the analysis of polysemy. The implications of rival processes are only very briefly discussed in that article and

---

[7]   It may not have escaped the reader's attention that I have avoided the use of
the term 'morpheme' as far as possible. The theoretical problems involved
with this term are notorious and need not be repeated here.

summarized in the final remark that "we should ... develop a more sophisticated theory of how word-formation rules with competing affixes interact"
(1986:505). This is what I have tried to do in the foregoing chapters.

Before discussing these points in detail, I will briefly summarize the key
ideas of separationist theories, referring mainly to the work of Robert
Beard (e.g. 1981, 1987a, 1987b, 1988, 1990a, 1990b, 1995), who has developed the most sophisticated of these theories, so-called Lexeme-
Morpheme-Base Morphology (LMBM).

8.6.1. The separation hypothesis

Separationist theories aim at finding a principled solution to the frequently
observed mismatches between form and function in morphology. One affix
may often express a number of different grammatical or semantic functions, whereas one function is often expressed by a whole range of affixes
including zero. Consider, for example, English plural nouns which can be
marked by a number of different suffixes (e.g. *-s* as in *dogs, -en* as in *oxen,*
-Ø as in *sheep*). At the same time, these suffixes are used elsewhere in the
language to mark completely different categories. For instance, the suffix
-s expresses also third person singular on verbs (as in *works*) and genitive
case (as in *Mary's*), and the suffix *-en* is used for the purposes of verbal
derivation (*black - to blacken*). To complicate matters further for sign-
based theories, there appear to be affixes that are meaningless. Thus, the
suffix *-al* in words such as *syntactical,* or *dramatical* can be omitted without change of meaning, which is an indication of the meaninglessness of
-al in these derivatives. Similarly, in German compounds one often finds a
linking element (so-called *Fugenmorphem,* as in *Verwaltung-s-gebäude*
'administration building') that does not carry any meaning (see e.g. Wiese
1996a:143-147 for some discussion).

Although traditional sign-based approaches to morphology (called LMH-
theories by Beard, from 'Lexical Morpheme Hypothesis') acknowledge the
existence of such mismatches, ancillary theories are needed to explain
these violations of the assumed one-to-one correspondence of form and
meaning. For example, in order to account for the versatility of *-s* in English, LMH-morphologists would have to posit three homophonous suffixes
-s, each with its own function. Although this leads to a perhaps undesired
proliferation of suffixes, there are independent arguments for such an approach, namely that there are striking differences in behavior between
these three suffixes. One suffix *-s* attaches to verbs, the other attaches to

nouns, and the third (i.e. the clitic) attaches to noun phrases (hence -*s* on verbs is never interpreted as plural marking, for example). In addition, the nominal suffix and the clitic differ in their allomorphy due to haplology effects, i.e. the clitic has a zero-allomorph which surfaces after plural -*s* (e.g. *the boys'*). In a sign-based approach such differences between suffixes are expected.

Separationist theories solve the problem in a more principled way by strictly separating meaning and form in morphology by postulating the independence of lexical derivation from its morphological spell-out. In this view, morphological asymmetry results from using several spelling operations to express a single derivation or from a single spelling operation used to express several derivations (Beard 1995:47-48). The central claim is that "the dissociation of derivation and morphology in word formation and inflection accounts for asymmetries of affixal sound and meaning such as polysemy, synonymy, zero and empty morphology, which plague other approaches" (Beard 1990a:103).

Let us illustrate this with one of Beard's own examples, deadjectival nominalizations (Beard 1995:50-51). There are at least five suffixes which are used to mark such nouns in English, -*th, -ce, -ity, -ness,* and -*Ø*:

(7)   warm   warm-th
       intelligent   intelligen-ce
       readable   readabil-ity
       slow   slow-ness
       white   white-Ø

To account for these facts Beard assumes that there is only one rule of lexical derivation with five possible spell-out operations. The derivational rule does no more than transpose underlying qualitative adjectives into nouns. The crucial argument for the existence of such a unitary derivational rule is of course that the meaning of the different suffixes in (7) is identical. Note also that the restriction of the lexical derivational rule to non-relational adjectives holds for all suffixes. According to LMBM, the appropriate phonological spell-out of the derivational rule is done separately and is conditioned by different restrictions (such as the phonological make-up of the base, the semantics of the base, etc.). Hence Beard can state that "[a]ffixation [i.e. morphological spell-out, I.P.] truly operates on conditions that differ radically from those determining derivation (meaning)" (Beard 1995:51). No ancillary theories are needed to solve the mismatches: zero morphology is derivation without subsequent spell-out operations (see *white*~NOUN~), empty morphemes are spell-out operations without derivation (see *syntactic-al* above), and morphological asymmetry in general results from the multiple mapping of derivations and spell-out possibilities. All mismatches predicted by this model occur and other types of mismatches do not occur.

Having outlined the basic ideas of separationist theories, let us see how separationist theories deal with verbal derivation in English.

8.6.2. *Verbal derivation and the separation hypothesis*

In the foregoing chapters I have put forward a sign-based theory of verbal derivation where each class of derivatives has its own semantic and phonological properties. Separationist theories proposed completely different accounts. In this section, I will argue in detail that a sign-based approach is preferable.

Gussmann (1987) claims that there is a derivational rule ("the uniform semanto-syntactic formula whereby adjectives become verbalized", Gussmann 1987:82), with the meaning 'make (more) X', where X stands for the adjective. The pertinent spell-out operations include the affixes *eN-, be-, -en, -ify, -ize, -ate* and Ø. However, such an account can neither account for the differences in meaning between the different affixes, nor can it explain the polysemy of individual affixes.

To save the separationist approach (also with regard to denominal verbal derivation) one could perhaps postulate a number of different derivational rules such as stative, inchoative, causative, ornative (cf. Szymanek 1988:180-181), mapped onto the morphological spell-out rules in complex ways. This solution leads, however, to a proliferation of derivational rules for which there is no independent evidence. Thus, I fail to see how the derivational rules can be motivated, if not through their manifestation in speech. Szymanek (1988) proposes that the derivational categories are ultimately grounded in cognitive concepts. While this may well be the case, a direct connection between the cognitive categories and the derivational categories can be excluded in view of the abundance of differences between the derivational categories across languages. The derivational categories can therefore only be motivated by making reference to the individual signs in the specific language.[8] The fact that semantic categories like causation play a role in so many languages speaks for the universality of the concept, but not necessarily for the separation hypothesis. It is thus unclear to me how many derivational rules one would have to propose in order to account for the many different interpretations of our derived verbs, and how the selection of these rules can be independently justified. In sum, Gussmann's separationist account of verbal derivation should be rejected.

In a more recent treatment of verbal derivation, Beard (1995: chapter 8) offers another solution within the separationist framework. He argues that *-ize, -ify, -ate,* and Ø are spell-out operations of two different derivations, the transposition of nouns into verbs and the transposition of adjectives into verbs. In his theory, transposition is a lexical derivation without semantic content which only changes the syntactic category of the base. Transposition thus contrasts with so-called functional derivation, which has a semantic effect on the base. Agentive *-er* as in *baker* and locative *-ery* as in *bakery* are examples of functional derivation.

With regard to de-adjectival verbal derivation, the change of category is performed by the neutralization of the adjectival feature [gradable] and the assignment of the feature [+/- transitive]. According to Beard, the causative and inchoative meanings of *-ize, -ify* and *-ate* derivatives result from the feature [+/- transitive] via so-called correspondence rules, which are required to interpret this feature in semantics. The correspondence rules are given in (8) and (9) (taken from Beard 1995:181-182):

(8)   If the output of a verbal transposition is marked [- transitive] assign it the predicate structure [BECOME (XY)] and coindex Y with the R-representation [i.e. the semantic representation, I.P.] of the base.

---

[8]   Beard (1990b) gleans independent evidence for the postulation of the derivational category 'deadjectival nominalizations' from the fact that across languages, competing processes all entail feminine gender. Impressive though this may be, feminine gender (at least in German) is not only characteristic of deadjectival nominalization but also of deverbal nominalization, a fact that considerably weakens Beard's argument. But what does it tell us that all kinds of nominalizations tend to adopt a certain gender? In my view it tells us that certain derivational processes share certain linguistic properties, no more, no less. Even under a separationist approach such similarities are not entailed by the theory.

(9)   If the output of a verbal transposition is marked [+ transitive] as-
        sign it the predicate structure [CAUSE (XY$_i$ [BECOME (Y$_i$Z)])]
        and coindex Z with the R-representation [i.e. the semantic repre-
        sentation, I.P.] of the base.

Beard (1995:182) acknowledges the problem that there are zero-derived
verbs such as *to hammer* or *to brush* that have meanings "even more specific" than predicted by the correspondence rules in (8) or (9). According
to his analysis such instrumental meanings can be predicted from the semantic representation of the noun, which specifies its natural function as
being an instrument. This functional feature is then selected for the verbal
meaning.
    Leaving technical details of semantic representation aside, there are a
number of problems with the assumption of transposition and with correspondence rules such as (8) and (9). First, as Beard himself admits, the
correspondence rules are necessary to interpret the newly assigned feature
[+/- transitive]. However, the introduction of correspondence rules makes
transposition practically indistinguishable from functional derivation. If
semantically empty transposition needs to be enriched by semantic correspondence rules I can see no reason why the semantic effect should not be
directly encoded as in functional L-derivation. To complicate matters further, it seems that for the semantic interpretation of instrumental verbs like
to hammer, correspondence rules are equally needed. Thus I fail to see by
which other mechanism "all features denoting anything other than the natural function may be ignored when the noun is used in a verbal context"
(Beard 1995:183). Taking these problems seriously means that the semantics of verbal derivation cannot be reduced to a unitary transposition rule
but must involve semantically different derivations, at least for instrumental verbs such as *to hammer* and causative/inchoative verbs such as *crystal-
lize*. Hence, the crucial assumption of affix synonymy needs to be given up.

    Second, as shown in the previous chapters, the semantics of *-ize/-ify* and
-ate are much more complex than suggested by Beard's correspondence
rules. They cannot be explained by semantically empty transposition, even
if the transposition is enhanced by the correspondence rules in (8) and (9).
Furthermore, the clear semantic differences between *-ify* and *-ize* on the
one hand, and *-ate* on the other are unaccounted for. In essence, Beard's
approach suffers from a superficial semantic analysis.
    Third, under the assumption that zero-derivation and overt suffixation are
indeed completely synonymous, it would be surprising if the kinds of more

specific meanings (such as instrumental) we frequently observe with converted verbs were confined to this sub-class of derived verbs. But this is exactly what the data show. In a sign-based approach this fact is naturally accounted for, since each class of derivatives has its own semantic and phonological properties. This brings us to the the crucial argument for separationist approaches to morphology, the assumed existence of total synonymy of affixes. If affixes are sound-meaning entities they should behave like other sound-meaning entities, i.e. lexemes. With lexemes one can never observe complete synonymy. Hence, sign-based theories predict approximate synonymy of affixes, whereas "LMBM predicts absolute, not approximate synonymy among morphological forms" (Beard, 1995:78, see also Beard 1990b).

It was already pointed out at the beginning of this chapter that the assumption of absolute affix synonymy is problematic. Upon closer inspection, putatively synonymous affixes have turned out to show subtle differences in meaning (e.g. Malkiel 1977, Riddle 1985, Doyle 1992). Crucially, this is also the case with regard to verbal derivation in English. Although there is undoubtedly a certain amount of overlap in meaning between the different verb-deriving processes, the detailed semantic analysis in the foregoing chapters has shown that the meaning of -ize and -ify derivatives on the one hand clearly differs from that of -ate derivatives, and the semantics of all kinds of overtly suffixed derived verbs markedly differ from that of converted verbs. In sum, the meanings of the different processes are similar to each other, but still far from being identical. This parallels the situation of lexemes, which in general can only have near synonyms. Only -ify and -ize seem to show the kind of absolute synonymy envisioned by Beard, and we have argued that this is a case of phonologically-conditioned suppletion.

Another argument against Beard's theory is that the verb-deriving affixes quite clearly exhibit polysemy. Hence, Beard's claim that LMH theories tend to produce too many cases of homonymous affixes or involve arbitrary decisions between homonymy and polysemy does not hold in our case. In the sign-based, output-oriented model proposed in this book, the polysemy of the derivatives follows from the same semantic mechanisms that are responsible for the polysemy of non-complex signs, i.e. simplex lexemes. Furthermore, the separationist model cannot explain the polysemy peculiar to the invidual processes. In a separationist model, it is unclear why an individual affix should spell out just the derivational categories it does and not others. For example, why should one verbal suffix spell out different meanings that are related in a specific way? In a sign-based model this follows again from the mechanisms of semantic extension that are characteristic of polysemy in general, i.e. also of the polysemy of simplex lexemes.

Another drawback of a separationist account of derived verbs in English concerns the kinds of restriction that govern the choice of the individual affix. Beard argues that semantic and syntactic restrictions may govern the choice of a particular spell-out operation. For example, null marking in deadjectival nominalizations (see again (7) above) is restricted by the semantic property of its base word (it must be a color term, Beard 1995:50). If affixation is a purely phonological spell-out process, it is strange that its application depends on non-phonological properties of the base word. Beard is right to assume (and chapters 4 through 8 have provided ample evidence for this) that indeed many different kinds of properties together may be responsible for the choice of a particular affix. But this is an argument for a sign-based approach, because (only) in a sign-based approach phonological and non-phonological information is not separated.

My last argument against separationist morphology is output-orientedness. Beard's theory is essentially a process-oriented model of morphology, making crucial use of traditional rule mechanisms. This study has however demonstrated the empirical and theoretical superiority of output-oriented approaches to morphological processes over rule-based ones. For example, I proposed that in verbal derivation, reference to the syntactic category of the base word is superfluous. This seems not possible in Beard's approach, where for example two transpositional rules are needed to take care of denominal and deverbal affixation. Notably, output-oriented accounts necessarily stress the sign character of complex formations.

To summarize, we have seen that the properties and peculiarities of verbal derivation in English are impossible to explain in a morphological theory that completely separates form and meaning. Exisiting separationist accounts erroneously assume absolute affix synonymy and do not adequately handle the polysemy of individual affixes. The distribution and productivity of the different verb-deriving processes can only be predicted on the basis of the semantic and phonological properties of each class of complex verb, which is impossible to account for under a separationist model in which the mapping of form and meaning is essentially coincidental.

9. Conclusion

This book started out with the statement that the mechanisms responsible for the productivity of morphological processes are still ill-understood. After having clarified the notion of productivity and how it can possibly be measured, a broad range of suffixes were investigated in order find out more about the machinery necessary to deal with their combinatorial properties. The gist of the argument was that most of the responsible factors lie with the individual properties of a given process and that more general mechanisms can be severely restricted.

We then narrowed our focus down to one of the most intriguing problems in derivational morphology, the nature of rival processes, with basically the same conclusions emerging. The close inspection of the structural properties of the individual verb-deriving processes revealed that the productivity and distribution of these processes fall out once these properties are correctly described.

On the theoretical level, the foregoing study has argued for a sign-based, output-oriented model of derivational morphology, and against theories that want to separate meaning and form in morphology. Coming back to the general, i.e. not rule-specific, restrictions proposed in the literature (and summarized and discussed in chapter 3.3.), it seems that only the last three hold up against the empirical evidence: the unitary output hypothesis, blocking, and stratal constraints. The unitary output hypothesis is inherent in an output-oriented approach and need not be commented on in more detail. Token-blocking (but not type-blocking) is certainly a relevant factor restricting productivity, but it was argued that it is much less a structural than a processing constraint. Stratal constraints are also relevant in some areas of derivation but contra earlier claims by Gussmann (1987), for example, they seem to be of minor influence when it comes to verbal derivation. Nevertheless, further investigation of the stratal constraints is needed to clarify their nature and relevance.

This book has also made a contribution to methodological issues pertaining to the study of word structure. Thus, the most important insights into the nature of the verbal derivation were gained on the basis of the analysis of large numbers of neologisms. By restricting the data in this way it was possible to arrive at significant generalizations concerning the properties of possible words that go beyond what can be found in earlier treatments. The *OED on CD* turned out to be a powerful tool for this kind of approach and allowed the coverage of a broad range of data. Furthermore, it was demonstrated that the *OED* can be used even for measuring the productivity of a given process, provided that one is aware of its shortcomings. The application of Baayen's text-corpus-based measures to derived verbs as manifested in the Cobuild corpus indicated that these statistical measures are useful for the determination of the productivity of overt affixation, if employed carefully, and if complemented by a qualitative investigation.

Returning to the central problem of productivity, this study, like many others before, has argued that the productivity of a given morphological process can largely be predicted on the basis of the process's peculiar structural properties and restrictions. However, I have also demonstrated that even in a seemingly well-described language like English surprisingly little is known when it comes to the exact formulation of these properties. The foregoing study can therefore be read as a case study laying out a possible research agenda for future in-depth investigations of other derivational processes in English and other languages.

References

Adams, Valerie
    1973   *An Introduction to English Word-formation*. London: Longman.

Akmajian, Adrian—Richard A. Demers—Robert M. Harnish
    1979   *Linguistics: An Introduction to Language and Communication*. Cambridge: MIT Press.

Alber, Birgit
    1998   "Interaction between Morphology and Stress Assignment in Optimality Theory", in Wolfgang Kehrein—Richard Wiese (eds.) *Phonology and Morphology of the Germanic Languages*, 113-141. Tübingen: Niemeyer.

Alderete, John
    1995   "Faithfulness to Prosodic Heads". Ms., University of Massachusetts. Rutgers Optimality Archive.

Algeo, John
    1971   "The Voguish Uses of *non-*", *American Speech* 46, 87-105.

Allen, Margaret
    1979   *Morphological Investigations*. PhD thesis, University of Connecticut.

Anderson, Stephen R.
    1988   "Morphology as a Parsing Problem", *Linguistics* 26, 521-544.
    1992   *A-morphous Morphology*. Cambridge: CUP.

Anshen, Frank—Mark Aronoff
    1981   "Morphological Productivity and Phonological Transparency", *Canadian Journal of Linguistics* 26, 63-72.
    1988   "Producing Morphologically Complex Words", *Linguistics* 26, 641-655.

Anshen, Frank—Mark Aronoff—Roy Byrd—Judith Klavans
    1986   "The Role of Etymology and Word-length in English Word-formation", ms., SUNY Stonybrook/IBM Thomas Watson Research Center, Yorktown Heights, NY.

Archangeli, Diana
    1997   "Optimality Theory: An Introduction to Linguistics in the 1990s", in Diana Archangeli—Terence Langendoen (eds.) *Optimality Theory: An Overview*, 1-32. Oxford: Blackwell.

Archangeli, Diana—Terence Langendoen (eds.)
1997   *Optimality Theory: An Overview*. Oxford: Blackwell.

Aronoff, Mark
1976   *Word Formation in Generative Grammar*. Cambridge: MIT Press.
1980a   "Contextuals", *Language* 56, 744-758.
1980b   "The Relevance of Productivity in a Synchronic Description of Word Formation", in Jacek Fisiak (ed.) *Historical Morphology*, 71-82. The Hague—Paris—New York: Mouton.
1983   "Potential Words, Actual Words, Productivity and Frequency", in Shirô Hattori—Kazuko Inoue (eds.) *Proceedings of the XIII International Congress of Linguists, August 29-September 4, 1982, Tokyo*, 163-171. Tokyo: Permanent International Committee on Linguistics.
1994   *Morphology by Itself*. Cambridge: MIT Press.

Aronoff, Mark—Roger Schvanefeldt
1978   "Testing Morphological Productivity", *Annals of the New York Academy of Science: Papers in Anthropology and Linguistics*, vol. 318, 106-114.

Aronoff, Mark—Sridhar, S. N.
1983   "Morphological Levels in English and Kannada; or, Atarizing Reagan", in John F. Richardson—Mitchell Marks—Amy Chukerman (eds.) *Papers from the Parasession on the Interplay of Phonology, Morphology, and Syntax*, 3-16. Chicago: Chicago Linguistics Society.
1987   "Morphological Levels in English and Kannada", in Edmund Gussmann (ed.) *Rules and the Lexicon*, 9-22. Lublin: Catholic University.

Baayen, Harald
1989   *A Corpus-based Study of Morphological Productivity. Statistical Analysis and Psycholinguistic Interpretation*. Doctoral dissertation, Vrije Universiteit, Amsterdam.
1992   "Quantitative Aspects of Morphological Productivity", in Geert Booij—Jaap van Marle (eds.) *Yearbook of Morphology 1991*, 109-149. Dordrecht—Boston—London: Kluwer.
1993   "On Frequency, Transparency and Productivity", in Geert Booij—Jaap van Marle (eds.) *Yearbook of Morphology 1992*, 181-208. Dordrecht—Boston—London: Kluwer.
1994   "Derivational Productivity and Text Typology", *Journal of Quantitative Linguistics* 1, 16-34.

1995 "Review of *Analogy and Structure*, by Royal Skousen, Dordrecht: Kluwer, 1992", *Language* 71.2, 390-396.

1997 "Stem Productivity in Lexical Processing, or, how Complex Simplex Verbs can be", paper presented at the 19. Jahrestagung der Deutschen Gesellschaft für Sprachwissenschaft, 26.-28.2.1997, Heinrich-Heine-Universität Düsseldorf.

Baayen, Harald—T. Dijkstra—Robert Schreuder

1997 "Singulars and Plurals in Dutch: Evidence for a Parallel Dual Route Model", *Journal of Memory and Language* 36, 94-117.

Baayen, Harald—Rochelle Lieber

1991 "Productivity and English Word-formation: a Corpus-based Study", *Linguistics* 29, 801-843.

1997 "Word Frequency Distribution and Lexical Semantics", *Computers and the Humanities* 30, 281-291.

Baayen, Harald—Rochelle Lieber—Robert Schreuder

1997 "The Morphological Complexity of Simplex nouns", *Linguistics* 35, 861-877.

Baayen, Harald—Richard Piepenbrock—Hedderik van Rijn

1993 *The CELEX Lexical Data Base* (CD-ROM). Philadelphia: Linguistic Data Consortium, University of Pennsylvania.

Baayen, Harald—Antoinette Renouf

1996 "Chronicling the Times: Productive Lexical Innovations in an English Newspaper", *Language* 72.1, 69-96.

Baker, Mark

1988 *Incorporation. A Theory of Grammatical Function Changing.* Chicago: Chicago University Press.

1992 "Review of *A-morphous Morphology*, by Stephen Anderson, Cambridge: CUP, 1992", *Language* 69, 587-590.

Bard, Ellen G. —Dan Robertson—Antonella Sorace

1996 "Magnitude Estimation of Linguistic Acceptability", *Language* 72.1, 32-68.

Barker, Chris

1995 "Episodic *-ee* in English: Thematic Relations and Newword Formation", in *Proceedings of Semantics and linguistic theory SALT 5 Conference.* Cornell University.

Bauer, Laurie

1983 *English Word-formation.* Cambridge: CUP.

1988 *Introducing Linguistic Morphology.* Edinburgh: Edinburgh University Press.

1992   "Scalar Productivity and *-lily* Adverbs", in Geert Booij—Jaap van Marle (eds.) *Yearbook of Morphology 1991,* 185-191. Dordrecht—Boston—London: Kluwer.

1993   "Review of Thomas Becker *Analogie und morphologische Theorie*", in Geert Booij and Jaap van Marle (eds.) *Yearbook of Morphology 1992,* 264-268. Dordrecht—Boston—London: Kluwer.

1994   "Productivity", in Ronald E. Asher and John M. Y. Simpson (eds.) *Encyclopedia of Language and Linguistics,* Vol.7, 3354-3357. Oxford—Aberdeen: Pergamon and Aberdeen University Press.

Beard, Robert

1981   *The Indo-European Lexicon. A Full Synchronic Theory.* Amsterdam: North-Holland.

1987a   "Lexical Stock Expansion", in Edmund Gussmann (ed.) *Rules and the Lexicon,* 24-41. Lublin: Catholic University.

1987b   "Morpheme Order in a Lexeme/Morpheme-based Morphology", *Lingua* 72, 1-44.

1988   "On the Separation of Derivation from Morphology: Toward a Lexeme-morpheme-based Morphology", *Quaderni di Semantica* 9, 3-59.

1990a   "The Nature and Origins of Derivational Polysemy", *Lingua* 81, 101-140.

1990b   "The Empty Morpheme Entailment", in Wolfgang Dressler, Hans Luschützky, Oskar E. Pfeiffer, and John Rennison (eds.) *Contemporary Morphology,* 159-169. Berlin: Mouton de Gruyter.

1995   *Morpheme-Lexeme Base Morphology.* Albany: State University of New York Press.

Becker, Thomas

1990   *Analogie und Morphologische Theorie.* München: Wilhelm Fink.

1993a   "Morphologische Ersetzungsbildungen im Deutschen", *Zeitschrift für Sprachwissenschaft* 12.2, 185-217.

1993b   "Back-formation, Cross-formation, and 'Bracketing Paradoxes' in Paradigmatic Morphology", in Geert Booij and Jaap van Marle (eds.) *Yearbook of Morphology 1993,* 1-25. Dordrecht—Boston—London: Kluwer.

Beckman, Jill N.
1998   *Positional Faithfulness*. Ph.D. dissertation, University of Massachusetts, Amherst.

Benua, Laura
1995   "Identity Effects in Morphological Truncation", in Jill Beckman, Laura Walsh-Dickey, and Suzanne Urbanczyk (eds.) *Papers in Optimality Theory* (University of Massachusetts Occasional Papers 18), 78-136. Amherst: GLSA.
1997   Transderivational Identity. Phonological Relations between Words. Ph.D. dissertation, University of Massachusetts, Amherst.

Berg, Donna Lee
1991, 1994 *A User's Guide to the Oxford English Dictionary*. Oxford—New York: Oxford University Press.

Berschin, Helmut
1971   "Sprachsystem und Sprachnorm bei spanischen lexikalischen Einheiten der Struktur KKVKV", *Linguistische Berichte* 12.39-46.

Blank, Andreas
1997   "Wege zu einer kognitiven Wortbildungslehre am Beispiel des Französischen und Italienischen", paper presented at Philipps-Universität Marburg, April 22, 1997.

Blevins
1995   "The Syllable in Phonological Theory", in John A. Goldsmith (ed.) *Handbook of Phonological Theory,* 206-244. Oxford: Blackwell.

Bloomfield, Leonard
1933   *Language*. New York: Holt.

Bochner, Harry
1993   *Simplicity in Generative Morphology*. Berlin—New York: Mouton de Gruyter.

Bolinger, Dwight
1948   "On Defining the Morpheme", *Word* 4, 18-23.

Booij, Geert E.
1977   *Dutch Morphology. A Study of Word Formation in Generative Grammar*. Lisse: de Ridder.
1979   Semantic Regularities in Word Formation", *Linguistics* 17, 985-1001.

1983   "Rezension von Plank, Frans *Morphologische (Ir-)Regularitäten. Aspekte der Wortstrukturtheorie*, Tübingen: Narr, 1981", *Zeitschrift für Sprachwissenschaft* 2, 251-264.

1986   "Form and Meaning in Morphology: The Case of Dutch 'Agent Nouns'", *Linguistics* 24, 503-517.

1987   "Lexical Phonology and the Organisation of the Morphological Component", in Edmund Gussmann (ed.) *Rules and the Lexicon*, 43-65. Lublin: Catholic University.

1992   "Morphology, Semantics and Argument Structure", in Iggy M. Roca (ed.) *Thematic Structure: Its Role in Grammar*, 47-64. Dordrecht: Foris.

1994   "Lexical Phonology: A Review", in Richard Wiese (ed.) *Recent Developments in Lexical Phonology* (Arbeiten des Sonderforschungsbereichs 'Theorie des Lexikons' Nr. 56), 3-29. Düsseldorf: Heinrich-Heine-Universität.

1996   "Autonomous Morphology and paradigmatic relations", in Geert Booij and Jaap van Marle (eds.) *Yearbook of Morphology 1996*, 35-53. Dordrecht—Boston—London: Kluwer.

1998   "Phonological Output Constraints in Morpholgy", in Wolfgang Kehrein—Richard Wiese (eds.) *Phonology and Morphology of the Germanic Languages*. Tübingen: Niemeyer.

Booij, Geert E. and Jaap van Marle (eds.)
1992   *Yearbook of Morphology 1991*. Dordrecht—Boston—London: Kluwer.

Booij, Geert E.—Jaap van Marle (eds.)
1996   *Yearbook of Morphology 1995*. Dordrecht—Boston—London: Kluwer.

Botha, Rudolph P.
1968   *The Function of the Lexicon in Transformational Generative Grammar*. The Hague: Mouton.

Bréal, Michel
1897, 1904 *Essai de sémantique*. Paris: Hachette.

Brown, A. F.
1963   *Normal and Reverse English Word List*. 8 vols. (Prepared at the University of Pennsylvania under a Contract with the Air Force Office of Scientific Research (AF 49 (638)-1042)).

Burgschmidt, Ernst
1977   "Strukturierung, Norm, und Produktivität in der Wortbildung",
         in Herbert E. Brekle and Dieter Kastovsky (eds.) *Perspektiven
         der Wortbildungsforschung. Beiträge zum Wuppertaler
         Wortbildungskolloquium vom 9.-10. Juli 1976*, 39-47. Bonn:
         Bouvier.
Burzio, Luigi
1994   *Principles of English Stress.* Cambridge: CUP.
Butterworth, Brian
1983   "Lexical Representation", in Brian Butterworth (ed.) *Langua-
         ge Production (Vol.2): Development, Writing and other Lan-
         guage Processes*, 257-294. London: Academic Press.
Bybee, Joan—Carol Lynn Moder
1983   "Morphological Classes as Natural Categories", *Language* 59,
         251-270.
Bybee, Joan—Dan Slobin
1982   "Rules and Schemas in the Develoment and Use of English
         Past Tense", *Language* 58, 265-289.
Cannon, Garland
1987   *Historical Change and Word-formation.* New York: Lang.
Caramazza, Alfonso—Alessandro Laudanna—Cristina Romani
1988   "Lexical Access and Inflectional Morphology", *Cognition* 28,
         297-332.
Carstairs, Andrew
1990   "Phonologically Conditioned Suppletion", in Wolfgang U.
         Dressler, Hans Luschützky, Oskar E. Pfeiffer, and John Ren-
         nison (eds.) *Contemporary Morphology*, 17-23. Berlin—New
         York: Mouton de Gruyter.
Carstairs-McCarthy, Andrew
1988   "Some Implications of Phonologically-conditioned Suppleti-
         on", in Geert Booij and Jaap van Marle (eds.) *Yearbook of
         Morphology* 1, 67-94. Dordrecht— Boston—London: Kluwer.
1992   *Current Morphology.* London: Routledge.
1993   "Morphology without Word-internal Constituents: A Review
         of Stephen R. Anderson's *A-morphous Morphology*", in Geert
         Booij and Jaap van Marle (eds.) *Yearbook of Morphology
         1993*, 209-233. Dordrecht—Boston—London: Kluwer.
Casali, Roderic F.
1997   "Vowel Elision in Hiatus Contexts: Which Vowel Goes?",
         Language 73, 493-533.

CED
1970   *A Chronological English Dictionary*. Ed. by Thomas Finkenstaedt, Eberhard Leisi, and Dieter Wolff. Heidelberg: Winter.

Chandler, Steve
1993   "Are Rules and Modules Really Necessary for Explaining Language?", *Journal of Psycholinguistic Research* 22, 593-606.

Chapin, Paul
1967   *On the Syntax of word-derivation in English*. PhD thesis, MIT, Cambridge.
1970   "On Affixation in English", in Manfred Bierwisch and Karl E. Heidolph (eds.) *Progress in Linguistics*, 51-63. The Hague: Mouton.

Chitashvili, Revas J.—Harald Baayen
1993   "Word Frequency Distributions", in L. Hrebícek and G. Altmann (eds.) *Quantitative Text Analysis*, 54-135. Trier: WVT.

Chomsky, Noam
1957   *Syntactic Structures*. The Hague: Mouton.
1973   "Conditions on Transformations", in Stephen R. Anderson and Paul Kiparsky (eds.) *A Festschrift for Morris Halle*, 232-286. New York: Holt, Rinehart and Winston.
1993   "A Minimalist Program for Linguistic Theory", in Kenneth Hale and Samuel J. Keyser (eds.) *The View from Building 20*, 1-52. Cambridge: MIT Press.

Chomsky, Noam—Morris Halle
1968   *The Sound Pattern of English*. New York: Harper and Row.

Clark, Eve
1981   "Lexical Innovations: How Children Learn to Create New Words", in W. Deutsch (ed.) *The Child's Construction of Language*, 299-328. London: Academic Press.

Clark, Eve—Herbert Clark
1979   "When Nouns Surface as Verbs", *Language* 55, 767-811.

COBUILD
1987   *Collins COBUILD English Language Dictionary*. London—Glasgow: Collins.

Colen, Alexandra
1980/81 "On the Distribution of *un-*, *de-* and *dis-* in English Verbs Expressing Reversativity and Related Concepts", *Studia Germanica Gandensia* 21, 127-152.

Coleman, John
1998   *Phonological Representations. Their Names, Forms and Po-
         wers*. Cambridge: Cambridge University Press.
Corbin, Danielle
1987   *Morphologie dérivationelle et structuration du lexique*. 2
         Vols. Tübingen: Niemeyer.
Coseriu, Eugenio
1952   "Sistema, norma y habla", in Coseriu, Eugenio (ed.) *Teoría de
         lenguaje y lingüística general*, 11-113. Madrid: Gredos.
Cowart, Wayne
1997   *Experimental Syntax: Applying Objective Methods to Sen-
         tence Judgments*. Beverly Hills—London: Sage.
Crystal, David
1991   *A Dictionary of Linguistics and Phonetics*. (3rd edition). Ox-
         ford: Blackwell.
Cutler, Anne
1981   "Degrees of Transparency in Word Formation", *Canadian
         Journal of Linguistics* 26, 73-77.
Danielsson, Bror
1948   *Studies on the Accentuation of Polysyllabic Latin, Greek, and
         Romance Loanwords in English with Special Reference to
         those Ending in* -able, -ate, -ator, -ible, -ic, -ical, *and* -ize.
         Stockholm: Almqvist and Wiksell.
Derwing, Bruce—Royal Skousen
1989   "Morphology in the Mental Lexicon: A New Look at Analo-
         gy." in Geert Booij and Jaap van Marle (eds.) *Yearbook of
         Morphology 1989*, 55-71. Dordrecht—Boston—London:
         Kluwer.
1994   "Productivity and the English Past Tense: Testing Skousen's
         Analogy Model", in Susan Lima, Roberta L. Corrigan, and
         Gregory Iverson (eds.) *The Reality of Linguistic Rules*, 193-
         218. Amsterdam—Philadelphia: Benjamins.
Di Sciullo, Anna-Maria—Edwin Williams
1987   *On the Definition of Word*. Cambridge: MIT Press.
Don, Jan
1993   *Morphological Conversion*. Utrecht: OTS, Rijksuniversiteit.
Downing, Pamela
1977   "On the Creation and Use of English Compound Nouns",
         Language 53, 810-842.

Doyle, Aidan
  1992   "Suffixal Rivalry: A Case Study in Irish nominalizations", in
          Geert Booij and Jaap van Marle (eds.) *Yearbook of Morpho-*
          logy 1992, 35-55. Dordrecht— Boston—London: Kluwer.
Dressler, Wolfgang U.
  1988   "Preferences vs. Strict Universals in Morphology: Word-based
          Rules", in Michael Hammond and Michael Noonan (eds.)
          Theoretical Morphology, 143-154. San Diego—London:
          Academic Press.
Dressler, Wolfgang U.—Lavinia Merlini Barbaresi
  1994   *Morphopragmatics. Diminutives and Intensifiers in Italian,*
          German, and other Languages. Berlin: Mouton de Gruyter.
Dressler, Wolfgang U.—Hans Luschützky—Oskar E. Pfeiffer—John
          Rennison (eds.)
  1990   *Contemporary Morphology*. Berlin: Mouton de Gruyter.
Emonds, Joseph
  1966   "A Study of some very Confusing Suffixes: Or, Phonetic Re-
          gularities in some Words Derived from Romance Tongues",
          ms., MIT.
Fabb, Nigel
  1988   "English Suffixation is Constrained only by Selectional Re-
          strictions", *Natural Language and Linguistic Theory* 6, 527-
          539.
Fowler, H. W.
  1929, 1959   *A Dictionary of Modern English Usage*. Oxford: Clarendon
          Press.
Frauenfelder, Uli—Robert Schreuder
  1992   "Constraining Psycholinguistic Models of Morphological
          Processing and Representation: The Role of Productivity", in
          Geert Booij and Jaap van Marle (eds.) *Yearbook of Morpho-*
          logy 1991, 165-183. Dordrecht—Boston—London: Kluwer.
Funk, Wolf-Peter
  1986   "Toward a Definition of Semantic Constraints on Negative
          Prefixation in English and German", in Dieter Kastovsky and
          Aleksander Szwedek (eds.) *Linguistics across Historical and*
          Geographical Boundaries. In Honor of Jacek Fisiak on the
          Occasion of his Fiftieth Birthday, 876-889. Berlin—New
          York: Mouton de Gruyter.

Gauger, Hans-Martin
  1971   *Durchsichtige Wörter. Zur Theorie der Wortbildung.* Heidel-
          berg: Winter.
Giegerich, Heinz J.
  1985   *Metrical Phonology and Phonological Structure.* Cambridge:
          Cambridge University Press.
  1992   *English Phonology.* Cambridge: Cambridge University Press.
  1998   *Lexical Strata in English. Morphological Causes, Phonologi-
          cal Effects.* (to appear 1999, Cambridge: Cambridge Univer-
          sity Press)
Goldsmith, John
  1990   *Autosegmental and Metrical Phonology.* Blackwell: Oxford.
Golston, Chris—Richard Wiese
  1996   "Zero Morphology and Constraint Interaction: Subtraction and
          Epenthesis in German Dialects", in Geert Booij and Jaap van
          Marle (eds.) *Yearbook of Morphology 1995,* 143-159. Dor-
          drecht— Boston—London: Kluwer.
  1998   "The structure of the German root", in Wolfgang Kehrein—
          Richard Wiese (eds.) *Phonology and Morphology of the Ger-
          manic Languages,* 165-185. Tübingen: Niemeyer.
Gussmann, Edmund
  1987   "The Lexicon of English De-adjectival Verbs", in Edmund
          Gussmann (ed.) *Rules and the Lexicon,* 79-101. Lublin: Ca-
          tholic University.
Hale, Kenneth—Samuel J. Keyser
  1993   "On Argument Structure and the Lexical Expression of Syn-
          tactic Relations", in Kenneth Hale and Samuel J. Keyser (eds.)
          The View from Building 20. Cambridge: MIT Press, 111-176.
Halle, Morris
  1973a   "Prolegomena to Theory of Word Formation", *Linguistic In-
          quiry* 4, 3-16.
  1973b   "Stress Rules in English: A New Version", *Linguistic Inquiry*
          4, 451-464.
Halle, Morris—Karuvannur P. Mohanan
  1985   "Segmental Phonology of Modern English", *Linguistic Inquiry*
          16, 57-116.
Halle, Morris—Samuel Keyser
  1971   *English Stress.* Harper and Row: New York.
Halle, Morris—Jean-Roger Vergnaud
  1987   *An Essay on Stress.* Cambridge: MIT Press.

Hammond, Michael
1984   *Constraining Metrical Theory: A Modular Theory of Rhythm and Destressing*. Ph. D. Thesis, University of Califormia, Los Angeles.

Harris, Zelig
1951, 1960   *Methods in Structural linguistics*. (4th impression, entitled *Structural Linguistics*). Chicago: University of Chicago Press.

Haspelmath, Martin
1995   "The Growth of Affixes in Morphological Reanalysis", in Geert Booij and Jaap van Marle (eds.) *Yearbook of Morphology 1994*, 1-29. Dordrecht—Boston—London: Kluwer.
1996   "Word-class Changing inflection and Morphological Theory", in Geert Booij and Jaap van Marle (eds.) *Yearbook of Morphology 1995*, 43-66. Dordrecht—Boston—London: Kluwer.

Hayes, Bruce
1982   "Extrametricality and English Stress", *Linguistic Inquiry* 13, 227-276.

Hogg, Richard—Christopher B. McCully
1987   *Metrical Phonology: a Coursebook*. Cambridge: CUP

Inkelas, Sharon
1989   *Prosodic Constituency in the Lexicon*. PhD thesis, Stanford University.
1993   "Deriving Cyclicity", in Sharon Hargus and Ellen Kaisse (eds.) *Phonetics and Phonology 4: Studies in Lexical Phonology*, 75-110. San Diego: Academic Press.

Inkelas, Sharon—Cemil Orhan Orgun
1995   "Level Ordering and Economy in the Lexical Phonology of Turkish", *Language* 71, 763-793.

Ito, Junko—Armin Mester
1998   "Markedness and Word Structure: OCP Effects in Japanese", Ms., University of California at Santa Cruz.

Jackendoff, Ray
1975   "Morphological and Semantic Regularities in the Lexikon", *Language* 51, 639-671.
1977   *X-Bar syntax. A Study of Phrase Structure*. Cambridge: MIT Press.
1983   *Semantics and Cognition*. Cambridge: MIT Press.
1990   *Semantic Structures*. Cambridge: MIT Press.
1991   "Parts and Boundaries", *Cognition* 41, 9-45.

Jaeger, Jeri J. —Alan H. Lockwood—David L. Kemmerer—Robert D. van Valin—Brian W. Murphy, —Hanif G. Khalak
   1996   "A Positron Emission Tomographic Study of Regular and Irregular Verb Morphology in English", *Language* 72.3, 451-497.

Jakobson, Roman
   1962   *Selected Writings 1: Phonological Studies*. The Hague: Mouton.

Jespersen, Otto
   1942   *A Modern English Grammar. On Historical Principles*. Part VI Morphology. London: Allen & Unwin.

Jucker, Andreas H.
   1994   "New Dimensions in Vocabulary Studies: Review Article of the *Oxford English Dictionary (end edition)* on CD-ROM", *Literary and Linguistic Computing* 9, 149-154.

Kager, René
   1989   *A Metrical Theory of Stress and Destressing in English and Dutch*. Dordrecht: Foris.
   1997   "Rhythmic Vowel Deletion in Optimality Theory", in Iggy Roca (ed.) *Derivations and Constraints in Phonology*, 463-499. Oxford: Clarendon Press.

Kaplan, Ronald M. —Joan W. Bresnan
   1982   "Lexical-functional Grammar: A Formal System for Grammatical Representation", in Joan W. Bresnan (ed.) *The Mental Representation of Grammatical Relations*, 173-281. Cambridge: MIT Press.

Karius, Ilse
   1985   *Die Ableitung der denominalen Verben mit Nullsuffigierung im Englischen*. Tübingen: Niemeyer.

Kastovsky, Dieter
   1986   "The Problem of Productivity in Word Formation", *Linguistics* 24, 585-600.

Kenstowicz, Michael
   1996   "Base-Identity and Uniform Exponence: Alternatives to Cyclicity", in Jacques Durand and Bernard Laks (eds.) *Current Trends in Phonology: Models and Methods*, 363-393. Salford: European Studies Research Institute.

Kettemann, Bernhard
   1988   *Die Phonologie Morphologischer Prozesse im Amerikanischen Englisch*. Narr: Tübingen.

Kiparsky, Paul
   1982a   *Explanation in Phonology.* Dordrecht: Foris.
   1982b   "Lexical Morphology and Phonology", in The Linguistic
            Society of Korea (ed.) *Linguistics in the Morning Calm*, 1-91.
            Seoul: Hanshin Publishing Co.
   1983   "Word-formation and the Lexicon", in Frances Ingemann (ed.)
            *Proceedings from the 1982 Mid-America Linguistics Confe-
            rence*, 3-29. Lawrence: University of Kansas.
Kouwenberg, Silvia
   1997   "Papiamento Non-affixational Derivational Morphology",
            paper presented at the Annual Conference of the Society for
            Pidgin and Creole Linguistics, London, University of West-
            minster, June 26-28, 1997.
Kulak, Manfred
   1964   *Die semantischen Kategorien der mit Nullmorphem abgeleite-
            ten desubstantivischen Verben des heutigen Englischen und
            Deutschen.* Unveröffentlichte Dissertation, Universität Tübin-
            gen.
Laskowski, Roman
   1981   "Die Semantik slawischer desubstantivischer kausativer Ver-
            ben", *Zeitschrift für Slawistik* 26,19-25.
Laudanna, Alessandro—Cristina Burani
   1985   "Adress Mechanisms to Decomposed Lexical Entries", *Lin-
            guistics* 23, 775-792.
Leben, William
   1973   *Suprasegmental Phonology.* PhD thesis, MIT, Cambridge.
Lehnert, Martin
   1971   *Rückläufiges Wörterbuch der Englischen Gegenwartssprache.*
            Leipzig: VEB Verlag Enzyklopädie.
Lepschy, G.
   1981   "Le parole dello sciacallo", *Journal of the Association of the
            Teachers of London* 32, 65-71.
Liberman, Mark—Alan Prince
   1977   "On Stress and Linguistic Rhythm", *Linguistic Inquiry* 8, 249-
            336.
Lieber, Rochelle
   1980   *On the Organization of the Lexicon.* PhD thesis, MIT, Cam-
            bridge. (Published 1981 by IULC, Bloomington, republished
            1990 by Garland, New York).

1981   "Morphological Conversion within a Restrictive Theory of the Lexicon", in Michael Moorgat, Harry van der Hulst, and Teun Hoekstra (eds.) *The Scope of Lexical Rules*, 161-200. Dordrecht: Foris.

1983   "Argument-linking and Compounds in English", *Linguistic Inquiry* 14, 251-85.

1988   "Phrasal Compounds in English and the Morphology-Syntax Interface", in Diane K. Brentari, Gary Larson, and Lynn MacLeod (eds.) *Papers from the Parasession on Agreement in Grammatical Theory* (*CLS* 24.2), 202-222. Chicago: Chicago Linguistics Society.

1992   *Deconstructing Morphology*. Chicago and London: University of Chicago Press.

1996   "The Suffix *-ize* in English. Implications for Morphology". Ms. (to appear in Steven G. Lapointe, Diane K. Brentari, and Patrick M. Farrell (eds.) *Morphology and its Relation to Phonology and Syntax*. Stanford: CLSI).

Lieber, Rochelle and Harald Baayen

1993   "Verbal Prefixes in Dutch: a Study in Lexical Conceptual Structure", in Geert Booij and Jaap van Marle (eds.) *Yearbook of Morphology 1993*, 51-78. Dordrecht—Boston—London: Kluwer.

Lipka, Leonhart

1977   "Lexikalisierung, Idiomatisierung und Hypostasierung als Probleme einer synchronischen Wortbildungslehre", in Herbert Brekle and Dieter Kastovsky (eds.) *Perspektiven der Wortbildungsforschung*, 155-164. Bonn: Grundmann.

Mahn, Lothar H.

1971   *Zur Morphologie und Semantik englischer Verben auf -IFY mit Berücksichtigung französischer und deutscher Entsprechungen*. Tübingen: Narr.

Malkiel, Yakov

1977   "Why Ap-*ish* but Worm-*y*?", in Paul. J. Hopper (ed.) *Studies in Descriptive and Historical Linguistics*, 341-364. Amsterdam—Philadelphia: Benjamins.

Manelis, Leon—David A. Tharp

1977   "The Processing of Affixed Words", *Memory and Cognition* 5, 690-695.

Marchand, Hans
    1964   "Die Ableitung desubstantivischer Verben mit Nullmorphem
            im Englischen, Französischen und Deutschen", *Die Neueren
            Sprachen* 63, 105-118.
    1969   *The Categories and Types of Present-day English Word-
            formation*. Second edition. München: Beck.
    1973   "Reversative, Ablative, and Privative Verbs in English, French
            and German", in Braj B. Kachru, Robert B. Lees, Yakov
            Malkiel, Angelina Pietrangeli, and Sol Saporta (eds.) *Issues in
            Linguistics: Papers in Honor of Henry and Renée Kahane*,
            636-543. Urbana: Univesity of Illinois Press.
Marcus, Gary—Ursula Brinkmann—Harald Clahsen—Richard Wiese—
            Steven Pinker
    1995   "German Inflection. The Exception that Proves the Rule",
            Cognitive Psychology 29, 189-256.
Marle, Jaap van
    1985   *On the Paradigmatic Dimension of Morphological Creativity*.
            Dordrecht: Foris.
    1986   "The Domain Hypothesis: The Study of Rival Morphological
            Processes", *Linguistics* 24, 601-627.
    1988   "On the Role of Semantics in Productivity Change", in Geert
            Booij and Jaap van Marle (eds.) *Yearbook of Morphology
            1988*, 139-154. Dordrecht—Boston—London: Kluwer.
    1992   "The Relationship between Morphological Productivity and
            Frequency: A Comment on Baayen`s Performance-oriented
            Conception of Morhpological Productivity", in Geert Booij
            and Jaap van Marle (eds.) *Yearbook of Morphology 1991*,
            151-163. Dordrecht—Boston—London: Kluwer.
Mayerthaler, Willi
    1977   *Studien zur theoretischen und zur französischen Morphologie*.
            Tübingen: Niemeyer.
McCarthy, John J.
    1995   "Extensions of Faithfulness". Ms. University of Mas-
            sachusetts. Rutgers Optimality Archive.
McCarthy, John J. —Alan Prince
    1993a   "Generalized Alignment", in Geert Booij and Jaap van Marle
            (eds.) *Yearbook of Morphology 1993*, 79-153. Dordrecht—
            Boston—London: Kluwer.

1993b   *Prosodic Morphology I: Constraint Interaction and Satisfaction.* Ms., University of Massachusetts, Amherst, and Rutgers University. Rutgers Optimality Archive.

1995   "Faithfulness and Reduplicative Identity", in Jill Beckman, Laura Walsh-Dickey, and Suzanne Urbanczyk (eds.) *Papers in Optimality Theory* (University of Massachusetts Occasional Papers 18), 249-384. Amherst: GLSA.

1998   "Prosodic Morphology", in Andrew Spencer, and Arnold M. Zwicky (eds.) *The Handbook of Morphology*, 283-305. Oxford: Blackwell.

Menn, Lise—Brian McWhinney

1984   "The Repeated Morph Constraint: toward an Explanation", *Language* 60, 519-541.

Minsky, Marvin

1975   "A Framework for Respresenting Knowledge", in Patrick Henry Winston (ed.) *The Psychology of Computer Vision*, 211-277. New York: McGraw-Hill.

Mohanan, Karuvannur P.

1986   *The Theory of Lexical Phonology.* Dordrecht: Reidel.

Neef, Martin

1996   *Wort-Design.* Tübingen: Stauffenburg.

Nespor, Marina—Irene Vogel

1986   *Prosodic Phonology.* Dordrecht: Foris.

Neuhaus, H. Joachim

1971   *Beschränkungen in der Grammatik der Wortableitungen im Englischen.* Unveröffentlichte Dissertation, Universität des Saarlandes, Saarbrücken.

1973   "Zur Theorie der Produktivität von Wortbildungssystemen", in Abraham P. ten Cate and Peter Jordens (eds.) *Linguistische Perspektiven: Referate des VII. Linguistischen Kolloquiums Nijmegen, 26.-30. September 1972*, 305-317. Tübingen: Niemeyer.

OED

1994   *The Oxford English Dictionary,* 2nd Edition, on Compact Disc. Oxford: Oxford University Press.

Orgun, Cemil Orhan

1996   *Sign-based Morphology and Phonology, with Special Emphasis on Optimality Theory.* PhD thesis, University of California, Berkeley.

Pater, Joe
   1995   "On the nonuniformity of weight-to-stress and stress preservation effects in English" Ms. (submitted for publication).
Rutgers Optimality Archive.

Paul, Hermann
   1880, 1995 *Prinzipien der Sprachgeschichte*, 10. Aufl. Tübingen:
Niemeyer.
   1896   "Über die Aufgaben der Wortbildungslehre", *Sitzungsberichte
der philosophisch-philologischen und der historischen Classe
der k. b. Akademie der Wissenschaften zu München*, 692-713.
(reprinted in Leonhard Lipka and Hartmut Günther (eds.) *ang*

Pinker, Steven
   1989   *Learnability and Cognition*. Cambridge: MIT Press.

Plag, Ingo
   1996   "Selectional Restriction in English Suffixation Revisited: a
Reply to Fabb (1988)", *Linguistics* 34, 769-798.
   1997   "The Polysemy of -*ize* Derivatives. The Role of Semantics in
Word-formation", in Geert Booij and Jaap van Marle (eds.)
Yearbook of Morphology 1997. Dordrecht—Boston—London:
Kluwer.
   1998   "Morphological Haplology in a Constraint-based Morphophonology", in Wolfgang Kehrein und Richard Wiese (eds.)
Phonology and Morphology of the Germanic Languages, Tü-
bingen: Niemeyer.

Plank, Frans
   1981   *Morphologische (Ir-)Regularitäten*. Tübingen: Narr.

Pollard, Carl—Ivan A. Sag
   1994   *Head-driven Phrase Structure Grammar*. Chicago: University
of Chicago Press.

Prince, Alan
   1983   "Relating to the Grid", *Linguistic Inquiry* 14, 19-100

Prince, Alan—Paul Smolensky
   1993   *Optimality Theory*. Ms. Rutgers University.

Pulleyblank, Douglas
   1997   "Optimality Theory and Features", in Diana Archangeli and
Terence Langendoen (eds.) *Optimality Theory: An Overview*,
59-101. Oxford: Blackwell.

Raab-Fischer, Roswitha
1994   "A Hyperinflation of Lexical Mega-monsters? Eine korpusge-
        stützte Analyse zum Gebrauch der Wortbildungselemente *me-
        ga-*, *ultra-*, und *hyper-* im heutigen Englisch", *Arbeiten aus
        Anglistik und Amerikanistik* 19, 83-111.
Raffelsiefen, Renate
1992   "A Non-configurational Approach to Word-formation", in
        Mark Aronoff (ed.) *Morphology now*, 133-162. Albany: State
        University of New York Press.
1993   "Relating Words. A Model of Base Recognition", *Linguistic
        Analysis* 23, 3-164.
1996   "Gaps in Word-formation", in Ursula Kleinhenz (ed.) *Inter-
        faces in Phonology*, 193-208. Berlin: Akademie-Verlag.
Rainer, Franz
1987   "Produktivitätsbegriffe in der Wortbildungstheorie", in Wolf
        Dietrich (ed.) *Grammatik und Wortbildung Romanischer
        Sprachen: Beiträge zum Deutschen Romanistentag in Siegen,
        30.09. - 3.10.1985*. Tübingen: Narr.
1988   "Towards a Theory of Blocking", in Geert Booij and Jaap van
        Marle (eds.) *Yearbook of Morphology* 1, 155-185. Dor-
        drecht—Boston—London: Kluwer.
1993   *Spanische Wortbildungslehre*. Tübingen: Niemeyer.
Renouf, Antoinette
1987   "Corpus Development", in John M. Sinclair (ed.) *Looking up:
        An Account of the Cobuild Project in Lexical Computing*, 1-
        40. London: Collins.
RHCD: Barnhart, Clarence L.
1947   *The American College Dictionary*. New York: Random
        House.
Riddle, Elizabeth
1985   "A Historical Perspective on the Productivity of the Suffixes -
        ness and -*ity*", in Jacek Fisiak (ed.) *Historical Semantics, Hi-
        storical Word-formation*, 435-461. New York: Mouton.
Roeper, Thomas
1987   "Implicit Arguments and the Head-Complement Relation",
        Linguistic Inquiry 18 (2), 267-310.
Rose, James H.
1973   "Principled Limitations on Productivity in Denominal Verbs",
        Foundations of Language 10, 509-526.

Ruf, Birgit
  1996   *Augmentativbildungen mit Lehnpräfixen. Eine Untersuchung
           zur Wortbildung in der deutschen Gegenwartssprache.* Hei-
           delberg: Winter.
Rubach, Jerzy
  1984   "Segmental Rules of English and Cyclic Phonology", *Lan-
           guage* 60:21-54.
Rubenstein, Herbert—Irwin Pollack
  1963   "Word Predictability and Intelligibility", *Journal of Verbal
           Learning and Verbal Behavior* 2, 147-158.
Russel, Kevin
  1997   "Optimality Theory and Morphology", in Diana Archangeli
           and Terence Langendoen (eds.) *Optimality Theory: An Over-
           view*, 102-133. Oxford: Blackwell.
Sanders, Gerald
  1988   "Zero Derivation and the Overt Analogon Criterion", in Mi-
           chael Hammond and Michael Noonan (eds.) *Theoretical Mor-
           phology*, 155-175. San Diego—London: Academic Press.
Scalise, Sergio
  1984   *Generative Morphology.* Dordrecht: Foris.
  1988   "The Notion of 'Head' in Morphology" in Geert Booij and
           Jaap van Marle (eds.) *Yearbook of Morphology 1*, 229-245.
           Dordrecht—Boston—London: Kluwer
Scarborough, Don—Charles Cortese—Hollis S. Scarborough
  1977   "Frequency and Repetition Effects in Lexical Memory", *Jour-
           nal of Experimental Psychology: Human Perception and
           Performance* 3, 1-17.
Schneider, Edgar W.
  1987   "Beobachtungen zur Pragmatik der verbbildenden Suffixe *-en*,
           -ify, und *-ize* im Englischen", *Sprachwissenschaft* 12, 88-109.
Schneider, Klaus Peter
  1997   *'Size and Attitude'. Expressive Wortbildung und diminutivi-
           sche Ausdrücke in der englischen Alltagskommunikation.* Un-
           veröffentlichte Habilitationsschrift, Philipps-Universität Mar-
           burg.
Schreuder, Robert—Harald Baayen
  1997   "How Complex Simplex Words can Be", *Journal of Memory
           and Language* 36, 118-139.

Schultink, Henk
1961   "Produktiviteit als morphologisch phenomeen", *Forum der Letteren* 2, 110-125.
1988   "Some Remarks on the Relations between Morphology and Syntax in Twentieth Century Linguistics", in Martin Everaert, Arnold Evers, Ring Huybreyts and Mieke Trommelen (eds.) *Morphology and Modularity*. Dordrecht: Foris.
Schütze, Carsten
1996   *The Empirical Base of Linguistics: Grammaticality Judgments and Linguistic Methodology*. Chicago: University of Chicago Press.
Segui, Juan—Maria Luisa Zubizarreta
1985   "Mental Representation of Morphologically Complex Words and Lexical Access", *Linguistics* 23,759-774.
Selkirk, Elisabeth
1982a   *The Syntax of Words*. Cambridge: MIT Press.
1982b   "The Syllable", in Harry van der Hulst and Norval Smith (Eds.). *The Structure of Phonological Representations* II. Dordrecht: Foris.
Sherrard, Nicholas
1997   "Questions of Priorities: Introductory Overview of Optimality Theory in Phonology", in Iggy Roca (ed.) *Derivations and Constraints in Phonology*, 43-89. Oxford: Clarendon Press.
Siegel, Dorothy
1971   "Some Lexical Transderivational Constraints in English", unpublished ms., MIT.
1974   *Topics in English Morphology*. PhD thesis, MIT, Cambridge. (published by Garland, 1979)
1977   "The Adjacency Condition and the Theory of Morphology", in M. J. Stein (ed.) *Proceedings of NELS 8*, 189-97. Amherst: Graduate Linguistics Student Association.
Sinclair, John. M. (ed.)
1987   *Looking up. An Account of the Cobuild Project in Lexical Computing*. London: Collins.
Skousen, Royal
1989   *Analogical Modeling of Language*. Dordrecht: Kluwer.
1992   *Analogy and Structure*. Dordrecht: Kluwer.
1995   "Analogy: A Non-rule Alternative to Neural Networks", *Rivista di Linguistica* 7.2, 213-231.

Smolensky, Paul
  1993   "Harmony, markedness, and phonological acticity", handout from talk given at Rutgers Optimality Workshop 1. Rutgers Optimality Archive.
  1995   "On the internal structure of the constrint component Con of UG", handout from talk at the University of Arizona, March 1995 Rutgers Optimality Archive.
  1997   "Constraint Interaction in Generative Grammar II: Local Conjunction", handout from talk given at the Hopkins Optimality Theory Workshop, University of Maryland, May 1997. Rutgers Optimality Archive.

SOED
  1955   *The Shorter Oxford English Dictionary on Historical Principles.* 3rd. ed. Revised and edited by C.T. Onions. Oxford: Oxford University Press.

SPE. See Chomsky —Halle (1968).

Spencer, Andrew
  1991   *Morphological Theory: An Introduction to Word Structure in Generative Grammar.* Cambridge: CUP
  1993   "Review of *Deconstructing Morphology*, by Rochelle Lieber, Chicago: The University of Chicago Press, 1992", *Language* 69, 580-587.

Stemberger, Joseph P.
  1981   "Morphological Haplology", *Language* 57, 791-817.

Stein, Gabriele
  1977   "The Place of Word-formation in Linguistic Description", in Herbert E. Brekle and Dieter Kastovsky (eds.) *Perspektiven der Wortbildungsforschung. Beiträge zum Wuppertaler Wortbildungskolloquium vom 9.-10. Juli 1976*, 219-235. Bonn: Bouvier.

Strauss, Steven
  1982   *Lexicalist Phonology of English and German.* Dordrecht: Foris.

Szymanek, Bogdan
  1980   "Phonological Conditioning of Word Formation Rules", *Folia Linguistics* 14, 413-425.
  1985   *English and Polish Adjectives. A Study in Lexicalist Word-formation.* Lublin: Catholic University.
  1988   *Categories and Categorization in Morphology*: Lublin: Catholic University.

Taft, Marcus
  1985 "The Decoding of Words in Lexical Access: A Review of the Morphographic Approach", in D. Besner, T.G. Waller, G.E. MacKinnon (eds.) *Reading Research: Advances in Theory and Practice, Vol.V*, 197-217. New York: Academic Press.
  1994 "Interactive-activation as a Framework for Understanding Morphological Processing", *Language and Cognitive Processes* 9 (3), 271-294.

Taft, Marcus—Kenneth I. Foster
  1975 "Lexical Storage and Retrieval of Prefixed Words", *Journal of Verbal Learning and Verbal Behavior* 14, 638-647.

Uhlenbeck, Eugenius Marius
  1962 "Limitations of Morphological Processes: Some Preliminary Remarks", *Lingua* 11, 426-32.
  1977 "The Concepts of Productivity and Potentiality in Morphological Description and their Psycholinguistic Reality", *Salzburger Beiträge zur Linguistik* 4, 379-392.

Urbanczyk, Suzanne
  1995 "Double Reduplications in Parallel", in Jill Beckman, Laura Walsh-Dickey, and Suzanne Urbanczyk (eds.) *Papers in Optimality Theory* (University of Massachusetts Occasional Papers 18), 499-531. Amherst: GLSA.
  1996 *Patterns of Reduplication in Lushootseed*. Ph.D. dissertation, University of Massachusetts, Amherst.

Vennemann, Theo
  1972 "Rule Inversion", *Lingua* 29, 209-242.
  1988 *Preference Laws for Syllable Structure*. Berlin—New York: Mouton de Gruyter.

Walinska de Hackbeil, Hanna
  1985 "*En*-prefixation and the Syntactic Domain of Zero Derivation", in Mary Nipokuj, Mary VanClay, Vassiliki Nikiforidou and Deborah Feder (eds.) *Proceedings of the 11th Annual Meeting of the Berkeley Linguistics Society, February 16-18, 1985*, 337-357. Berkeley: Berkeley Linguistics Society

Walker, John
  1924 *The Rhyming Dictionary*, revised by L. Dawson. London: Routledge.

Wellmann, H.
   1975   *Deutsche Wortbildung. Typen und Tendenzen in der deutschen
            Gegenwartssprache. Zweiter Hauptteil: Das Substantiv.* Düs-
            seldorf: Schwann.
Webster's Third
   1961   *Webster's Third New English Dictionary of the English Lan-
            guage.* Addenda Section 1981. Ed. by Philip Gove. Spring-
            field: Merriam-Webster.
Whaley, C. P.
   1978   "Word-nonword Classification Time", *Journal of Verbal Le-
            arning and Verbal Behavior* 17, 143-154.
Wiese, Richard
   1996a   *The Phonology of German.* Oxford: Clarendon Press.
   1996b   "Prosodic Alternations in English Morphophonology: A Con-
            straint-based Account of Morpheme Integrity", in Jacques Du-
            rand and Bernard Laks (eds.) *Current Trends in Phonology:
            Models and Methods*, 731-755. Salford: European Studies Re-
            search Institute.
   1996c   "Phrasal Compounds and the Theory of Word Syntax", *Lin-
            guistic Inquiry* 27, 183-193.
Williams, Edwin
   1981a   "Argument Structure and Morphology", *The Linguistic Review*
            1, 81-114.
   1981b   "On the Notions 'Lexically Related' and 'Head of a Word'",
            Linguistic Inquiry 12, 245-274.
Williams, Theodore
   1965   "On the *-ness* Peril", *American Speech* 40, 279-286.
Wójcicki, Adam
   1995   *Constraints on Suffixation. A Study in Generative Morphology
            of English and Polish.* Tübingen: Niemeyer.
Wurzel, Wolfgang Ulrich
   1976   "Zur Haplologie" *Linguistische Berichte* 41,50-57.
Yip, Moira
   1996   "Identity Avoidance in Phonology and Morphology", Ms.,
            University of California, Irvine (to appear in Steven G. La-
            pointe, Diane K. Brentari, and Patrick M. Farrell (eds.) *Mor-
            phology and its Relation to Phonology and Syntax.* Stanford:
            CLSI).

Zimmer, Karl E.
    1964   *Affixal Negation in English and other Languages: an Investigation of Restricted Productivity* (Supplement to *Word* 20).
Zipf, G. K.
    1935   *The Psycho-Biology of Language*. Boston: Houghton Mifflin.

Appendix 1: 20th century neologisms from the *OED*

The following sections contain lists of 20th century neologisms of derived verbs as listed in the *OED* (excluding forms derived by prefixation or parasynthesis). The spelling is adopted from the *OED*.

1. *-ize* derivatives (N= 284 types)

absolutize	academicize	accessorize	acidize
acronymize	adjectivize	aerosolize	Anglicanize
anodize	anthropologize	bacterize	banalize
Baskonize	Bolshevize	Bonderize	bovarize
bovrilize	cannibalize	capsulize	casualize
channelize	chemicalize	choriambize	chromicize
cinematize	compartmentalize	comprehensivize	computerize
containerize	contextualize	conveyorize	Coslettize
crofterize	Cubanize	customize	cyclize
Czechize	Daltonize	dieselize	digitalize 1
digitalize 2	dimensionalize	diploidize	discretize
ecize	ecphorize	embolize	empathize
epimerize	epoxidize	eroticize	erotize
eschatologize	factionalize	fantasize	fascistize
faucalize	Filipinize	finalize	finitize
Fletcherize	fluoridize	fractionalize	functionalize
funicularize	ghettoize	glamorize	glottalize
grammaticalize	heparinize	Hitlerize	Hollywoodize
Hooverize	hormonize	hospitalize	Hurrianize
hypophysectomize	indigenize	infinitize	instantize
institutionize	interiorize	interpolymerize	intransitivize
Jordanianize	jumboize	Kenyanize	ketonize
labilize	lactonize	lairize	laminarize
lateralize	lateritize	lemmatize	leucotomize
levantinize	lexicalize	lobotomize	Locarnize
Lukanize	luminize	luteinize	lyophilize
lysogenize	Malayanize	Manchesterize	Maoize
Marxize	masculinize	McLuhanize	mediocritize
Mendelize	metamorphosize	metasomatize	metastasize

metathesize

moisturize

multimerize

nativize

niggerize

notarize

opsonize

orthonormalize

pantheize

Parkerize

pelletize

phagocytize

photosensitize

pinealectomize

polygonize

Powellize

preservatize

prisonize

protectionize

quantize

radioize

reflexivize

rhematize

Romanianize

ruggedize

saucerize

scenarioize

sensibilize

slenderize

sorbitize

Stalinize

structurize

subitize

technicize

texturize

tolerize

transitivize

Turkicize

vasectomize

micronize

Mongolianize

musicalize

negritize

nodalize

nuclearize

optionalize

palletize

parameterize

passivize

Pelmanize

phlorizinize

photosynthesize

plasticize

polyploidize

premunize

pressurize

privatize

psychedelicize

quaternize

radiumize

regionalize

rhythmicize

routinize

saccharinize

Scandinavianize

scotomize

sherardize

sloganize

Sovietize

staticize

strychninize

subtopianize

technologize

thematize

topicalize

traumatize

tyndallize

velarize

miniaturize

monochromatize

mutagenize

nephrectomize

nodulize

oligomerize

orchidize

panchromatic

*parathyroidec-
tomize*

patinize

permanentize

phonemicize

physicalize

podzolize

Poplarize

prenasalize

primitivize

productionize

psychiatrize

Quislingize

randomize

relativize

rigidize

rubberize

salvationize

scapolitize

segmentalize

silanize

solodize

spheroidize

strategize

studentize

synergize

tectonize

thermalize

topologize

tribalize

vacuumize

vellumize

modularize

motorize

Namierize

Nigerianize

nonentitize

operationalize

orthogonalize

pancreatectomize

parfocalize

peasantize

permeabilize

photoisomerize

pidginize

polemicize

posterize

prepolymerize

prioritize

proletarize

publicize

racialize

reflectorize

renovize

robotize

rubricize

satellize

sclerotize

semanticize

simonize

solubilize

spoonerize

structuralize

subalternize

Taylorize

tetrazotize

thymectomize

transistorize

trypsinize

valorize

vernalize

verticalize	Vietnamize	virtuize	visceralize
vitaminize	weatherize	winterize	zabernize
Zambianize	zeroize		

2. -*ate* derivatives (N=72)

alluviate	automate	cannulate	cavitate
centuriate	citrate	coventrate	cybernate
disproportionate	dissonate	eluviate	escalate
exflagellate	fidate	fluoridate	fluorinate
formate	formylate	gelate	hæmagglutinate
hydroborate	hydroxylate	hyperventilate	inactivate
instantiate	intrapolate	iodinate	lenate
mercurate	metalate	methan	metricate
nitrogenate	nitrosate	nodulate	notate
olate	parcellate	passivate	pathosticate
patriate	perseverate	pervaporate	phosphate
phosphorylate	plasticate	predate	preferentiate
pupariate	quantitate	radio'activate	re'mediate
respirate	re'valuate	rotavate	seriate
silylate	solate	solvate	sonicate
spatulate	speciate	stereoregulate	structurate
sulphonylate	summate	tambourinate	Tarviate
tosylate	um'bilicate	vagulate	xanthate

3. -*ify* (N= 23)

ammonify	aridify	artify	bourgeoisify
gentrify	jazzify	karstify	massify
mucify	mythify	Nazify	negrify
opacify	passivify	plastify	probabilify
sinify	syllabify	technify	trustify
tubify	youthify	yuppify	

4. Conversion (N=488)

access	*ace*	*angel*	*apex*
arbitrage	*archive*	*audition*	*autopsy*
back-track	*bad-mouth*	*ball*	*ballock*
bay	*birdie*	*bish*	*bleep*
blip	*blitz*	*blockhouse*	*bloodhound*
bloop	*blouse*	*bogey*	*bonk*
boob	*boogie*	*boot*	*bootstrap*
bop	*born*	*bose*	*bot*
bottleneck	*brash*	*broadside*	*buffalo*
bug	*burlap*	*burp*	*caddy*
cairn	*camouflage*	*camp*	*caption*
carbon	*cartwheel*	*caterpillar*	*catfoot*
cantrifuge	*chauffeur*	*chuff*	*chutter*
clink-clank	*clipper*	*clone*	*clonk*
cobber	*cobweb*	*cocoa*	*coiffure*
cold-call	*cold-cream*	*compartment*	*compère*
composite	*concertina*	*contango*	*co-star*
courier	*coxswain*	*crayfish*	*crescendo*
crew	*cross-reference*	*cross-ruff*	*cue*
deke	*dingo*	*doll*	*dolomite*
dual	*duct*	*eel*	*eyeball*
fast-talk	*filmset*	*filthy*	*finger-post*
fink	*fish-tail*	*fission*	*flair*
flibbertigibbet	*flipper*	*format*	*fountain*
frontage	*frou-frou*	*garage*	*gas*
gavel	*gel*	*genotype*	*getter*
gig	*gillie*	*girder*	*goal*
gong	*goof*	*gramophone*	*grandmother*
gubble gurk	*gussy*	*guts*	*ham*
hands-up	*hau-hau*	*highball*	*high-hat*
highlight	*hightail*	*hip*	*hobday*
holster	*hoosh*	*hostess*	*hydroplane*
hype	*hypo*	*indemn*	*interface*
isograft	*jackal*	*japp*	*jazz*
jeep	*jerry*	*jet*	*jigger*
jinker	*jitter*	*jitterbug*	*jive*
juke	*junction*	*jungle*	*karyotype*
kayo	*keeper*	*keyboard*	*keynote*

keypunch	*keystone*	*kip*	*Klondike*
kyoodle	*la-di-da*	*lady's-maid*	*lager*
lagoon	*lair*	*la-la*	*landmark*
larder	*leaflet*	*lection*	*leisure*
lens	*lethal*	*leverage*	*lightning*
limehouse	*limelight*	*loon*	*lorry*
lyddite	*magic*	*main*	*main-line*
mallein	*manger*	*manslaughter*	*man-trap*
marcel	*marconi*	*marmalade*	*mat*
matrix	*megaphone*	*microdot*	*microfilm*
microwave	*mike*	*milestone*	*minimax*
minor	*monger*	*mothball*	*moue*
mousse	*multiple*	*multiplex*	*multistage*
muscle	*mush*	*nanny*	*nap*
napalm	*necropsy*	*newspaper*	*niblick*
niff	*nitride*	*nix*	*noodle*
norm	*nose-dive*	*nosh*	*nostril*
nymph	*oboe*	*off-centre*	*oink*
ooh	*option*	*opus*	*orbit*
orgasm	*ormer*	*oscillograph*	*package*
packsaddle	*pallet*	*panhandle*	*pamsy*
pantograph	*pastiche*	*pelican*	*peneplain*
periscope	*pern*	*petal*	*phagocyte*
phase	*phoney*	*photometer*	*picot*
pigment	*pike*	*ping-pong*	*pin-point*
pip	*piston*	*plateau*	*plink*
plock	*plotch*	*pogrom*	*pole*
politic	*polychrome*	*polygraph*	*pompadour*
ponce	*pong*	*poof*	*potmanteau*
postcard	*pot-hole*	*potlatch*	*premature*
première	*pressure*	*pretty*	*pring*
prodnose	*profiteer*	*propagand*	*propaganda*
proposition	*pundit*	*punk*	*purée*
puss	*pussy*	*pussyfoot*	*put-put*
putter	*quarterback*	*quarter-deck*	*quick-step*
quiff	*quinine*	*racketeer*	*radio*
radius	*rag*	*ranger*	*rat-hole*
ratio	*razz*	*razzle*	*reamer*
recap	*recce*	*recon*	*reflux*
remainder	*retrofit*	*rev*	*rhubarb*

rice	*riff*	*ritz*	*roger*
roll-call	*romatic*	*roocoocoo*	*rosette*
roster	*rough-house*	*rouseaboout*	*roustabout*
rowdy-dow	*rubbish*	*rumba*	*rummy*
rune	*runnel*	*rustproof*	*safety-pin*
samba	*sap*	*satellite*	*satire*
saucer	*sauna*	*sausage*	*saxophone*
scam	*scapegoat*	*scat*	*scooter*
screef	*script*	*scrum*	*scrutineer*
secretary	*sequence*	*serotype*	*set*
sherry	*shicker*	*shill*	*shimmer*
shimmy	*shiv*	*short-cut*	*shush*
sickle	*side*	*side-step*	*sirocco*
siwash	*skeeter*	*skip*	*skull*
slash	*sleeper*	*sleuth*	*snoek*
sod	*soft-pedal*	*somatotype*	*S.O.S.*
souvenir	*spasm*	*special*	*spotlight*
sprount	*spruce*	*sprue*	*squiz*
steam-roller	*Stellenbosch*	*stockpile*	*stooge*
stop-watch	*stork*	*streamline*	*stretcher*
strobe	*stunt*	*summit*	*supercharge*
supercoil	*sweet-talk*	*synapse*	*tab*
tailspin	*tangent*	*tango*	*tank*
tarmac	*tart*	*taxi*	*tea-table*
tee	*telemeter*	*temp*	*tender*
terrier	*threshold*	*thunk*	*tick-tock*
time-table	*toadstool*	*toast*	*tock*
toff	*tolerance*	*tom*	*tom-cat*
tonk	*torque*	*towl*	*trailer*
tremor	*trial*	*trigger*	*tripper*
tu-whit	*tweedle*	*twos*	*ultracentrifuge*
underseal	*vacuum*	*vamp*	*vector*
verbal	*video*	*volplane*	*volt*
wank	*watchdog*	*water-ski*	*waymark*
weasel	*wee*	*wee-wee*	*wham*
what-the-hell	*whee*	*whiplash*	*white-ant*
whomp	*whoofle*	*whoom*	*widdle*
wink	*winkle*	*witch*	*woodshed*
wow	*wrong-foot*	*wrong-slot*	*xerox*
yabby	*yacker*	*yacket*	*yomp*

york	*young*	*yo-yo*	*yuck*
zap	*zeep*	*zephyr*	*zero*
zing	*zipper*	*zither*	*zizz*
zonk			

5. Converted verbs that are semantic rivals to potential derivatives with at least one of the overt suffixes

5.1. Deadjectival derivatives (N=17)

born	*camp*	*cruel*	*dual*
filthy	*hip*	*indemn*	*lethal*
main	*multiple*	*phoney*	*polychrome*
pretty	*romantic*	*rustproof*	*skinny*
young			

5.2. Denominal derivatives (N=62)

archive	*cairn*	*camouflage*	*carbon*
caption	*compartment*	*cold-cream*	*composite*
crew	*cross-reference*	*cue*	*dolomite*
doll	*format*	*garage*	*gas*
gel	*highlight*	*hip*	*holster*
lethal	*indemn*	*marmalade*	*matrix*
mothball	*mousse*	*multiplex*	*necropsy*
nitride	*norm*	*package*	*pastiche*
peneplain	*phagocyte*	*picot*	*pigment*
pike	*pogrom*	*pothole*	*proposition*
propagand	*purée*	*quiff*	*quinine*
rustproof	*satire*	*scapegoat*	*script*
sequence	*set*	*sprue*	*streamline*
supercoil	*synapse*	*tab*	*tarmac*
timetable	*torque*	*video*	*volplane*
waymark	*zero*		

6. Verbal derivatives that are only attested as participles or verbal nouns

6.1. -izing *and* -ized *(N=62)*

œstrogenize	adrenalectomize	agenize	calorize
crofterize	dolbyize	drumlinize	editionize
elasticize	fetalize	hepatectomize	heterochromatize
hominize	hormonize	hyalinize	immunosympa-thectomize
impotentize	infantilize	insulinize	iodinize
laterize	migmatize	molarize	mullitize
myxomatize	nembutalize	nephenilize	nitridize
parathyroidecto-mize	paternalize	pearlize	phenolize
pinealectomize	pinocytize	polytenize	pupinize
radappertize	reggeize	reserpinize	rhodanize
rigidize	roboticize	rodingitize	Sanforize
scholasticize	Schreinerize	Shavianize	solonize
solutionize	somatize	spatio-temporalize	sympathectomize
tanalithize	Tebilize	telomerize	terminalize
Trubenize	unilateralize	vacuolize	virilize
weaponize	yotize		

6.2. -ating *and* -ated *(N=15)*

arpeggiate	deuterate	elasticate	illuviate
lenticulate	mentholate	nimbate	pifflicate
piliate	pomellate	pseudobrecciate	thoriate
tritiate	vacuolating	wobbulate	

6.3. -ifying *and* -ified *(N=7)*

desertify	interestify	nancify	pansify
partify	societify	theatrify	

Appendix 2: Hapax legomena from the Cobuild corpus

The following sections contain lists of hapaxes of derived verbs in *-ize*, *-ate* and *-ify*, extracted from the Cobuild word list, Cobuild corpus of July 1995 (c. 20 million tokens).

1. *-ize* (N=80)

academicize	*aerobicize*	*aerolize*	*aluminiumize*
anthologize	*anthropomorphize*	*apostasized*	*arabize*
archaize	*astrologize*	*attitudinize*	*austrianize*
bilingualize	*botanize*	*canadianize*	*carbonize*
chiropodise	*christianize*	*civilianize*	*climatize*
collateralise	*colonialise*	*communize*	*containerise*
corporealize	*craterize*	*diarize*	*directionalize*
divisionalize	*dormitorize*	*elasticize*	*eroticize*
eternalize	*euphemize*	*euthanize*	*federalize*
feminize	*finlandize*	*firmanize*	*fluoridize*
fractionalize	*globalize*	*gourmandize*	*hellenize*
historicize	*imperialize*	*instrumentalize*	*interiorize*
iodize	*italicize*	*licize*	*luminize*
martyrize	*matize*	*matrize*	*medicalize*
metastasize	*minimalise*	*monetize*	*mongrelize*
musicalize	*nominalize*	*normandize*	*palatalize*
parametize	*parenthesize*	*perennialize*	*proletarianize*
psychedelicize	*robotize*	*romanize*	*secularize*
securitise	*semicivilize*	*sensibilize*	*siliconize*
thermostabilize	*vampirize*	*ventriloquize*	*vitalize*

2. *-ate* (N=69)

acidulate	*agglomerate*	*agglutinate*	*annuate*
apostemate	*caffeinate*	*calvulate*	*cavitate*
coaginate	*concatenate*	*conciliate*	*conglomerate*
contemplate	*decrepitate*	*depilate*	*derogate*

dilacerate	emerate	excrutiate	exsanguinate
exsiccate	exsultate	extirpate	fecundate
flortate	flotate	granulate	grasseate
gratinate	imbricate	immolate	infratiate
ingurgitate	inhabitate	inspissate	itinerate
lactate	lancinate	macerate	mancipate
marvelate	masticate	obumbrate	odinate
particulate	passionate	patinate	pendulate
perorate	predestinate	profilgate	propitate
reconciliate	relicate	rotavate	rusticate
speciate	spectaculate	susurrate	syllabicate
triangulate	triplicate	triturate	ulcerate
unduate	variate	vitiate	vituperate
vociferate			

3. *-ify* (N=16)

citify	commodify	emulsify	frenchify
funkify	humidify	hypocrify	matify
nannify	nitrosify	ossify	russify
scarify	stampify	vinify	vivify

Author index

Subject index

Affix index